THE TRUTH

Real Stories and the Risk of Losing a Free Press in America

Bob Gabordi

authorHOUSE

AuthorHouse™
1663 Liberty Drive
Bloomington, IN 47403
www.authorhouse.com
Phone: 1 (800) 839-8640

Published by AuthorHouse 07/08/2020

ISBN: 978-1-7283-6604-3 (sc)
ISBN: 978-1-7283-6603-6 (hc)
ISBN: 978-1-7283-6605-0 (e)

Library of Congress Control Number: 2020912134

Print information available on the last page.

DEDICATION

For Jessica, who lets me sing her to sleep at nights and feed her breakfast in the mornings. No matter how old she gets, she will always be her Daddy's little girl.

ACKNOWLEDGEMENTS

To begin, I thank every journalist I've ever worked with, from those at the very beginning to those who were so kind when it ended.

That said, I've tried to make a list of the top 10 influencers on my career, but 10 quickly became 15, then 20 and so on. I did the same with the people who I enjoyed working with the most – and the process only repeated itself.

But I do need to publicly acknowledge a few people, especially regarding this book.

My wife, Donna Hamernick-Gabordi, encouraged me, listened to me read passages and even tried to help edit it, which was way outside her comfort zone. She has been there at every turn, as have our children – now all grown – and their spouses and significant others.

Then there is the group outside of my family.

Mara Bellaby tops that list. Not only did her quick-thinking help save my life when I had a stroke Nov. 9, 2018, but also she has been a constant visitor and supporter. She has encouraged me to keep writing. She is one of the very few people I entrusted early on to read what would eventually become the introduction and she convinced me I had a story to tell. She took over at FLORIDA TODAY, reluctantly I'd say, when I no longer could be there and has performed fabulously.

Thanks to Tom Curley, associate general counsel at Gannett Co. for his help in obtaining rights to reprint materials from The Bulletin in Norwich, Conn., the Asheville Citizen-Times, the Tallahassee Democrat and FLORIDA TODAY and the Gannetter. His uncle, also named Tom, was my first Gannett editor back in Norwich in the early 1980s. I'm deeply indebt to the Curley family.

I am likewise deeply indebted to the Gannett Company over the years. All of the Gannetts, before the spin and afterwards, before the merger and after. We have always believed in each other and that has allowed me to pursue my dreams and feed my family.

I also thank Les Smith, Lee Wolverton, Andrea Copley-Smith and Jim Heady of HD Media LLC., for their support in gaining rights to reprint materials produced during my time as executive editor of The Herald-Dispatch.

Jim Spanner, publisher of the Parkersburg News and Sentinel and The Marietta Times, helped me gain rights to reprint materials from my first job as a senior editor in Marietta.

Thanks, too, to Kim Bates, managing editor of The Blade for a quick turnaround to get reprint rights approved for a photo that published on The Blade's front page, a special nod to her for remembering The Other Ohio project.

Mickey Johnson and Fran Allred helped me edit the manuscript. They were both with me at The Herald-Dispatch in Huntington and when I heard about their book-editing company, We Edit Books, it was only natural I would turn to them for help. If you are even thinking about writing a book, keep in mind that the writing is the easy part; editing is a bear. Their website is weeditbooks.com and I highly recommend it.

FOREWORD

Mark Truby, chief communications officer Ford Motor company

I was a 26-year-old college dropout making $10 an hour as a reporter in Huntington, W.Va., when I met Bob Gabordi. I worked the night shift – 3 to 11 p.m. – listening to the police scanner, running out to school board meetings, and typing up obituaries. Good news was in short supply.

Huntington, a once-thriving river town at the heart of the Tri-State Area of Kentucky, Ohio, and West Virginia, has endured more than its share of setbacks and sadness. Often as not, the "big story" in Huntington is a heartbreaker – another factory closing or school consolidation or opioid abuse epidemic. Those great flat barges taking on coal from the mountains of West "By God" Virginia didn't ply the Ohio River that flowed past Huntington with the same regularity that they once did.

One of my first assignments at The Herald-Dispatch was to cover the annual memorial ceremony in remembrance of those lost when a Southern Airways charter carrying the Marshall University football team went down on a hillside just west of Huntington. It was the crash memorialized in the movie "We Are Marshall." The tragedy occurred in 1970, but the community still struggled with the weight of the unfathomable event a quarter century later. It remains the biggest sports-related disaster in U.S. history. The victims included 37 players, 12 coaches and university staff members, five flight crew members, and 21 townspeople. Seventy children lost parents.

The newsroom of The Herald-Dispatch was just as you'd imagine. Page proofs, grease pencils, stacks of phone books, and crisscross directories littered desks. The smell of Camel cigarettes and photo-developing chemicals filled the air, as did the cacophony of gruff banter, ringing phones, and clacking keyboards. I loved it. When Bob Gabordi rolled into town as our young hotshot editor, I was skeptical. First of all, I was suspicious of our parent company, Gannett, which was often derided for its bottom-line focus, cost-cutting, and formulaic journalism initiatives. And Bob seemed to my idealistic (and naive) eye to be a company man right down to the Gannett baseball cap.

Far from being too corporate, Bob turned out to be a ballsy newsman with a big-hearted belief that great local journalism could lift a community up and even help change its destiny. Bob loved the big story as much as anybody, but more than that, he wanted to leave Huntington better than he found it. Soon after he arrived, the small but skilled staff at The Herald-Dispatch began punching above its weight with in-depth take-outs and investigations on local politics, downtown development, business, and sports. And, as often seems to be the case with great editors, soon after Bob arrived, huge stories started falling from the sky, almost literally.

There was a fireworks disaster on the eve of Independence Day in 1996 – a national tragedy in our backyard. Bob demanded we cover it like The New York Times – investigative pieces, profiles of the victims, and a 100-inch reader on the poor brain-damaged teen who flicked the lit cigarette that sparked the fire that claimed nine lives.

Two months later, we learned President Bill Clinton had chosen little Huntington to embark on an old-fashioned, whistle-stop train tour to kick off his re-election bid. The Clinton campaign may have only chosen Huntington for its rail lines and proximity to crucial Ohio voters, but Bob decided it was our story to own. He somehow wrangled a spot on the train for a Herald-Dispatch reporter. "Don't screw it up, Truby," he said as I was about to board a passenger car filled with the likes of Britt Hume and Candy Crowley. The Herald-Dispatch chronicled every speech, rally, and kissed baby as Clinton's "21st Century Express" wended its way through the swing states of Ohio and Michigan as well as Indiana and Kentucky en route to the Democratic National Convention in Chicago.

That same year, Randy Moss, the greatest high school athlete in West Virginia history, transferred to Marshall after losing football scholarships at Notre Dame and Florida State as a result of off-the-field issues. Bob knew it was more than the story of Marshall lucking into landing possibly college football's best player. He could see it would be a time of redemption and healing some 26 years after the tragedy that left a proud town broken. The Herald-Dispatch didn't win a Pulitzer for its coverage of Marshall's 15-0 championship season in 1996, but it easily could have.

If it's true that a person's career comes down to a few moments, the one I keep like a faded Polaroid is the day I walked into Bob's office with a ridiculous request. One night in the newsroom of The Herald-Dispatch, I received a tip that a wealthy local couple had been arrested for murder while sailing in the Caribbean off the nation of St. Vincent and the Grenadines. If convicted of the shooting death of a popular local man, the penalty would be execution by hanging from stone gallows on a hilltop in St. Vincent. I wrote up a couple stories on the case but couldn't shake it. If it were any other editor, I would not have bothered, but I decided to march into Bob's office and ask him to send me to St. Vincent. Bob was a step ahead of me.

He somehow found money in the budget and convinced our publisher to send me and a photographer to the out-of-the-way archipelago. When we returned, we worked night and day for a week and published a three-day, book-length series titled "Prisoners in Paradise." Under Bob's guidance, the reporting helped expose corruption and holes in the case and the couple eventually won an acquittal. A few months later, Bob and I traveled together to Washington, D.C., to receive the National Press Club's top award for foreign correspondence.

After that big break, Bob helped me get a position at USA TODAY. I moved on to The Detroit News and eventually to Ford Motor Co., where I now serve as chief communications officer after completing international assignments in Europe and China. (I finally got that degree from Marshall while living in Germany.) I hope along the way I have been able to pay forward the gifts I received from Bob. He believed in me and challenged me to find my potential. He taught me to lift my gaze, take risks and try to make a difference rather than whining about the inevitable compromises and constraints of daily journalism.

I left newspapers with sadness and some regret in 2007. By this time, I was a senior editor at The Detroit News, but the handwriting seemed to be on the wall. I believed I had missed out on the heyday of newspapers and couldn't stomach a steady stream of staff cuts, bureau closings, and crafting memos about doing more with less. The rise of the Internet had seemed to suck all the juice out of the newspaper business. People no longer needed the paper to read the box scores, check their stocks, solve crosswords, check movie times, and find apartments to rent.

But Bob stayed in the fight – from Huntington to Asheville, N.C., to Tallahassee, Fla., to FLORIDA TODAY – for more than 40 years. He adapted and remained an inspiration to communities that needed a watchdog and a cheerleader. He used the prism of his life – his daughter who was born with developmental issues, his love of baseball, and the stroke he suffered – to bring humanity to the pages of the newspapers he edited. He's a living testament to the power of local journalism at a time when these vital institutions are in grave peril and he has the amazing stories to prove it.

Enjoy.

Mark Truby
Chief Communications Officer
Ford Motor Company

ASHEVILLE
CITIZEN-TIMES
50 cents

VOICE OF THE MOUNTAINS • CITIZEN-TIMES.com

Friday
May 16, 2008

PENLAND: Former reserve Capt. Guy Kenneth Penland also found guilty on same charges.

SENTENCING: Medford and Penland face a maximum penalty of 170 years in prison.

NEXT STEP: Former sheriff says no decision has been made on an appeal.

MEDFORD GUILTY

Former Buncombe County Sheriff Bobby Medford said Thursday he was disappointed in the jury's verdict that he was guilty on all 11 counts of using his position to extort money from gambling operators.

WHAT'S NEXT?

■ The Federal Probation Office will conduct a pre-sentencing investigation that could consider career backgrounds of former Sheriff Bobby Medford and former reserve Capt. Guy Kenneth Penland and any explanations they have of their crimes.

■ The presentencing reports go to prosecution and defense attorneys. A hearing would be held to resolve any differences. The reports go to the judge for use at his discretion.

■ Sentencing should happen in 4-6 weeks.

■ Medford and Penland will have 10 days after sentencing to decide whether to appeal.

MORE ON A4-5

■ People who knew Bobby Medford best recall a modest, dedicated lawman.

■ A look at people who have pleaded guilty in the federal government's investigation into the gal video gambling in Western North Carolina.

■ Highlights of the testimony and evidence.

WEB EXTRA

Visit CITIZEN-TIMES.com/videogambling for stories and multimedia related to the trial.

Ex-sheriff maintains innocence after conviction on all counts

ASHEVILLE — The government got its prize Thursday. A former sheriff who had been the target of a two-year public corruption investigation, who pocketed at least $300,000 in bribes and who once controlled the fate of a multimillion-dollar gambling empire now faces spending the rest of his life in prison. Bobby Lee Medford, Buncombe County's top lawman for more than a decade, was found guilty by a federal court jury.

Medford shuffled down the courthouse steps after the verdict, hobbled by a bad back and general poor health, and said he was "disappointed."

It could also be said that Medford was beaten from the start.

Prosecutors gave 12 jurors from throughout Western North Carolina a mountain of evidence during the 11-day trial, and jurors took barely two hours to return a verdict of guilty on all 11 counts related to extortion, money laundering and illegal gambling. Medford said he told the truth on the witness stand when he denied taking bribes. "Well, apparently some peo-

ple didn't believe it," he said. "Most people that know me, they know better than this. There is not much else I have to say. I still believe in the justice system."

Appeal considered

The jury of 10 men and two women got the case at 9:05 a.m. and was back in the courtroom with the verdict by 11:25.

Outside court, jurors declined to comment on their deliberations.

Judge Tim Ellis told jurors they were free to discuss the case but also said he believed they had a "duty of confidentiality" to each other.

Please see GUILTY on A5

Susan Carter, daughter of former volunteer Capt. Guy Penland, takes a break from court after a jury found Penland guilty on charges related to illegal gambling.

STORY BY JON OSTENDORFF/JOSTENDORFF@CITIZEN-TIMES.COM ◆ PHOTOS BY ERIN BRETHAUER/EBRETHAUER@CITIZEN-TIMES.COM

Sports, C1	Mountains, B1	TAKE5	Nation, A2	Today's forecast	Index
LAST DANCE: Asheville School track coach Doug Embler, who is leaving the school after 16 years, hopes to depart with a state title.	**HIKER'S DEATH:** John Bryant, whose skeletal remains were found in February in Macon County, died of a gunshot wound to the head.		**FOOD WORRIES:** Republicans, worried about steep losses in the fall elections, abandoned President Bush and voted to boost food stamps and farm subsidies. Page A2	Partly cloudy storms High 76, Low 54 **WEATHER, C10**	
Living, C1					
STAR WATCH: Madonna will have to wait another week to know whether a Malawian boy will permanently join her family.	**SERIOUS ACCUSATION:** A Madison County deputy has resigned after being accused of planting evidence. Page B1		**INSIDE TODAY'S TAKE5:** Indiana Jones is back with a new flick.		

Asheville Citizen-Times May 16, 2008

INTRODUCTION

GUARDIANS OF THE FIRST AMENDMENT

Buncombe (N.C.) County Sheriff Bobby Medford was one of the most vile, evil people I had ever met. He was a bully with authority, always a dangerous combination. He was a crook with a badge, which adds up to worse than just evil.

When the Citizen-Times in Asheville blared in headline type suitable for the start of World War III MEDFORD GUILTY on May 16, 2008, I was long since gone as executive editor of the newspaper in that beautiful mountain community.

But I quietly celebrated, anyway.

I suspect Medford might have been arrested and done significant time in prison without any media scrutiny. Perhaps. The government's investigation happened independently of the newspaper. The fact that the Citizen-Times had been investigating Medford's illegal activities, however, was not unknown or lost on government officials. I know that because I know it. That's about all I can say.

Medford was the one bad apple who could make the whole department look bad. I truly think he felt he was invincible, untouchable, more powerful – as he would say – than Jesus Christ in Buncombe County. In the end, he was just one bad apple, but he was bad to the core.

That's why I celebrated. He was convicted of a variety of public corruption charges related to an illegal gambling operation involving video games, often in backrooms at convenience stores, in the county. He was sent to the federal pen following a two-year government investigation. He is due to be released within the next couple of years.

The newspaper investigated Medford for at least that long. I might never know just how much the newspaper's investigation influenced the government's work, if at all, but I suspect there is a reason Medford tried to shut us down.

He wouldn't see our reporter at his office or come to the phone when we called there. He threatened to arrest our reporter – and suggested he could legally shoot her if she came to his house door – and as her editor when I challenged him on that, he said he would do the same to me.

I told him that I thought arresting me was a bad idea on multiple levels, but he could be sure that if he arrested a newspaper reporter or editor for asking questions it would only lead to more and more media outlets at his office asking questions. We wouldn't go away and the questions would not go away, even if we did.

In other words, we called the bluff of this schoolyard bully. He didn't scare me, and I told him so. In retrospect, he was kind of a pathetic character, the rooster who had once ruled the roost. His time was up, his power slipped away. Only he didn't know it yet.

We kept digging, of course, as did the feds. They got him first and better. Nowadays, he would probably call a press conference or just Tweet about "fake news" and blame the FBI investigation on a biased Justice Department influenced by biased media. But I worry about guys like Medford winning if independent news outlets run out of money or public support. What happens when the politicians – local and national – finally destroy our credibility for political gain?

I read an interview Medford gave not too long ago. He didn't sound rehabilitated. If anything, he was more belligerent. He sounded even worse than the mean bastard I remembered.

Harsh?

This was the same guy who once grabbed a rifle and stood on the courthouse steps threatening any protester who dared to try to enter to find out more about others he had locked up. That was my first week or so in Asheville. David Peyton wrote a column about it in my former newspaper, The Herald-Dispatch of Huntington, W.Va.

Bobby Medford was the type of person the Founding Fathers had envisioned when they created the First Amendment barring the government from making laws to interfere with a free press.

There are a lot of politicians these days who need to go back and reread that section of the Constitution. Hell, maybe they should read the whole thing while they are at it. It might serve them and their communities well to remember they have no business deciding who are their media favorites, who they dislike and who they can try to control.

It's not a new thing for politicians and government officials to dislike the press for doing its job. President Donald Trump is not the first to think of the media as the enemy. Union Gen. William T. Sherman thought journalists were nothing but a pack of spies. Richard Nixon had his famous enemies list that included some journalists but wasn't exclusively so. Lyndon Johnson once said that if he walked across the Potomac River the press would say the president couldn't swim.

Even Thomas Jefferson had harsh words when it came to press coverage of his presidency.

So, Trump didn't invent animosity with the press. But he has taken it to a new low, where he has applauded violence – he praised Montana U.S. Rep. Greg Gianforte for assaulting a reporter – and given leave to those who verbally attack the media at all levels.

Recently, I was awoken after midnight by a Tweet from the president of the United States. Angered by questions from reporters over the Corona Virus pandemic, Trump Tweeted:

"The Lamestream Media is truly out of control. Look how they work (conspire!) together. They are the Enemy of the People, but don't worry, we will WIN in November!"

I guess it is not realistic to hope politicians today would understand the role of the media as the Fourth Estate, empowered by the Founders to get in their business, to ask uncomfortable questions and tell the public their secrets. It has become kind of a standard playbook at all levels: scream fake news, question the credibility of media outlets, even try to taint reporters and editors' integrity and morality.

In politics, as in sports, only winning matters. Maybe that's all that ever mattered, but at least we used to at least give lip service to having ethics and morals that made how you won matter. Now? Even the Houston Astros got to keep their World Series rings.

Sadly, in America today, party matters more than country, and politicians are willing to tear down decades old – in some cases centuries old – institutions in the name of their own egos.

In some cases, even at the local level, politicians spend hundreds of thousands of dollars – in some cases millions of dollars - on video production and self-glorifying promotions to build their images; often this is taxpayers' money.

In Brevard County, Fla., for example, the local sheriff spent more than $512,000 on his media and community services department – far more than any other nearby county sheriff's office – while flooding social media with his own image. Meanwhile, he asked the county commission for a tax increase to support his expanding "critical needs" in funding.

He received the money, of course, because he is the most powerful politician in the county.

Of course, it is a legitimate government expense to hire communication specialists. No doubt, they are needed to ensure the public is well informed of government's messages. But some government officials attempt to control what the public knows and doesn't know about their operations at the public's expense.

Of course, media outlets and journalism doers – already weakened by frontal attacks by government – are in grave danger of surviving COVID-19. Revenue losses resulted in extreme job losses in the industry throughout the world in 2020. Gannett – the largest newspaper company in the United States and maybe the world – saw its stock dip below $1 per share and it reported a net loss in first quarter results.

It has instituted furloughs, even as many dozens of other news outlets around the world have closed, resulting in fewer people doing journalism, which means less truth telling.

This comes at a time when Americans are again marching in the streets, fighting against systemic racism and trying to understand the reality of a president who has used violence to clear a churchyard so he could stage a photo opp. He threatens the American people with our own military and mistakes toughness with violence against the people.

What's the future? That depends on what the public determines is the value. There are some who would celebrate the collapse of media outlets, the extinction of journalism as we have known it since the birth of freedom in the newly formed United States.

These very same people have rejected science, invented a new way to describe lying as alternative facts and praised dictators from other countries as "strong leaders."

But what about when the government knowingly (or by mistake, for that matter) arrests the wrong person? Who steps up if not the media? Or someone runs off with money from the public treasury? Or poisons a local water table? Or simply fails to fulfill its obligation to provide quality education, public safety, and good roads?

I reluctantly joined a Facebook conversation that suggested journalists were actually rooting for more people to die because it would make the president look bad. I asked for specifics and of course there weren't any. Our leaders are teaching their followers to disbelieve anything that might reflect poorly on their job performance. And that is very dangerous.

What happens – without a free and independent press – when infant mortality rates soar and there's no one to point out trends? When police abuse people because of their race or national origin? When a contractor wins a bid because they are somebody's friend or campaign contributor?

I've seen these things happen in communities large and small across the country.

But I digress. Back to Bobby Medford.

When I left Asheville in 2005 for the executive editor's job at the Tallahassee Democrat, which had been newly acquired by Gannett, Medford had not been arrested yet. One day, I got a phone call that I've never shared with anyone outside my family until now.

It was from a prominent public official in Buncombe County wanting to know what I knew, what our investigation had revealed, about Medford. For what purpose? That was never clear to me. But surely, the feds had to know what we knew and more. After all, their investigative authority and powers were strong, while ours, well, we had virtually no powers.

The truth is anyone who really wanted to know about his gambling operations could have found out. His perception of his own power kept him from trying to hide it too much. A letter to the editor published in the Citizen-Times back in the 1990s even hinted at it, saying the county deserved better.

The person on the other end of the phone asked that I keep his identity private, and I've always done so. I was reluctant to give away anything, but, in the end, I knew and trusted this guy, so we talked. I don't know how useful I was, but I felt as a citizen, anything I could do to bring out the truth about Medford and his corrupt ways, I should.

After all, that's what the First Amendment is about: providing checks on the government, giving voice to those without one. Those were days when a political bad actor couldn't just attack the newspaper as lacking credibility to counter reporting he or she didn't like. A politician couldn't just scream "fake news" to diffuse the impact of good reporting. That has been the Trump impact.

Things were different then.

Newsrooms were loud, smoky places when I first became a reporter in 1979. Police scanners blared. Phones rang unanswered and reporters and editors talked to each other – or, just as likely, yelled – across several desks.

When I retired 41 years later, they were much quieter with nice artwork, though probably still louder and definitely messier than most business offices. Scanners were silenced by police moving to secret digitized systems that kept the press out of touch with what they were doing in real time. No one smoked indoors, of course. Phones were required to be answered under penalty of nasty notes from editors like me.

And conversation, of course, largely was replaced by email or text, even between people sitting right next to each other. Even at lunch, we're on our phones, touching them an average of hundreds of times a day, or so I read – probably in an article on my phone.

One constant through the years though, mainly, is that the people who inhabit newsrooms are exceptionally smart. I never felt I measured up. Even as I moved up, I always felt at a disadvantage to smarter, more worldly colleagues. The higher I went, the more I felt overmatched. At editors' meetings, I sometimes wondered how and why they let me in. They were so smart.

When I became executive editor in Huntington, Associate Editor James E. Casto, who ran our editorial page, wanted to take me out to dinner. He insisted he would buy. He had an agenda. Why was it, he wanted to know, was I his boss. He was obviously smarter, more experienced, and knew the community very well.

I couldn't refute any of that.

"You know," I replied, "I kind of feel the way John Kennedy did when he was told there was cheating in Chicago that gave him the presidency over Richard Nixon. I'm not giving it back."

My colleagues in newsrooms were brave, too. They have been willing to take on the rich and powerful, often at great personal risk, to get at the truth and report local history. As an editor, I have sent reporters off to foreign countries potentially in harm's way, and I have gone myself. At times, though, I've wondered if we don't face more danger at home. If not physical danger, then certainly emotional abuse.

I once opened the door to my office to find a reporter involved in a tough investigative story curled up on the floor in the fetal position, crying, "I'm not as tough or as smart as you think I am." But she was.

Another time – for a story you'll hear more about later in the book – we had to get a U.S. official in Barbados to fly into neighboring St. Vincent to rescue our reporter who we believed was surely about to be arrested for his coverage on that island-nation. When we got him safely home, he begged to go back. Of course, we sent him back. I have no doubt whatsoever that his reporting played a major role in saving the lives of two West Virginians.

Who'll take on the bullies if American journalism is destroyed, either from economics or by simply screaming "fake news" and convincing enough people to believe them? Or if we allow the politicians to pick and choose which journalists are "friendly" enough to work with?

In writing this, my motivation is to take you inside the journalism profession, to show you real journalists – the guardians of the First Amendment. I'm telling you their stories. OK, these are my stories, told through my eyes. But stories like these happen in newsrooms every day – in American newsrooms and those around the world in places struggling to build free press traditions.

I have been to places like Pakistan, Turkey and Armenia, and worked with the International Center for Journalists to host dozens of more journalists from Kenya, Ghana, Uganda, Mali, Romania, Malaysia, Argentina, Syria, Ukraine, Russia, Georgia and, of course, Turkey, Armenia and Pakistan, where I have been most involved.

These are places that still hold American journalism and press freedoms as aspirations. What is the cost of allowing that to die?

I tell stories that I have been personally involved with over the years, as a reporter or editor. But these stories do not belong to me or the media; they belong to the communities in which I have lived and to the people whose lives were played out in them. Real people telling true-life tales about real people.

There is nothing fake about that. Only people whose motivation is to control the narrative for their own purpose can oppose this kind of journalism. Sometimes that purpose is power or money. Sometimes the purpose is less easy to define, such as their personal legacy or what the neighbors might think.

In explaining why I'm writing this now, there are two factors. One is that I retired as an active editor and believe that I can express myself freely. The other is best explained by a story. Before I do, I should warn you that you'll be required to have patience as you read this book. I love to go off on tangents and tell stories. OK, so here we go, my motivation for writing this:

It was during one of Trump's visits to Florida and thousands of people were gathered to support him. He pointed at members of the media huddled together behind a roped-off area and told the audience that they were dishonest. The media, in other words, was to blame that not everyone agreed with Trump.

Those people are to blame. Oh, how many times throughout history have we heard those words uttered by a demagogue about one group or another.

I had journalists who I was responsible for in that group, people who had never done or said anything untoward about Trump. Yet in front of an amped-up crowd, he blamed them for some ill in his mind.

Trump's approach to the media has trickled down to the local level. Very quickly, Americans have turned on our own Constitution and its guarantee of a free press. Either they don't understand what that could mean, or they do and just don't care. We have already put political parties before allegiance to the country, and that's just one step from not caring about what the country is supposed to stand for. Winning is more important than leading or governing well.

This has all happened before, of course. As I said earlier, Trump didn't invent this nor will he be the last to follow the script. First, use your own popularity to destroy the credibility of the press. It is simple from there. Control what the people know, and you control the people. Adolf Hitler did this as a first order of business when he took power in Germany.

I spoke to a woman not long ago who was born in the 1920s in Germany. She was a child when the Nazis rose to power. She saw the trucks loaded with people, Jews, being hauled away.

"But I had no idea what that was about, what was going on," she said. "We didn't know."

And, no one was left to tell them. The credibility of the German press, once considered one of the most independent in the world, had been destroyed.

I'm not suggesting Trump is a Nazi, only that he is following the Nazi script to destroy the press and the First Amendment.

In case you've forgotten, the First Amendment doesn't belong to the press; it belongs to all Americans. Lose it and we lose what America stands for around the world: hope and freedom. I know, I have been to places where America is still an aspiration. I've been to places where people get arrested and shot for what they write and sometimes what they refuse to write. Talk about fighting for freedom, aspiring to the American dream. A Pakistani journalist – badly bandaged and on crutches after being released from the hospital for a beating he took for what he wrote – told me he considered himself free to write what he wanted. "We're as free as our courage takes us," he said. More on that in a later chapter.

Journalists don't get into this business expecting to be loved. No one becomes a journalist expecting riches or celebrity, either. Livable wages and celebrity treatment are, generally speaking, relatively new developments.

As for pay, I started off at a group of weekly newspapers making $115 a week, or $5,980 for the year, and no one bothered tracking the hours we put in. I answered the phones when the receptionist was out. I helped paste up pages in the production area. I wrote stories and took my own photos. I had to buy a camera to get the job.

When I got my first job at a daily newspaper, the pay was much higher: I earned $175 per week, or $9,100 annually. It was my dream come true, working for the hometown Norwich (Conn.) Bulletin, now called just The

Bulletin. I had won an award from its rival newspaper, The Day of New London, for journalism when I graduated high school in 1974 in Ledyard. But now I was playing for the other team.

A couple years into the business, with both my wife and me working, we bought our first house. It was an old Shaker meeting house. We put on a new roof, replaced the straw with real insulation, and put in a wood-coal burning stove and new hearth to keep the costs down.

But things didn't go smoothly. One day I had to run outside and talk the electric man into not turning off our power. I gave him a check for the overdue bill, and he promised to hold onto it until payday. By then we had a baby inside the house, so I was desperate. I'm not sure what we would have done if he had not shown mercy.

So, no. Money was not the attraction.

Journalists never expect to be popular, either. As the nation came to grips with the coronavirus, people got angry at the media for "overhyping" the disease that has killed tens of thousands of people. Many took coverage of the virus as a way to embarrass the president, who initially had downplayed its impact in the United States.

The lack of popular support is never truer than when we bring bad news about public officials. People think bad news sells. But as I recall, single-copy sales of newspapers went down the day the headline was that President Clinton had been impeached by the House. People get angry at journalists when we bring news of corruption and other wrongdoing by popularly elected officials. Few editors or reporters would win popularity contests running against the people we write about.

Despite that, I've always felt it was part of the job as editor of the local news organization to love the community we serve, to find out what makes it what it is, and help it to be successful. My children have teased me that I would love living anywhere, and maybe that is true. But I tell young editors not to expect the love to be returned. You will love them more than they love you. It is fundamental to our jobs. After all, sometimes we must tell our communities bad news. But there is a lot to love about American towns and cities and, besides, it was my job or so I felt to fit in, and when we must bring bad news to do so with love.

I have been the senior editor in a bunch of unique places: Appalachian communities like Marietta, Ohio, Huntington, W.Va, and Asheville, N.C., nestled in the mountains; the Florida capitol, Tallahassee; and my dream job in Melbourne, Fla., home of FLORIDA TODAY.

I inherited supervision of the newsrooms at the Treasure Coast newspapers, too, when I was executive editor at FLORIDA TODAY.

Huntington and Tallahassee had major college sports programs, which I loved. But college sports were almost an afterthought in Asheville and maybe not even that along the Space Coast of Florida. Yeah, these places are different in many ways, but they all had in common that people loved living in them. They deserved news organizations that reflected them. That meant a commitment to diversity in the news operations.

By the way, I first visited FLORIDA TODAY in 1994 as part of the initial Gannett Management Development program for newsroom executives. I set becoming editor at FLORIDA TODAY as one of my career goals. It only took me 21 more years to achieve that goal, moving from Tallahassee to FLORIDA TODAY in 2015. I love being back near the beach, the sunrises and the smell of the salty ocean water.

My career path was filled with zigs and zags. I left daily newspapers after Norwich for a couple roles at corporate, moving to Rosslyn, Va., in October 1984. It started as a two-week loan to corporate. After a couple extensions, I was hired permanently by Gannett New Media in March 1985 – you know, as permanent as things get in the news business.

We spent 6 ½ years living in suburban Washington, D.C., while I worked at Gannett New Media and then Gannett News Service, where I landed in 1988, in the early days of USA TODAY. During my GNS days, I worked with Gannett newspapers in the Northeast and South regions, visiting most to try to understand their news needs. I think that's what made me so sensitive to learning what made communities tick in my 26 years as a senior editor.

Passes to get me into the SEC and Senate and House press areas. I imagine security is tighter these days.

Later in my tenure at GNS, I moved back into a reporting role at my request, becoming a national business reporter, covering the Security and Exchange Commission and Congress and writing business features. More zigs and zags.

Gannett New Media was our company's first foray into what became known first as online media and then digital media. I worked updating the news online when files were transferred over phone lines at 300 baud. Later, I was promoted to director of special projects and helped edit and publish USA TODAY books.

Two of those book projects stand out. One was our first instant book, a travel book based on USA TODAY published articles within two weeks of the invasion of the U.S. Embassy in Beirut. Let's be honest: None of us knew what we were doing, not me as the overall editor, not the designer who was an amazing newspaper designer, no one. Not even Al Neuharth, CEO of the company, who took a big hand in our book publishing.

We made deadline, and 10,000 copies of the bright yellow book were printed. We got back the proofs, called blues, and I approved them, so did my boss, Nancy Woodhull, and her boss, Neuharth, who loved the book when it was in the proofing stage.

But he hated it in actual print. Newspapers, of course, filled every inch of our pages with type and photos and would never publish blank pages.

White space in newspapers meant space was available to place an ad. It was treasured, like gold. You just didn't leave white space.

Books, on the other hand …

I picked up the ringing phone in our small apartment on Edsall Road in Alexandria and Woodhull was on the other end of the call. It was the weekend and she almost never called on the weekend. I knew it was serious. She wanted me to come to the office – Neuharth's office. We were all meeting there. The books had been delivered and the CEO was not happy. Not to worry, she said. We'll fix it.

Sure, I said, and hung up the phone. Then I ran to the bathroom and threw up. I thought for sure I was going to be fired. I heard one of the kids ask Donna why Daddy was crying. Here we were with two little ones, trying to buy a house, hundreds of miles from home, and I was being called into the CEO's office, I was sure, to be fired.

I promised myself no matter what ever happened in my career, my kids would never see or hear Daddy cry again over a job. I kept that promise.

Turns out, Neuharth decided to take the blame. It was a quick fix, after all. We just re-edited the book over the course of the rest of the day, added blank pages and shipped it back to the publisher. Every one of the first 10,000 copies were destroyed and 10,000 more were printed. No one outside our small group needed to know what happened, he said.

It just took money, and the book was really being done as a marketing tool for the newly launched national newspaper, which is why Neuharth took such a big hand in it.

When we were finished, he apologized again for the drama and said he should have caught the problem. I'm not sure why he felt that way. My guess is, despite his well-earned reputation as an ass, he sensed an opportunity to nurture young editors. It would not be the last time the man who titled his autobiography "Confessions of a S.O.B" would show kindness to me and my family. He was a tough boss, but he also had a heart and after this I would have jumped through a fiery hoop for the man.

The second book that stands out was based on his travels to all 50 states, the famous "Buscapade: Plain Talk Across the USA". I traveled a little on the bus, which he rode only for short distances. In between, he flew on the luxury company jet. I was on board the bus for Rhode Island, where I introduced him to Gov. Edward DiPrete and got a big hug and kiss from Frances Segerson, assistant director of public information for the governor's office. Fran had been my first editor at the Cranston Herald, the weekly that gave me my first full-time journalism job. I learned a lot from her professionalism and journalism. I was terribly saddened to learn that she died in 2009 while on vacation in Spain.

When I was greeted warmly by the governor and then hugged by Fran, Neuharth turned to me and joked, "Hey, you're big in this town, aren't you?"

I tried to talk him into going over to Adler's Design Center and Hardware, where my college friend Harry Adler, who was in my wedding party, helped run the place. But there wasn't time.

I did a few other states on the bus, too. I went to New Hampshire, where after an extremely long day, Neuharth wanted me to cover a small-town parade for a paragraph or two in his column. He sent Ken Paulson, his chief of staff and later one of my predecessors at FLORIDA TODAY, to tell me to cover the parade.

"Really, Ken?" I pleaded. "Man, what for?"

Because the chairman wants it covered, Paulson replied.

"Well, then, maybe the chairman should go cover it," I said.

I'm still grateful Paulson never relayed that conversation to Neuharth. So much for jumping through fiery hoops.

Somehow, I ended up on the bus for Chicago, too. We went to Wrigley Field. I guess that was Paulson's way of saying thanks for the hard work.

My main function during the travels was to plan for the printing and distribution distribution of the book. We did a hardcover coffee-table-sized book, with his columns and other remembrances from all 50 states. In addition to editing it, along with many other people, I cut the deal with Waldenbooks, which agreed to buy outright 20,000 copies of the book, non-returnable or refundable. Book deals were often done on consignment, which meant we'd have to take back any books not sold. But not this one. I still have the metal plate used to stamp the hardcover title on the front of the book.

**Metal plate from the book, Buscapade: Plain Talk Across the USA.
I oversaw the printing at Arcadia Graphics in Tennessee.**

Neuharth was so pleased by the Waldenbooks' deal and how book projects were going that he took me to a World Series game on a corporate jet as a reward.

That trip seemed surreal to a young man from small towns in eastern Connecticut. We flew from Washington Dulles airport to St. Louis to watch the game and I would have slept in my own bed in Virginia that night had weather not forced us to divert to Newark, New Jersey. I came home with a bag of World Series trinkets, gifts from Neuharth for my kids.

Of course, it didn't start off so well. I was worried about the "alone time" with the chairman and what I would talk about. I asked my friend, Phil Pruitt, who knew Neuharth much better than I, what I should talk about. Relax, he said. You love baseball. He loves baseball. Talk about baseball. Neuharth was a Yankees fan, Pruitt said, so I brought up the Yankees who rehired Billy Martin for the fifth time and fired him again in the 1988 season. We were in a limo on the way to the airport and Neuharth was sitting straight across from me. A pained look came over his face.

"I wish you hadn't brought that up," he said, and then stayed silent for the rest of the car ride.

Nice.

Sometime around then I began to realize how much I missed community journalism. I began lobbying to go to a newspaper in a real community. I wanted to make a difference in a community as a daily journalist. Instead of moving me to a newspaper, I was moved to Gannett News Service, as a news editor for the regions. That got me into dozens of newsrooms to visit and try to understand their key issues. At GNS, we covered Congress and the federal agencies for the newspapers in our regions, and we played traffic cop to help with content sharing among our newsrooms.

GNS had once been the prize gem of the company, before USA TODAY came along. I was back in a newsroom, one of the finest in the country, but I was still pushing to go to a community newspaper.

In the early 1990s, I began a two-year stint of being a reverse loaner. Mostly, as a company, loaners came to corporate for USA TODAY, which was a great deal. Great experience for the journalist, cheap labor for USA TODAY. But I was being sent first to Jackson, Tenn., then Springfield, Va., and finally North Hills, Pa.

This was an amazing experience for me and, of course, I fell in love with every community I visited. Each was special. I remember walking through the pressroom in Jackson when one of the pressmen stopped me. "You're a Yankee, ain't ya?" he asked, though it was more of an accusation.

"Yep, I am. How'd you know?

"Just the way you walk."

At lunch in Jackson a pretty waitress asked me if I wanted a little extra ice when I ordered tea on a hot day. But I misunderstood her accent, and thought she said ass instead of ice. I said no thank you, but remember thinking Jackson was a friendly place.

As news delivery systems change from printing presses and paper carriers to all manner of electronic devices, I worry it comes at a cost. Communities are losing ownership of the local news outlet, and strong editors who live in and love them. It is more than printing presses and mastheads that might disappear.

I've often said news people are the only performing artists who never get to hear the audience applaud. We look for public approval in other ways. Until digital came along, we only had two ways of measuring how the audience thought we were doing, neither very precise nor personal.

One was circulation numbers, which moved up and down for lots of reasons, including internal things like service and external factors like changes in the economy. The second was the occasional market study or research, which because of their nature, were expensive and had validity only when measured over time.

Few people called the newsroom in those days to react to stories, if they could find the phone number and if we answered the phone. Email – when it came into existence – was seldom used for things like that.

So, the only feedback we ever got was internal, from colleagues and in journalism contests. I hated stories that won awards but had no positive impact in the community. I think most journalists found that frustrating.

I had a hard time breaking through, getting a job at a daily newspaper and when I did, I was completely overwhelmed by how brilliant the journalists were who already worked there. Take my first daily newsroom in Norwich, Conn. I don't know that I was ever surrounded by more motivated, passionate or talented people. They were dedicated to the mission of telling local people what was happening and helping the community become a better place to live.

That remained the case throughout my career: in large newsrooms like USA TODAY and Gannett News Service to small ones, like The Marietta (Ohio) Times. It was true in 1979 when I started in Norwich and in 2019 when I walked away from it all at FLORIDA TODAY.

And it just creeps me out when I read and hear people saying journalists are anything but committed public servants dedicated to fairness and truth telling.

I hope by taking you inside real newsrooms, to give you a chance to see through the eyes of real journalists that we can create a better understanding of what the First Amendment stands for and how a free press functions.

For more than 40 years, I had a ringside seat as an editor and reporter. I was part of the old ink-and-paper set who banged on a manual typewriter to make words and later helped lead the transition to digital – by force in some cases. What matters to me is the journalism, not the delivery mechanism. Understanding that, I think, is essential to understanding what is happening in journalism today.

I was interviewed over the phone by a reporter for Editor & Publisher magazine when I was executive editor of the Tallahassee Democrat. I had gained a reputation as helping to lead the transition to digital. The reporter asked if I thought journalism would have a better chance of survival if all the old ink-and-paper journalists went away. Maybe we should just bite the bullet and fire the old guard, he suggested.

"Gee, I hope not," I replied.

And as if the technological transition was not enough to deal with, we have come under constant attack by politicians with a vested interest in controlling how Americans think. Let's be honest, politicians have never liked the press. But we are not the enemy of the American people. Nothing could be further from the truth.

Certainly, there have been presidents who have been angry at their treatment by the media, but rarely have presidents truly believed or said aloud that we were guilty of treason.

I write this to show how things work. Sure, I write through my own perspective, but I've tried to tell it as honestly as possible. This is my story, and it is true to my best ability. Of course, it is colored by my biases and I make no claim of total objectivity.

I've never thought total objectivity was possible – or even desirable – in journalism or the recording of history. That's why we debate it and have more than one person telling it. This is a collection of my views of the stories that comprised my journalistic career, or at least the ones I've chosen to share.

That doesn't mean there is anything "fake" or untrue. It is my best effort to seek the truth as truthfully and honestly as I humanly can, without regard to political allegiance, vested interests, or personal gain. That is the best we can hope from any telling of events by humans, flawed as we are. That is what makes journalism an honorable pursuit, not some unobtainable notion of objectivity.

I hope you'll come away with a better understanding of the local press in cities and towns across the country.

Let me be clear: This is not an answer to one president, but it is a response to a feeling he has helped create that the American media is dishonest. It is a response to an attempt to discredit journalists and a response to the most objectionable T-shirt I ever saw.

The shirt was being worn by a man at a Trump rally in Minnesota. It contained the words: "Rope. Tree. Journalist. Some Assembly Required." The picture of the man wearing the shirt and the two women smiling at him went viral, of course.

Instead of arguing about whether the press is good or bad, about whether the First Amendment is good or bad, I thought I would just share my stories and let you pass your own judgment about what kind of people bring you the news every day, and the value that has to freedom in a country whose greatness emanates from how free its people feel.

"MY NAME IS JIMMY"

By: Bob Gabordi

By: Bob Gabordi

As the sunshine resplendently reflected off the silvery wings of Air Force One, the small crowd inside the Air National Guard airport suddenly grew more attentive. Outside the heavily guarded gates, along Airport Road, scores of men, women, and children waited for but a glimpse of the smiling face of the transplanted Georgian now President of the United States, Jimmy Carter. Many had stood for hours waiting in below freezing temperatures just to see the Presidential motorcade speed by. Some carried signs, hoping to catch the President's eye, but most just hoped that they might actually see the most powerful man in the world.

But at last the wheels of the official plane touched down upon Rhode Island soil, and President Carter appeared at the doorway beginning the first leg of his campaign-style trip through three New England states. Carter, who remained in the Ocean State for little more than three hours, arrived in Warwick on Friday February 16, escorted by Rhode Island's senior U.S. Senator, Claiborne Pell.

Airport Security Tight

As one might expect, for a Presidential affair, security was extremely heavy. Local and State Police, combined with Secret Service agents, estimated to be in the hundreds, made up the security force. Two arrests were made in connection with possible threats on Mr. Carter's life. It was later determined, however, that neither of the two men posed an actual threat to the President's safety.

But even Secret Service agents have a sense of humor. After being detained for more than thirty minutes by a zealous guard at the Air National Guard station at Green State Airport, I entered the main building and presented my "press credentials." These credentials were obtained after the White House staff ran security checks on every member of the press. Additionally, one day before the President's arrival, each member of the press was required to present proper identification before receiving a press pass. Only members of the press and the families of military personnel were permitted inside the gates. The general public, for security reasons, was considered "off-limits." The guard, however, was unimpressed with my press pass and ordered me to remain where I was. He informed me that if I proceeded, he would sound the alarm and I would be arrested. "Wait here," he said. "Anyone can get one of those passes," he explained. Being certain that I would be cleared, as well as being equally certain that I was not in the mood to be arrested, I followed his orders.

Thirty-five minutes later, a huge Secret Service agent approached me and asked why I was sitting inside when I had a press pass to cover the President's trip. I quickly explained to the crewcut individual my story. After showing the new man my identification, he turned to the civilian and muttered some comments that even the Quill would not print. He escorted me laughingly to my designated press area, apologizing for the inconvenience.

Finally, only two minutes behind the scheduled arrival time, the President and his official party arrived at the Airport. After some quick handshaking and "good to see you" he was ushered into an awaiting car and was off to the Rhode Island Group Health Association (RIGHA) in Providence.

President Jimmy Carter flashing his famous smile to the awaiting crowd at Green State Airport, Warwick.
Photo by Bob Gabordi

The President at RIGHA

Carter arrived at RIGHA two minutes early and was greeted by prominent members of the Rhode Island Democratic party and officials of the health center. Handshaking here was again the norm while the President met briefly with doctors, nurses, and patients. The President first went to the pediatrics section where he was greeted by a small number of children. Carter asked one little girl her name and the girl replied Michelle. He then asked, "Do you know what my name is?" Michelle did not answer and the President helpfully replied, "My name is Jimmy."

The President went from the pediatrics ward to the urgent visit unit," the name given to the areas for patients waiting for surgery, and at one point offered encouragement to a patient by speaking about his wife's operation. Last year to remove a small growth. Carter continued through the health center until he reached the lobby. At the lobby it was more "handshaking and question answering. Nineteen minutes after he first entered the building, Carter left for his nationally televised press conference at the Cranston Hilton.

I Hope He Brings a Shovel

Traffic enroute to the Hilton was heavy so I turned on the CB to see if any "good buddie" had a suggestion for a faster route. There was no suggestion for me, but one man made a suggestion for the President.

"All I know," the man advised, "is that Carter better bring a shovel to help dig us out. I bet they don't get all this snow down in Georgia. He probably never saw it before."

Apparently, the man was unaware that the President's shovel had arrived the night before, disguised as an executive declaration of Rhode Island as a major disaster area, freeing millions of dollars to the state in the wake of the "blizzard of '78."

Outside the Hilton a large number of people had gathered, some of the same crowd as at the airport had traveled to the Hilton, but few actually saw Carter outside his car.

The President arrived at the Hilton at three o'clock and immediately was given about twenty-five minutes of "free time" to prepare for a national broadcast.

During this time, I hid in the press room pretending to prepare my notes. Actually, I was hanging out amazed at the "electronic communications media" working. The equipment those people use is practically unbelievable. Their phones were supplied for "to call in stories "long distance." I tried to call my "mother" but could not figure out which button to push at which time. I was too nervous to ask for help.

After the national press conference, the President held a "regional press conference" which was little more than a campaign ploy for Senator Pell. Those in attendance were invited by the Senator. Curiously, Rep. Richard Senator Chafee did not come. The general public again, was not invited to see "the people's President."

The "regional" was actually anti-climactic. Carter had already made his point. He "likes" Pell. For me, it was the end of a long, but fulfilling couple of days. After all was said and done, I went home very tired, yet very honored.

President Carter arriving with U.S. Senator Claiborne D. Pell, D-RI.
Photo by Bob Gabordi

This story appeared in The Quill, the Roger Williams College student newspaper, and was one of the great influences on my decision to become a journalist.

CHAPTER ONE

IN THE BEGINNING...

I think I was born to be a journalist. At least it feels that way. Everything I did growing up seemed to point me in that direction, right from the start.

I don't remember being born, of course. And I didn't have a notepad or a recorder, so I cannot swear to the facts. But I've heard the story enough to know my birth was quite an event. The umbilical cord was wrapped around my neck and a limb, maybe a leg. I was blue and possibly purple. It was a close call, but I apparently lived, thank God.

At least that's my mother's version and, like so many of my mother's stories, I have no real reason to doubt them. But I'm never really sure that I should believe them either. One thing I know for sure: If I had a notepad and laptop, I would have documented my birth, so we'd know what happened. I would have had strong opinions about whatever it was, too, because that's what I do.

Let's be honest. It was MY mom the old journalist was talking about when he said: "If your mother says she loves you, check it out."

My mom was 4 feet, 10 inches tall, or thereabouts. She got up to 92 pounds once, but, of course, she was pregnant. And it occurs to me that despite her diminutive stature and the fact that she has been dead for 27 years, I probably was afraid of her. I probably still am.

Maybe that's why I've never written about her, not in 41 years as a writer and journalist. Oh, once when I was invited to hospice and they released helium-filled balloons with messages to loved ones, I complained in a column that the skyward balloons were going the wrong way. But that was just one line in a column.

Maybe because her exploits were so unnatural, I thought no one would believe them. As a journalist, I've learned it is important not only to tell the truth, but also to tell the truth in a way people believe you. That's been my promise in this book as well, so I've had to leave out a lot of stories about my mom I've wanted to share. No one would believe them.

Wait, this is not supposed to be about my mom. I'm not even comfortable talking about her with people I know, let alone writing about her for total strangers to read. Maybe I'm afraid she'll put a curse on me. I am 100 percent sure that if she could, she would, for writing about her.

I've never been too afraid for my safety in doing my job in telling the truth, not even when people threatened me, which happened twice, not when I've been pulled over and held at gunpoint by police officers, which happened once, not when I've gotten calls from deranged people, which happened I don't know how many times, and not when I've found myself in the middle of people shooting at each other, which thankfully happened just once.

I've traveled three times to Pakistan and to Turkey and Armenia once each, none of which are known for being overly friendly to journalists. Sure, at times I was a little nervous, but I was never too afraid to go or to do my job. The Turkish soldier who ordered me to stop taking photos in downtown Ankara by pointing his gun at me startled me a little, but only a little.

But my mom scared me as far back as I can remember.

Of course, even she'd admit that she had a temper on her like nobody's business. My point is I inherited that temper and had to learn the hard way to control it. Believe me, many times I wish I had taken notes about some of the stuff she did when I was growing up. What a book that would have made.

Like the time this tiny woman chased down a trucker who cut her off in traffic. I was in the car and heard every uttered expletive with my own ears. We didn't use car seats back then and if we had seat belts they probably weren't accessible. I'd guess they were tucked in the backseat crack, between the seat and the back of the car.

Imagine being the trucker. Here comes this crazy speck of a woman, driving like mad, to catch you at the next light, rolling down the passenger side window with one hand and gesturing with her middle finger with the other, saying all kinds of words.

It was just one of the times I thought I might die, collateral damage in my mom's war against people who cross her.

There are a lot of other mom stories I could tell, but I won't. I will tell you my mom was the biggest influence on my life, though she was not influential in my decision to become a journalist, except in a general way. She never really understood what I did. When I covered the real estate industry for Gannett, which created and owns USA TODAY, she told people I worked in the real estate division for USA TODAY, helping, I suppose, to acquire property for the new national newspaper.

The truth is I first started thinking about journalism when I was very young but got serious about it in the eighth grade. I only took one journalism course and that was my senior year in high school.

In no particular order, the people who influenced me the most were Diane Chaney and Ellen Madison, teachers at Ledyard High School in Connecticut, though for quite opposite reasons; Dr. Robert Gaucher, principal at Ledyard High School; and Jimmy Carter, president of the United States. Also, very important in my life was the teacher of that one and only journalism class, Norma Walrath, a magnificent teacher who also was the advisor to the student newspaper, the Colonel, the year I was editor-in-chief.

Oh, I'd throw in Jim Miller, too. He beat me out for president of the Student Senate my senior year at Roger Williams College, which enabled me to take the editor's job at The Quill, our student newspaper. That was the steppingstone to my career.

Madison, who taught English, has long since apologized indirectly for her comments to me at Ledyard High School. She once said she didn't know what I planned to do for a living, but it certainly wouldn't involve writing. Obviously, even if you don't like my writing, she was wrong. Writing and editing has paid the bills for a long time and helped put my kids through college. Truth is she was a great teacher and I've always admired her, though I'm glad she was wrong about my writing.

It has been my second greatest love. The hater who posted on a blog that said the only reason I was a newspaper editor was that I wasn't a good enough baseball coach to earn a living from it was right, as was the guy who called me a frustrated Little League coach in a suit, except that I rarely wear suits.

I turned to journalism in earnest when I realized I would never be good enough to play second base for the New York Mets. I turned to coaching at about the same time. I wrote an autobiography once that started off saying that I told Donna before we married that three things would always be important to me: my family, my journalism, and the New York Mets, and, when the Mets are winning, not necessarily in that order.

But I thought about Madison's words when things got tough in trying to get my first job, then again when things would get hard at work, kind of a reverse incentive. And, in fairness, there is a picture of me somewhere with a jacket over my head trying to take a nap in her classroom. You can understand where she'd get the idea that I lacked motivation.

Diane Chaney, on the other hand, taught Latin and was advisor to the student newspaper. She wasn't that much older than her students and I totally had a crush on her. So, I took Latin and signed up for the student newspaper. She told me I had a talent for this kind of thing – newspaper work, not Latin. And she was the first person to suggest it might be something I consider as a career.

It was an option, she said, and maybe a better one than going down to Electric Boat or the summer job that I had for two weeks as the screwdriver operator at the place that made those glass bar lights. I quit that job – right before they fired me for telling one of the bosses to, well, you know what I said. After all, I was my mother's son. That job, by the way, convinced me that I might be college material after all. I accepted Roger Williams' invitation to enroll.

Chaney was killed in the summer before my senior year in high school in a motorcycle crash in Jamaica. She obviously affected a lot of us. We planted a tree in her honor in front of the school. I keep meaning to check if it is still there.

Gaucher was a great influence on me in many ways and he taught me everything I ever would need to know about the First Amendment. I wrote something critical of him. I think it had to do with school policy prohibiting students from wearing bell-bottom jeans. I thought the policy was goofy and clearly stepped on our Constitutional rights to free expression in our clothing.

I mean it was the early 1970s and people were marching in the streets over the war in Vietnam, racial inequity, and sexual freedom. Women were burning their bras and going shirtless, which as a teenage boy, was fine with me. But my big issue, apparently, was bell-bottom jeans.

Of course, I got called down to "The Office" and I figured I was going to be suspended or given detention or told we just couldn't print that kind of stuff in the school newspaper. I figured on a Constitutional battle. I figured I'd stand behind my words and was prepared to argue that men had died in war to protect my right to publish such criticism.

I was already a hero, in my own mind.

What I didn't figure was Gaucher being such a stand-up guy. We talked for quite some time about the First Amendment and what it means. My words hurt, he said, and I should remember that words always matter because they are so powerful. That said, he never said we couldn't publish the column. In fact, it had already been released for publication.

But I should know, and would have known if I had taken the time to speak with him prior to publication, that the ban on bell-bottoms came from his bosses on the school board and he thought the whole issue to be a silly waste of time.

I left his office feeling contrite and humble, but with a stronger respect for the First Amendment. It had just allowed me to criticize the most powerful person in my world and be wrong.

Jimmy Carter came into my life four years later when I was a senior at Roger Williams. He had the habit as president of trying to escape the clutches of the Washington press corps as often as possible. I was sitting at my desk as editor of The Quill when I got a phone call inviting me to his press conference in Providence. The president wanted to make sure the local press was given the chance to attend. Oh, and by the way, would I be interested in spending a few minutes with him afterward?

Of course, I replied. I tried hard not to act as giddy as I felt. I took my camera and shot a photograph. I really don't remember much from the interview. It would be wrong to try to tell you more about it. But two things: It cemented my decision to pursue journalism and I remember thinking that journalism really matters.

I was a college senior majoring in political studies, editing the college newspaper and because of that was able to talk to the president of the

United States. I was wowed and overwhelmed, but I really tried not to let on.

It would not be the only time the Carter family would intersect with my career.

I had already figured out that I would lean, politically speaking, toward the Republican Party. In my final semester in college, I did an internship working with Jim Reynolds, a Republican candidate for U.S. Senate, who would lose to incumbent Democrat Claiborne Pell in what was a solidly Democratic state. It was an ass whipping.

Reynolds was a novice and while the campaign was sprinkled with professionals, most were like me, political newbies. My goal was mainly educational when I started working with Reynolds: I wanted to see what real politics was like from the inside. Keep in mind I was a political studies major. A close friend did the same internship, except in the Pell campaign, and ended up working for him for years.

Reynolds might have been a newcomer to politics, but he was tough and played to win. Providence Mayor Buddy Cianci was rumored to be interested in forcing a primary by jumping into the race against Reynolds. Cianci was a tough guy, too. I would have loved to have been a fly on the wall when Reynolds and Cianci met face-to-face.

All I know is Cianci didn't get into the race, though later he was forced to resign from the mayor's office when he pleaded nolo contendere to federal charges brought against him. The charge had to do with an alleged assault on a man who Cianci thought was having an affair with his estranged wife. The man and Cianci's wife denied the affair.

But Reynolds must've had "something" on Cianci, that's all I know. The rumor was it had to do with a woman other than Cianci's wife. I don't know how Reynolds got it, and I really don't know if he threatened to use it should Cianci get in the race, but he didn't get in. End of story. Except, he wasn't particularly helpful to Reynolds in the campaign.

I graduated that spring, but Reynolds asked me to join the campaign full-time and assume additional media duties. My heart was set on being a journalist, but I was young and learning, so I stayed on with him.

Two things stand out: A woman in the campaign said to me that sex is a big factor in every campaign and that I shouldn't be shocked by that. I wasn't, but I can honestly say I also have no direct knowledge of the matter.

The second big revelation was that the media wrote us off early on, which was a little bit of a surprise, but then it felt as if they set about proving they were right. They were. But it still seemed unfair and not at all what I thought was their proper role. I tried to remember that as a lesson in not influencing the outcomes of elections.

It was the second time in my life I remembered being disappointed in the behavior of my future colleagues. The first was when I was a little kid. My new stepfather, Chief Petty Officer Richard J. Tourville, was coming home aboard the USS Intrepid in the late 1960s from his second tour of duty in Vietnam.

I guess I had expected big banner news headlines, brass bands, and celebrations on the dock. None of that happened. I remember thinking it was wrong at the time – I must've been in fifth or sixth grade. I remember thinking it was not like the movie clips of the big parades that greeted returning servicemen after World War II. I filed that away for the future, too.

By the way, the USS Intrepid is a grand old ship, with a history stretching back to World War II. Commissioned in August 1943, the Intrepid was an Essex-class carrier that is now a floating museum in New York City. My sons, Alex and Rob, and Rob's wife, Tracie, joined me on a visit to the ship for my 60th birthday.

Sons Alex and Rob and me standing in front of the USS Intrepid on my 60th birthday. Photo by Tracie Alexander Gabordi

But back to Election Day 1978. Reynolds, of course, got significantly more votes than the media polls had predicted, but still lost in what could only be called a massive landslide, 75 percent to 25 percent. Polls in the closing days of the campaign showed Reynolds with 10 percent of the vote. Pell would serve a total of six terms in the Senate, retiring after 36 years.

During the campaign, I had gotten friendly – for lack of a better word – with M. Charles Bakst, the Providence Journal's legendary political columnist. To be honest, I thought he was kind of an ass, but I was a kid and he was the very best at what he did, so I don't think he cared what I thought. One day, I asked to talk to him, seeking career advice. My fault for asking his opinion. But I did, violating one of my own rules through the years: Don't ask the question if you don't want to hear the answer.

I asked Charlie how I could get back on a journalism track after the campaign.

"You can't," he said. "You're damaged goods. No one will ever hire you." And he just walked away.

That conversation is why I accepted a job with a group of weeklies in January, primarily covering Cranston, R.I., where future Gov. Ed DiPrete was the Republican mayor. I liked and respected DiPrete and it broke my heart years later when he pleaded guilty to bribery, extortion, and racketeering and was sentenced to a year in prison.

His plea was part of a deal in which charges against a family member were dropped. I always felt he took the deal to protect his family. I guess we'll never know, but I will tell you that I never believed this was anything but dirty Rhode Island politics.

My stay in Cranston was brief, but memorable, though not from a journalism standpoint. I thumbed through some of my old articles and jeez, I was not very good. Advice to veteran reporters, throw away your first articles. You'll gag trying to reread your work. At least I did.

Donna and I were living in Cranston, of course, with me working as a reporter, but she was still going to Roger Williams and commuting every day to Bristol. We couldn't afford a second car, so she was doing the bus thing. I would pick her up in Providence to avoid bus transfers.

One evening in my rush I locked my keys inside the newspaper office. That meant I couldn't unlock the front door to the building to get out and I couldn't get back inside the newspaper office to get the keys. I was trapped. None of this would have been a big deal if I had had a cell phone, but, you know, it was 1979 and, well, no one had cell phones.

I tried to force open a window, but thrust my left hand through the glass, nearly severing my index finger. Blood was gushing out of my body. The broken window set off the alarm, which caused Cranston police to show up. That probably saved my life. The officer knew me from work, and he rushed me to the emergency room. Apparently, before I passed out, I asked him to call the Providence bus terminal to alert Donna. Instead, he just went and got her and brought her to the hospital. Thank goodness for that officer.

We had only been married a couple weeks. Oh, what a trouper Donna was going to have to be.

CHAPTER TWO

YOU CAN CALL ME BOB

Norwich is a grand old city connected to New London and Groton via the Thames River. It was there that I wanted to work, and I applied and applied for job after job.

Now before we go any further, I think we should discuss my name. Everyone calls me Bob, except close family members, who still call me Bobby. Unless you are related, please call me Bob.

Now I think Robert is a fine name, and mom was partial to it, especially in my bylines when I first started working. In fact, she called the newspaper that hired me for my first full-time job as a reporter at a daily. Wait, let me repeat that so it sinks in: she called the newspaper that hired me for MY FIRST FULL-TIME JOB to get a correction because my byline listed me as Bob Gabordi.

She called the main number, which transferred her to the newsroom clerk, who transferred her to the copy desk chief, who transferred her to my direct editor. I'm sure that all this transferring was done just to make sure the largest possible number of my colleagues heard the story about the crazy woman who called to get my byline corrected.

Somehow, she ended up with the managing editor, a fellow named Jim Docker, who called me in to talk about it.

Of course, Docker had explained that the newspaper's policy was to use the name the reporter wished to be known by, to which my dear mother replied:

"Well, it's wrong, and I should know, I named the little bastard."

**(From left to right) My Aunt Gloria, Grandfather Angelo
and my mother, Evelyn. All three died relatively young,
and shared great passion for their family.**

Of course, Docker insisted that I immediately change my byline to Robert Gabordi to avoid any further calls on the matter from the crazy lady. But, at least for a while, Docker referred to me as the "little bastard." It was an inside joke and Docker, thank goodness, thought it was funny.

I should probably tell you that it wasn't Docker's first encounter with my mom. More on that in a bit.

Now I felt like a journalist. I started work at that job on Dec. 10, 1979, and Donna and I had been married for six months. Roger Williams allowed Donna to finish her credits at a local community college, which enabled me to pursue my dream.

The weeklies in Rhode Island paid me $105 per week. I was happy and it was fun work, but I couldn't pay the bills – at least not all of them – especially once we got married. By the way, I was a Resident Assistant when Donna walked into the lobby on my first day on the job. That was the day I decided to marry her and three years later, I did. Our first date was to a New England Patriots game in Foxborough where the Patriots thumped the New York Jets on "Monday Night Football." It started snowing like hell while we were still in the parking lot for the 40-mile ride back to

Roger Williams. But we made it back to the dorm safely and I was deeply in love. And not just with Donna, either. That night cemented what would be a lifetime relationship with the Patriots, too. Did I mention I have a grandson named Brady?

OK, so back to Docker and my mom. I was eager to get a full-time job in which I could make more money than the $105 per week I was making before taxes. My dilemma was Donna was still in school. I went to the publisher of the weeklies and explained my situation. He offered to help, because he didn't want to lose me. I was a fine reporter, he said, and worth it.

But instead of a raise, he offered to go over my budget with me to see how I could make the $105 per week go further. That just pissed me off and I got more serious about my job hunt. In December, I got a call back from the Norwich Bulletin, near my hometown in Connecticut.

My interview, such as it was, with Docker took place more or less in a bar. Let me clarify, we were definitely in the bar, Billy Wilson's Aging Still. But the bar and the newspaper were kind of in the same building. The newspaper building wrapped around the bar. I wasn't much of a drinker in those days so most of what I remember from the interview was Docker being surprised with how well I did. He called me a "diamond in the rough." I wasn't sure what that meant, but he offered me a job on the spot: $175 a week to start. As with my old job, unlimited hours, meaning whatever it took to get the job done. That was before federal Labor Department rules were formulated to apply to reporters. I'm kind of glad about that, though. It meant I could cram two or three years of on-the-job learning into my first six months. Woohoo!

Oh, two things, Docker said, by the way: I'd be starting off in a bureau, about 45 miles north of Norwich working for a character named Don Bond, and could I please get my mom to stop calling him to get me the interview.

Good Lord! I had no idea she was doing that. Of course, Jim didn't really believe me that I had nothing to do with my mom's calls, until he got to know more about her. Then, it was totally believable.

I soon headed off to the Danielson bureau, covering the most northeastern towns in the state – Woodstock and Thompson. From there

I was promoted to the Groton bureau, covering the city of New London and soon was promoted to bureau chief.

I never measured up to the reporter who came before me as bureau chief in Groton, Nancy Gallinger, neither as a writer nor as a manager. But I kept getting promoted and moved. That would be the story of my career.

I was promoted from the Groton bureau to assistant city editor in the main office. Making the jump from bureau chief and respected young reporter to an editor's job was not easy. I knew reporting. Loved reporting. But I was consumed with wanting to be a senior editor and the career path of becoming a junior editor first made sense. When Gannett bought the Bulletin, Terri Gannett Hopkins became the publisher. She was from a different Gannett family than the namesakes of the company; at least she wasn't a direct descendant of Frank Gannett.

She called a lot of us into her office to meet one-on-one and talk about career goals. I was young and brash, I suppose, but I told her I wanted her job running things.

It was going to be an uphill climb.

In those days, obituaries were considered news and flowed through the news desk. Junior editors took turns editing the obits, which were taken over the phone by clerks. We took great care with obituaries, thinking – as I had been taught to do – for most people, it was their last chance to get their name published in the newspaper.

For most, they only were in the newspaper when they were born, graduated high school, got married and died. Most liked that just fine. The thing you didn't want to do is screw up somebody's obituary.

So, there I was reading obit copy for the first time and was surprised by the number of large funeral services planned. Large as in massive Christian burials, which, of course, should have read Mass of Christian burials.

The paper came out with these embarrassing errors that I should have caught. It was my fault. The next day, my new editor, Tom Curley, was standing over me inviting me to his office. After a good lecture, he said to me that he wasn't sure what to do with me: He'd demote me, he said, but I was already so junior I was editing obituaries. There wasn't much lower to go. He'd fire me, he said, but I was too smart with too much upside potential for that. So, the tongue lashing would have to do, he said.

Ironically, it was the first time an editor ever told me I was smart and could have a big career in the business. Obviously, I never forgot the lecture.

Let's back up a bit. I warned you good stories get me off track. Let's go back to the Danielson bureau, where I worked under, as I said earlier, a character named Don Bond. I learned a lot about being a boss by watching him and making a mental note that was not how I would do things. And I didn't. Except once or twice or no more than a handful of times.

One of those times actually involved him. As I began to advance in management and moved up to various senior editor roles, years after leaving The Bulletin, I bumped into Bond. It was during a phone call to a former colleague and Bond just wanted to say hi.

"I keep waiting for the announcement that you are coming back here," he said.

"Bondo," I replied without a second's hesitation, "you better hope that doesn't happen. That would be your signal to pack up your shit and kiss your ass goodbye."

I have little doubt I was serious, though I was trying to sound funny. I also know that was terribly unfair.

Bond was the type of person – as a reporter – you could love and hate at the same time. Looking back, I see that he was enormously talented and a royal pain in the ass. I have no doubt he made me a better journalist. I'm only surprised I wasn't killed in the process.

I was just starting out in the bureau, covering the towns of Woodstock and Thompson in the northeastern corner of Connecticut. Together, they were 110 square miles of mostly woods. The combined population was less than 18,000. I joked that I reported on the activities of lots and lots of trees and winding New England roads.

One day in January with the temperatures reaching 18 degrees, Christopher Labonte, 3, wandered away from his Thompson home with the family dog, 11-year-old Mitzi, a beagle crossbreed.

It set off a huge community search. State police and other first responders were aided by a massive number of volunteers.

State police set up headquarters in a small camper trailer. Bond sent me out to cover the search with instructions not to come back until it was over one way or the other. It was bitterly cold. When I needed to, I'd return to my car to get warm.

When the sun went down, it felt hopeless. Not just for me ever getting warm again, but the search had grown grim. It was hard to imagine this little boy being found alive.

Information was scarce but whatever was available would come from the state police trailer. I went to the door and knocked, hoping to be invited in for a minute or two of warmth, even if there was no news. I looked through the window and there was Bond yucking it up with the troopers, drinking coffee and smoking a cigarette.

An officer came to the door and quickly left. Bond came next and told me in no uncertain terms to go away, that he would handle the cop shop and any information to be had from there. I was not to come back until he called for me.

The truth is it was probably a good idea for him to handle the cops. He was more experienced and had worked cops for his whole career. I was more effective working people stories out on the search. He had the personality of a bad gunman in a John Wayne movie.

But he could have explained that. And he could have let me get warm for a minute. I would tell him that later and he just shrugged it off, saying he didn't think the cops wanted me inside the trailer and they might have kicked him out, too, meaning we'd lose our inside connection. He was probably right about that, too, and as it turned out, that was very important to us.

After 18 hours, little Christopher was found six miles from his home in Burrillville, R.I., alive and cuddled up to his dog, which probably saved his life. Bond knew the boy had been found first because he was in the trailer. So, he was right to have wanted someone inside the cop shop. If only he had not been such an ass about it.

That would not be the only big story I would handle during my Danielson stint. Two others did not involve trying to stay warm. One got incredibly hot.

How do I best describe my five years working for my hometown daily? Thrilling? For sure. Educational? No doubt. Amazing? Absolutely.

But maybe the best single word to describe the place from the perspective of 40 years is crazy. The Bulletin has dropped Norwich from its official name to reflect the importance of its regional status, especially for Northeastern Connecticut, which is where I got my start.

Again, let's backtrack. A few months after I started at The Bulletin, a guy named Al Neuharth walked in and said the Gannett Company had just purchased the place, but not the bar, Billy Wilson's Aging Still, which the Oat family retained. I don't know why I was in the main office that day, but I was and could tell employees had mixed emotions about losing the bar.

It had a special place in the hearts of employees. I was interviewed there, as I mentioned, and that should have been a clue.

But from time to time, editors would have a few drinks in the bar and then challenge employees to snake races up the stairway on your belly. One of the copy editors had the nickname Snake, I'm told, because he was really good at the game.

On the other hand, there is a reason not to mix drinking with a business known for deadline stresses. It never happened to me, but I heard that on occasion senior people might drink too much and come up to the newsroom and fire someone. Not to worry, I was told, because you would get the rest of the night off and they would hire you back the next day, usually with a token raise.

Getting fired was always a worry, especially in the family-owned newspaper days. I was sure I was going to get canned one time for smashing the front of a company car into one of those majestic gray-stone walls that lined the twisting, narrow roads in small-town Eastern Connecticut.

I got called into Publisher Donald Oat's office that time, and I know I was shaking when I went in. I should say the Oats were always good to me – the publisher especially. He always took an interest in me – though I wasn't sure why. After he sold The Bulletin to Gannett, we decided to do a feature story on him, and he asked for me to write it.

On the day I was called into his office, instead of firing me, he just wanted to make sure I was OK. It had been snowing hard and I was headed to what had been reported as a possible house fire, so I was probably driving too fast.

Anyway, there was little damage to either the car or me, and the house fire was minor, too, so all's well that ends well, I guess.

I won my first journalism award while working at The Bulletin, and for a long time, it was my only award. It was not for writing, but for photography and before all the photojournalists I've tormented over the years fall out laughing, I should admit it was a lucky shot. Not for the borough of Danielson, which was ablaze, but for me.

I got a call from Bond that there was a fire and I should get out to cover it. I think Donna and I had settled down for the night in our apartment. "Look out the window; you'll see it. Head toward the flames," he said. "Grab your camera, shoot a bunch of film and we'll send someone to pick it up. Move!"

The phone rang again as soon as we hung up. It was one of the photographers from the main office telling me how to bracket the F stops or something like that. I raced down the steps and – like Bond had said – followed the flames. It wasn't hard to do. I felt the heat as soon as I walked outside. It looked like the whole downtown was on fire. I picked up the camera and started shooting, one roll and then another.

I was loading a third roll when the car pulled up next to me. It was one of the guys from the bureau. "Gimme what you got. Gotta go. Trying to make press start and they're holding the page," he yelled out of the rolled down window. I ran over and handed him the film. "You've got 30 minutes. Call in what you got," he said.

I worried that I didn't have much and doubted I would get more. I remember thinking what if my film is blurry? What if the film is blank? What if I exposed it in trying to load the camera?

I don't remember what I got for copy, but called it in on time. The copy editor said it was good enough, but if I got more to call back in 15 minutes and I could help write a cutline for the photo. I did, but the photo almost didn't need a cutline. At least not much of one. It had big, billowing, and gorgeous flames.

It makes me sad that I loved that shot so much. It won a first-place award in some contest or another, but the fire was only a few blocks from my home. I couldn't help but wonder and worry about people who lost their jobs in the flames, who could've lost their lives. It was the journalist's job – my job – to document whatever happened, to question official and unofficial accounts of news events so that we would know the truth of what happened and why.

I was up the rest of the night doing exactly that and then thinking about the responsibility involved in that. Keeping that in mind would serve me well in my career, and in the next major fire I covered, it was almost prophetic.

I had been on the job in Danielson for about four months when a fire was reported in the tiny town of Sterling. The Revere Textile Mill, which employed more than 200 and stood in the town for more than 100 years, was on fire. The flames turned the entire sky orange and could be seen 16 miles from Danielson.

Sterling is roughly 27 square miles. Its population in 1980 was about 1,900. It is double that today. The textile mill was the only visible means of support for many who lived there.

I don't recall how I got this assignment or why I was asked to stay on the story after the initial blaze, but I was, and I'm grateful for that, because I learned so much about local journalism on this story.

The chief of the fire department was Charles Rabbit, who had the unfortunate nickname of Bunny, of course. I learned that when I went to his front door, knocked and was greeted by his wife, who called to him saying, "Bunny, the reporter is here to see you."

I needed to regain my composure quickly. Rabbit was very professional in his demeanor and approach and I was at his home on important and serious business. I had no proof, but I thought I knew who started the fire. I certainly didn't have enough information to write a story about it, though enough to mention in a story about the fire. I just want to tell someone who was in position to do something with what I knew.

The night before at the fire scene, a plant security guard came up to me, asked which media outlet I worked for, and proceeded to tell me a story, saying I would want to take notes. He was making his rounds, he said, when he saw a flash come from one of the distant buildings through a window. He then noticed a man running toward a chain-link fence. The man, he said, climbed over the fence and escaped in the darkness.

The guard would retell that story to investigators later.

I was standing near a crowd of onlookers, many of whom had worked at the mill and were watching their livelihoods burn. It is hard to overestimate what that plant meant to the economy of that small town and the lives of those people. The plant would never be rebuilt, of course, at least not there. The townspeople and the state didn't just shrug their shoulders in collective resignation to their fate. They fought back and my job was to document their efforts.

Now, I told the police and Rabbit that I suspected the security guard was lying. I had no proof, of course, but his story was just too pat, too neat, too much to be true. The security guard would eventually be suspected of setting the fire, but before he could be prosecuted, he was charged and convicted in an unrelated manslaughter in the death of Kimberly Gagne, 17.

At the very least, he was believed to have known how the fire started, whether a stray cigarette or whatever.

Alan Gaumond, who worked for Northeast Security, was convicted of first-degree manslaughter in Gagne's death. According to published reports, he admitted to smashing her head with a 47-pound rock after she tried to make him stop selling drugs to her friends.

The night of the fire, if nothing else, he was guilty of failing to do his job as watchman. Police investigated his story of the man running away from the building. Police believed the man, if he even existed, had nothing to do with starting the fire.

When I left my apartment in Danielson, I could see the orange sky from flames at the textile plant. Rabbit's firefighters did all they could to contain the fire, which destroyed the mill complex. Their effort was heroic, although it was hampered by the failure of the sprinkler system.

The New York Times, in an article dated Sept. 15, 1985, noted the opening of a new industrial park on land adjacent to where the mill had been. The park was a way for the 200 former Revere employees – of whom 175 had come from Sterling Village – to find employment. Most of the other textile jobs in New England had already moved South before heading overseas.

I had traveled with the town's selectmen – a kind of three-person ruling tribunal with duties typical of what you might see belonging to both a town council and mayor's office elsewhere – for meetings with economic development officials in Hartford.

This was government in action, and I had a great view from the backseat of the car. They even brought me into meetings with state officials. I took notes on it all as they worked to get funding to build a new industrial park.

How had it happened? I guess the politicians cared more about governing in those days than adding up votes. There was only a relative handful of votes in the whole town, probably not enough to make a difference in most statewide elections, so somebody must've really cared about what happened to Sterling the night of the big fire.

As for the selectmen, well, I got to see them up close, too close probably, on the loose in the big city of Hartford. Some tales are best left untold, even 40 years later.

I would have one more memorable, shocking-to-me, story before being transferred to the Groton bureau. I was assigned to cover a Ku Klux Klan rally. Yes, the Klan. In Connecticut. In the late 1970s and early 1980s, Imperial Wizard Bill Wilkinson attempted to show his "pro-white" and "pro-Christian" movement was gaining ground in the North.

The Klan wanted and got media attention. Wilkinson was very good at getting publicity and preying on people looking for someone to blame for the deep economic troubles and political weakness we were feeling as a nation at that time. So, the Klan came to the very rural town of Scotland in Windham County and scores of journalists – me included – were assigned to write stories about it. It was all part of his marketing efforts and he was very good at that.

It was September 1980. Gas prices had jumped from about 36 cents per gallon in 1970 to about $1.19 in 1980 and had jumped about 33 cents in a year. It was the first time in our history we were paying more than a buck for a gallon of gasoline.

America was officially in a recession, with inflation at more than 12.5 percent and the fed rate – used by financial institutions to set interest rates – at 18 percent. The jobless rate was 7.2 percent and would get worse before it got better.

Worse than all that, America's morale and standing were in decline. In 1979, the president, Jimmy Carter, who was one year away from losing to Ronald Reagan in one of the most one-sided defeats by an incumbent in history, gave a speech that told Americans that we – and our values – were to blame.

Well, someone had to be blamed, right? Wilkinson and the Klan made it easier for white Americans to digest. It wasn't all of us, just those people – the blacks, immigrants, Jews, people of Middle Eastern descent. He told us why we were hurting and whose fault it was. Membership in the Klan was growing, he said. But he wouldn't give specifics.

So, he rented some farmland in Scotland, Conn, for his rally. I remember one press conference that had more than 55 journalists there. I'm sure they, like me, had been told by their editors to go. But so many journalists covering what amounted to a domestic terrorist, provided exactly what he wanted: publicity. It made no sense. Again, I made a mental note: This is not how I would do things when I became the editor.

The day before the rally, some of us had been able to go back and forth on the rally site relatively easily. We'd get stopped and questioned by some Klansmen, but my being Catholic wasn't a reason to keep me out. The question was asked, however. Sometimes, they poke us with a pointed stick, like kids playing war in the backyard. But their guns were real, and these were no kids. These games were ugly and no fun at all.

My colleague, Antar Makansi, who was of darker skin than my olive Italian heritage gave me, hitched a ride on a horse. He chatted for a while with a woman who was taking part in the rally.

"Then she offered to take me in. That was on the Saturday, the open and friendly day of the event," he recalled in a recent exchange of Facebook messages with me. "On Sunday, when the PR stopped, I was prevented from entering the site."

Seeing Antar on that horse riding onto the site was one of my strongest memories from that weekend. It was funny, in the something-is-wrong-with-this-picture kind of way, not the jovial way.

Police searched cars entering the area. I recall one car's trunk filled with guns. That was not a jovial image either. This was the symbol of what the Klan stood for: hate and a chance to hell raise.

There was one more not-so-jovial memory. Honestly, I don't remember who did what first. I'm not sure anyone knows. But I was standing with a photographer near an intersection with various groups marching – or in the case of the bikers, riding – toward each other. Shots were fired. I don't think they were fired at anyone, and no one was hit that I knew of, but I quickly jumped behind one of those gray stone walls New England small towns are famous for, grateful to the forefather who erected it.

Later, as I was typing my story, I recall an editor screaming in my ear that my story lacked "color." Frustrated, angry, and still a bit shaky from the day's events, on deadline, I said words I knew my mother would have used. A cleaned-up version went like this: "Color? Do you want to know the shades of the leaves falling from the trees? Color? I'm still shaking as I type."

I would run into that editor again years later when Gannett purchased the newspaper he worked at. I had been loaned to the new team, brought in to – among other duties – assess employees and help decide who we would keep. We had a good laugh over that encounter in Scotland. He was a good editor. We kept him.

With a Personality of Its O

By ROBERT GABORDI
Bulletin Staff Writer

WILLIMANTIC — The first one-man grand jury investigation into the Christmas Eve 1973 hit-and-run death of Kevin B. Showalter in New London heard 107 witnesses during 26 sessions from July to December 1977 to reach a "probable" conclusion on the driver of the hit-and-run vehicle.

Throughout the 1977 proceedings, the recently constructed Superior Courthouse in Willimantic was the scene of a running game of hide and seek with court and law enforcement officials and witnesses trying to dodge the prying eyes of reporters.

The cast of characters involved in the first grand jury would have done justice to either a True Confession magazine story or an episode of Perry Mason, but instead was allegedly the basis for an episode of the Lou Grant newspaper-based show.

The reconvening of the grand jury during the last month has resurrected the confusion, rumors and secrecy that dogged the first installment, and brought back together some of the leading players in the first court drama, along with new characters associated with the alleged new information on the case.

But, perhaps nothing has remained as much the same during the two sets of hearings as the role of the media. It's a simple role, one of waiting basically, but at times it is as complex as a father-to-be in the maternity waiting room — day after day, after day.

Called to investigate the alleged confession of a 31-year-old carpenter at General Dynamics-Electric Boat, Paul C. Hansen of East Lyme, the present Showalter one-man grand jury has seen

a glimpse of who is walking into the hearing room; day to day, it is the same routine.

Everyone is afraid they will be suspected of being a "source." The secrecy of the proceedings is so guarded that many of the people who work at the courthouse, whose presence during the hearings is required, do not know from day-to-day when the grand jury will be in session.

"I really didn't know it was on for today until you guys (the press) showed up. It shows how much they tell me," one court official remarked.

There is the waiting, the walking up and down the courthouse foyer where stone blocks from a floor (there are exactly 226 stone blocks on the floor).

Passing the time while witnesses are secluded inside the grand jury room is the major preoccupation of the press. One way is to "make up" witnesses. The only problem is that sometimes the real witnesses seem even more unbelievable.

Sometimes the search for the tid-bits of information is less than successful. After a young woman testified, a reporter tracking down her identity tried to trace her car registration number. The car's registration proved to be of no help. But at least it gave the reporter something to do.

On some occasions, things happen outside the courthouse to attract reporters' attention.

Once a reporter from a local newspaper lent a hand in directing traffic outside the courthouse after a would-be Willimantic school bus bandit abandoned the bus in the middle of a city street. The thief, it seems, forgot to release the emergency brake and the smoke from the overheated brake caused him to flee.

For some, who have written about, investigated, or in some other manner been connected with the Showalter hearings, this has been a chance to

pected her to look much older,

Another person, a courthouse shown on television news broad escort Mrs. Showalter. He rela that a member of his family as know her? What is she like?"

Hansen is the man who gave opening of the grand jury which two years ago that former New Harvey Mallove was the "more driver" of the hit-and-run car.

Hansen believes that after spe drinking, he might have been th death car. By all accounts, he is likes to be alone, and shys away His decision to come forward to thought to stem from long-held nightmares.

There seems little reason to di a suspect, but the lack of a signif witness testimony presented in t appears to do just that. Little is Hansen's background, but rumor motivation and private life.

Satti, the State's Attorney for ty, is the man responsible for br to the grand juror. The direction case, the point he is trying to ma knowledge he is trying to bring him and apparently him alone. T after hearing several days of tes still has no idea what this is all a

Satti's office, and the state's at have been publicly criticized by t mother. On several occasions, sh his ouster from the case. Evidenc brought to the present hearings b

CHAPTER THREE

JOURNALISM LIMITS – SHOWALTER CASE

My strongest and most lasting memories of covering the Showalter hit-and-run mystery was of a sore backside. This was the most high-profile local story of the decade in eastern Connecticut, and I was assigned to cover the second session of a one-man grand jury investigation in October 1980.

The one-man grand jury is a tool used in only a few states and is purely investigative in scope. It is pretty heady stuff, but my head was not the body part that was most valuable to my journalism right then.

Sitting on the cold, hard floor while witnesses testified, then getting up and trying to talk to them as they came and went, usually brushing by you, looking for tiny pieces of information. My journalism was comprised of trying to figure out not only what they told the one-man grand juror, Superior Court Judge Joseph F. Dannehy, but also what they might be willing to tell me about it. That was my entire existence. Morning to night, all day long, sitting, getting up and chasing, then sitting again. Over and over.

The truth is they would say very little. The truth is, while I didn't know it at the time, they had very little to say. No one believed Paul C. Hansen was the mysterious hit-and-run driver, except maybe Paul C. Hansen. And that meant that hour after hour we sat on that floor, knowing there was not likely to be anything new and that we would have to go back, put a new top on an old story, and convince our editors we had to be there – just in case.

It got to be a hard sell. Everyone knew he wasn't the driver.

Hansen had come forward to confess to driving the car that killed Kevin Showalter, 21, of New London, on Christmas Eve 1973. That confession, the deranged ramblings of a deranged mind, caused this entire circus to come back together. But it was nothing more than a shell game, an attempt by the magician to draw your attention away from the hand actually holding the coin.

I would go home at night and want nothing more than to soak in a hot tub and nurse my sore rear end, and to think about this story, how I might break something loose, and dread the next day. So much of journalism depends primarily on two body parts: a brain for thinking analytically and a sturdy bottom for sitting and waiting for new developments.

I had been married just more than a year at that point, and I had to worry that my bride would think someone had stolen her husband's brain. Every night I would come home, crawl into the tub and have absolutely nothing to talk about because there was absolutely nothing new. I didn't even drink in those days, so I couldn't even find comfort in a beer bottle.

I guess that's how my editors felt, that someone had stolen my brain when I would argue to keep covering this fiasco.

On Christmas Eve 1973, when this story began, I was a high school senior. No doubt I was cooking for the family in our home in Gales Ferry, making our traditional Italian fish dishes, but guarding what I ate to make sure I could still make the 119-weight class. That became difficult, by the way, as a tri-captain for the state champion Ledyard wrestling team.

That was the most important thing in my life then, as it should have been.

Meanwhile, that night on a well-lighted Pequot Avenue in nearby New London, a young man was changing a tire on his girlfriend's car when another vehicle struck him and vanished into the night. A college student, Showalter died and the driver of the car that killed him was never charged, despite what would become the most expensive hit-and-run investigation in Connecticut history.

A prominent New London citizen became the most likely suspect in what many of us thought of as the most incredible cover up. Small town politics wanted this case to just go away, but the strong will of Kevin's mother, Lucille Showalter, and a herd of journalists over the years, would not let it.

The prominent citizen was former New London Mayor Harvey Mallove, a downtown merchant. He was close personal friends with presiding New London County Superior Court Judge Angelo G. Santaniello, who did nothing to remove himself from involvement in the case, even after Dannehy issued a ruling in 1973 that it was "more probable than not" that Mallove was driving the car that killed Kevin Showalter.

Even now, years later with most of the key players deceased, I hold out hope that someday the truth will become known. The bad guys are not supposed to win. The truth is supposed to prevail. I believed that then and I still do. It was unfathomable that it could turn out otherwise. But it did.

Ask me why we still need a free and vibrant press in America and my long answer always begins by telling about this case. The truth did not win in this case, but, with a free press, at least it had a fighting chance, Lucille Showalter had a fighting chance.

The time that Showalter was struck was fixed at 11:11 p.m. The girl with him, Debra Emilyta, said she did not get a good look at the car that pulled away. Neither did any other witness. They all said all they saw was vanishing tail lights in the darkness.

When Lucille Showalter showed up at the New London police station two weeks later to collect her son's personal belongings, she was told they were missing and that the case would never be solved. Go home, she was told. And that was supposed to be that. They didn't know Lucille Showalter very well.

I can understand why they could underestimate her. They were the police in 1970s' America and they had everything lined up. How do you investigate with no evidence? No one saw much of anything at the scene. Those who said they did saw things that weren't there.

Most people I knew thought former mayor Mallove was involved. Many thought he was guilty of the crime and orchestrating a magnificent cover up. Otherwise, why would he lie right from the beginning?

He said he passed the scene at 11:12 p.m., one minute after Showalter was struck and killed. He claimed to have seen a second car and that he saw Emilyta talking with an older man. No one else corroborated his story, not even Emilyta. There was no second car. Only Mallove, and the former mayor didn't even stop to see if he could help.

To look at Lucille Showalter you might judge her to be someone who people with authority might be able to push around. A single mother, bookish and academic by nature, and in her 50s at the time. Eventually, she scared the beans out of those who thought they could push her around. They called her crazy, suggested the death of Kevin, had pushed her over the edge. That's how you knew they – the powers that be – were afraid. They tried to discredit her by questioning her sanity and credibility. It is the same tactic "they" – the people in authority – always use when the truth scares them.

I tried to get to know her. I felt from the start she was being underestimated. I wasn't really sure by whom, but I thought of them as the people who knew what happened to Kevin and didn't want Lucille or anyone else to figure it out.

When I was assigned the story, I had been transferred to the Groton bureau of the Bulletin. I covered the city of New London, which included the U.S. Coast Guard Academy, city police, city government, and anything else that came up. The Day, based in New London, was the hometown newspaper. I covered New London for the readers who lived in Norwich and beyond.

I always felt if I could just focus on the Showalter story, I would break it. It got under my skin and became a passion. But it was hardly my only "big" story.

Others included an alleged bribery investigation – I say alleged only because a jury found the accused not guilty. I still have a transcript of a phone conversation from the case. I typed up the transcript on newsprint from the phone recording. We typed our stories in those days on the paper left at the end of rolls of newsprint and I used some of that to transcribe the recording. For whatever reason, I saved it in a plastic sheath to preserve it.

-3-

Massad—And the rest were all business.

████—Yeah. Well, anyhow, I just to make things ██ clear. I mean, what, what ████ Ted, what Ted, has. The stuff he was talking about is you know, I ████ called him and I asked him, I said, you know, I want to be able to give my word on this. Will you, what are you prepared to do? I mean are you prepared to do the things you told Carole. And he said ████ 'yes, *and he said*, no matter, no matter what. That yes, I'm prepared to do that.' So that takes care of his stuff. My stuff, as far as I'm concerned, the insurance and the commission on the sale of the other property that we're going to get—you got my word on that.

Massad—This is risky.

████—Huh?

Massad—It's risky.

████—It's not risky.

Massad—You know, I'm having a ███ heart attack over here.

████—Well, me too, pal. I mean honest. That's, that's the way I've done it. Tell you the truth, I like dealing with ████ better than anybody else ████ because when I nee d something, ████ always gets it. You know, whether he's got it or not. If he doesn't have it, he does ██ find it. You know, ███ it's not just because Willie's political, it's because they're good. Better tha n anybody else ████ around. Although I'm finding that Ron, oh shoot, I can't think of his ████ l ast name—that runs...

Massad—Steinman?

████—Huh?

Massad—Steinman?

████—No, the other, ███ the other guy ████

Partial transcript of telephone conversation between zone-change applicant and New London City Council member Stephen Massad. It was transcribed on old newsprint using a manual typewriter, just as we used to write our articles.

I was doing a lot of hunt-and-peck typing in the aftermath of my injury in Cranston. I wrote a lot about this story. Given what I knew about the case and the transcript, I was baffled by the verdict.

Stephen Massad was then a young New London City Council member. His full-time work was insurance and real estate. His vote targeted an issue regarding a new nursing home. He got a call from someone from the nursing home group who would later be acquitted in the case. On the phone, they talked vaguely about what others are prepared to do for Massad.

"So that takes care of his stuff," the caller tells Massad. "My stuff, as far as I'm concerned. The insurance and the commission of the sale of the other property that we're going to get – you've got my word on that."

Massad responded, that is "risky" and said, "You know, I'm having a heart attack over here."

A jury said not guilty, so I guess that's that. Anyway, one mystery at a time.

Once I was assigned the Showalter story in 1980, it would come to haunt me as a reporter. As I've said, it got under my skin. It woke me up at night. It taught me many lessons about being a journalist, one of which was not every story would have a happy ending – or, as in this case, any ending at all.

The pen might be mightier than the sword, but no pen could best a well-constructed small-town cover up. That's what this felt like, and to this day, I believe that to be the case. I saw others in my years as a reporter and editor, but few that could withstand the kind of media scrutiny that this one endured.

In 1975, reporter John C. Peterson wrote in the Norwich Bulletin the only other logical explanation of what could've happened:

"It almost seems as if the car which killed Kevin Bruce Showalter, and any evidence which might have helped to identify it, have vanished from the face of the earth."

But, of course, the car and evidence didn't just disappear on their own. The investigation was doomed from the start. It was botched so badly that I wondered if it wasn't botched on purpose.

New London police and other official investigators went down one empty rabbit hole after another, and Hansen's "confession" was just the latest. Everything "official" in New London County seemed only to divert attention away from what really happened. One thing was clear to me:

Whoever drove that car got a lot of help to prevent the truth from ever getting told.

To start, there was the missing evidence from the original investigation, including Showalter's personal belongings. That might have revealed something, maybe the color of the car that killed Showalter. That could be important, especially if Showalter's clothing revealed a bright yellow paint that matched the distinctive coloring of Mallove's car. So much of the investigation into this case went missing. It was either a cover up or some of the most official incompetence in history.

Reporters talk about the need to "own" a story, meaning he or she wants to be the journalist leading the way on coverage, being the first to report new information, and developing enough expertise to be the trusted voice on analysis and perspective pieces. But no one owned the Showalter story. It was too complicated, too involved, and too downright bizarre for that.

But it did own us. It wasn't just then, but forever, always moving forward. It got in your head and stayed there. Always. Even now, decades later. I thought I could be the one who found the missing piece of evidence that would bring this to conclusion, but that never happened. I would forever count this as a journalistic failure on my part.

Lucille Showalter would never let go of the investigation. She fought as long and hard as she could to ensure the investigation into her son's death didn't just "vanish from the face of the earth." At least we accomplished that: Kevin Showalter's mother knew the press wouldn't abandon the story, or her.

She pushed hard to keep the investigation alive. Judges, prosecutors, police officers, journalists – really anyone who would listen – all heard from Showalter, a history teacher at Mitchell College, where her son had gone to school.

I got to spend some time with her when the second one-man grand jury proceedings were ready to begin. One day, we were in her kitchen trading facts. I told her that I thought she had become something of a celebrity in the community and that I planned to write about that.

She wouldn't comment on that – on or off the record. But when my story appeared a month after the hearings, it related how the case had become almost like a TV soap opera in its appeal to the public.

"The greatest attraction to the public appears to be Mrs. Showalter," I wrote in a Nov. 23, 1980, article. "She has become, in an almost strange way, a celebrity. Her appearance at the courthouse to testify led one television reporter to say, 'Is that really her? After all I heard, I expected her to look much older, more drawn out.'"

When she died at age 79 in 2000, I had long since moved on in my career, serving as executive editor of The Herald-Dispatch in Huntington, W.Va. But I recall thinking that we had all failed this woman. She had gone to her grave without any of us telling her definitively who had killed her son. That made me cry.

No one knew for sure, but I believed that Mallove was driving his yellow Lincoln Continental when it struck Kevin Showalter and killed him on Christmas Eve 1973. It would have been nice to have seen if any color had rubbed off the offending vehicle onto Showalter's clothing.

After all, Mallove had admitted to driving by the scene one minute after the young man was killed and he made up a story about what he saw at the scene. No other witness could confirm Mallove's account. Maybe he didn't know he had struck Showalter, as some have suggested. Maybe he lied because he was scared that he would be wrongly accused. I don't know.

But that Mallove's distinctive car struck Showalter was nearly the conclusion of Dannehy's one-man grand jury conducted in 1977.

Dannehy heard from 107 people offering evidence in 26 sessions before issuing one of the most bizarre decisions I have ever heard from a judge. He concluded that while prosecution was impossible due to lost evidence and official incompetence, it was "more probable than not" that Mallove was responsible for the death.

In 2005, shortly after the suicide of Paul Hansen, David Burt, a reporter for The Day of New London, who covered the story when Dannehy first served as a grand juror, wrote this about the judge's bizarre "more probable than not" summary:

"Well, did he or didn't he? I surely don't know. I sometimes think Harvey himself went to his grave wondering whether he did it. I know I wonder still. I know thousands of people wonder still."

I think he raises a fair point. Maybe Harvey might not have even known for certain that he struck Kevin Showalter. But I suspect he knew, and he carried his lie to the grave.

Years later, when The Day tried to take another look into this never-solved case, it was told that the transcripts of Dannehy's investigation, all 3,000 pages and 26 volumes, had disappeared. It figured.

Dannehy's odd conclusion is only one part of this strange tale. The fact that a one-man grand juror was employed in the case is another. It was called to investigate because other traditional investigative tools failed. Dannehy's role was purely fact-finding. He had no power to issue an indictment.

When I came along in 1980, Dannehy was reconvening as the one-main grand jury because Hansen of nearby East Lyme had come forward to say he was driving the car that killed Showalter back in 1973.

Dannehy did not believe him. He said not a shred of evidence existed to tie Hansen to Showalter's death. It was, in other words, just another side show presented by New London County State Attorney C. Robert Satti. By the way, as so often happens in small towns, I knew Satti separately from this case. His son, John, was the toughest wrestler I had ever gone up against and he had dominated me my senior year. My brother, Lou, coached the state attorney's grandchildren.

Personal relationships were a concern in this case. In November 1980, Lucille Showalter tried unsuccessfully to have Satti removed from the case. In a letter to Satti, Dannehy, and numerous state and court officials, she claimed evidence of "probable criminal obstruction of justice" by Satti. She called the decision to bring the Hansen "confession" to Dannehy a "Satti diversion."

Dannehy seemed to feel the same way. A frustrated Dannehy concluded the Hansen confession "followed along the tortuous and often dark ways that led from false confessions, barroom boasts, a medium, a psychic, a clairvoyant with extra sensory perception, anonymous telephone calls, unsigned letters, common gossip, and, frequently, bare supposition to nowhere."

Hansen might have really believed he had struck and killed Showalter, but it was clear he was a sick man. When he killed himself in 2005, Hansen became one more casualty of this conspiracy that the locally powerful had perpetrated on the public. He didn't kill Kevin Showalter, but believing he did probably killed him.

At the end of the second grand jury, Dannehy had nothing new to report. Instead he asked and answered the only remaining question.

"What now, when only surmise, guess and conjecture remain?

"The end. The investigatory inquiry is closed. Out of all this reopened inquiry not one tangible piece of new evidence was established. Not one eyewitness appeared. No one came forward to prove evidence was wrongfully contaminated or altered."

For Lucille Showalter, there would be no giving up. In 1978 she was quoted as saying:

"I felt if the mystery of his death couldn't be solved, it would be as though he never existed. I knew there was a car and a driver. If I had to go to the ends of the earth to find them, I would."

I found a small article on the Internet published after Lucille Showalter's death. The occasion was the unveiling of an 18-by-24-inch oil painting of Mrs. Showalter by the New London Maritime Society, which she had founded.

The article quoted Vinnie Belbruno as saying about Showalter, her longtime friend:

"She was one of those people who had energy. She was tireless. She would stay up all night and do things that had to be done. I don't know when she slept."

Honestly, I don't think she did sleep. Until the day she died, she searched for the truth.

You would think that the least the world could do for a woman like that, a mother who fought with every breath she took to learn the truth about her son's death, would be to tell her who killed her boy. Sadly, all these years later, we cannot. I had believed that a righteous group of journalists could set the record straight in any case. But no longer. And never again. Moving forward I was less naïve, more pragmatic, and I guess that is a good thing.

But I will always regret not being good enough, my craft not being good enough, and me personally not smart enough to figure this one out. It was just the right amount of official corruption and incompetence to overcome the best of intentions.

We at least gave Lucille Showalter hope and I guess that is the best I can say about this story. Our journalism kept the fight for justice alive and gave her comfort in her fight. I guess that is something.

I've heard many people say this should be turned into a movie. Well, movies are supposed to have endings, happy or otherwise, and this just seems to never end. Now, I guess it never will.

This is how we were first introduced to Marietta, driving in with a newborn and three older children in the family car. Coming on via a bridge over the Ohio River, it was pretty enough to take your breath away. It still is.

CHAPTER FOUR

MARIETTA: FIRST AND ALWAYS

Jessica was only a few weeks old when we piled the kids into the car for the trip from Dale City, Va., to my first gig as a senior editor in Marietta, Ohio. The Marietta Times was a 12,000-circulation afternoon newspaper in a town built at the confluence of the Muskingum and Ohio rivers. I found it charming in 1992 and, as I learned on a return visit in 2020, it still is. The kind of place you want to live, to raise children, and even to grow old. My career dictated otherwise, but sternwheelers, red-brick streets, the local college in the center of town, a bike path that touches two major rivers – there is a lot to love here.

A confession. After my most recent visit, I had to rewrite this chapter. It just didn't feel right to mix in everything else with the story of a troubled police chief. Marietta was so much more than that and it deserves not to be defined by the actions of this one person. So, I've separated it into two distinct parts. Whether that feels right to the reader is for you to decide, but it makes me feel better. We'll tackle the Roger Phillis story and his impact on local journalism or vice versa next. It just didn't feel right including him in the story about Marietta, but I guess that was always part of the issue with Phillis.

Of course, I was going to take this job when it was offered. I was turning 35 and I had set a hard-and-fast deadline of being a senior editor by 35. The title was managing editor, which is typically the second-in-charge in the newsroom, but it was clear this was the chief news executive position.

By the way, a piece of advice to young people starting your career: Setting goals is fine, but never make them hard and fast. Too much stress.

Decisions shouldn't be made because you set a goal. This was a good decision but having a goal by a certain age should not have been a factor in accepting a job. It taught me to quit being so strict with myself.

I figured the job was being offered because I had been a good soldier, first being "loaned" from GNS to the Jackson (Tenn.) Sun as interim managing editor, then The Journal Newspapers in suburban Washington, D.C., as business editor and then helping to re-launch the weekly North Hills (Pa.) News Record as a daily. I also figured some people thought I had talent and brains, at least I hoped so, but I wasn't as sure that had much to do with this offer.

For two years, I had been pulled in so many different directions away from my family that two things happened: Phil Currie, Gannett senior vice president/news, sent a lot of roses to Donna to say thank you, and Danielle, who was still too young to know what was really going on, was telling our Dale City, Va., townhouse neighbors that her Daddy didn't live there anymore. We needed to settle down, together, in one place for a while.

By the way, I found a hand-written note from Phil one day in my boxes of memorabilia that was addressed to me and Donna on the birth of our fifth child, Alex, who was born in Marietta. Phil drew flowers on the letter written on the corporate letterhead, saying he would have sent real ones, but thought he was making me nervous.

In 1992, though, Donna was pregnant with No. 4, Jessica, who was due July 20. I had cut a deal with corporate that I could return to Dale City from North Hills by July 1. This kind of deadline is OK, by the way, and the time was up. On the day I was packing my car to drive back from western Pennsylvania I was invited by Phil to fly back on the corporate jet.

I couldn't, I said, because I had my car and needed to drive it back. Corporate would have someone drive it, he said.

But all my clothes were packed and all I had left was what I was wearing: dirty sweats. I protested, but Phil said no one would care what I was wearing and that a taxi would pick me up in two hours. Be ready. I was, of course.

I got on the plane wearing my baggy sweatshirt and pants and I was immediately ushered to the back where Gary Watson, newspaper group president, was sitting puffing on a cigarette. Sit down, he said.

"I really admired your work in North Hills," Watson began.

I almost fell over, then gulped, thinking he had barely said two words to me the whole time I was there. I assumed he barely knew I was alive. How could he now say he admired my work? I thought it might be a joke or a trick, but, thank goodness, it was one of the few times my internal filter worked, preventing me from blurting out my thoughts.

Watson went on to tell me that there was a job opportunity for me in Marietta. The paper needed a new editor and "people" in the company hoped the publisher, Emmett Smelser, and I could hit it off and make that happen. Any questions?

"Yes," I said, "where is Marietta?"

When I got home, it was hello, goodbye, and by the way we might be moving. After a few days, I jumped back on an airplane to Ohio to meet Smelser. The plan was for me to stay for two weeks, which would get me back home in plenty of time for Jessica's birth. None of us counted on her being born early, which, of course, she was on July 16, which is my birthday, and that of my father. Three generations of Gabordis born on the same day! It had to be some kind of record. I made it home with a couple days to spare.

On July 10, The Marietta Times announced me as the new chief newsroom executive in a front-page story. It was Robert C. Gabordi in the announcement, by the way. I knew that's how my mom would have wanted it.

Anyway, my purpose in Marietta on that first trip was to check out the place and spend some time with Smelser. The fact that I was a candidate for the top editor's job was a secret to the staff, although I'm not sure why. Still, I think they knew something was up. They were all very nice to me. I mean, they were all nice people, but they were especially nice to me.

I went there under the guise of helping while the previous editor was on loan to North Hills, and the visit went well. I found Emmett delightful and smart. He took me out on his boat to see the Ohio River when I said I was really hoping to get back closer to the ocean. He said I could look upriver and just pretend that it was ocean as far as you could see. At some point, I felt things switched from an interview to recruitment, and I knew I'd get the offer.

I asked a lot of questions of Emmett and corporate. I even asked about the weather, because I was concerned about lake-effect snowstorms I had heard about. Lake-effect snowstorms might not affect that part of the Ohio Valley, but I didn't know better. I grew up in cold, snowy weather and never liked it. I was told by Mary Kay Blake, who worked at corporate helping to arrange these editor moves, that the winter wasn't too bad in Marietta, a lot like Washington, but even more mild because the rivers were a mitigating influence.

The first year that seemed true about the weather. But 1994 was a different story and then some. Over a 31-day period at the start of the year, we had two major snowfalls – and I do mean major, the kind measured in feet, not inches – record minus-23-degree temperatures and a major flood. The Muskingum River migrated into our backyard on Second Street, which meant Front Street was swamped. We found a dead fish in our backyard when the water receded. That explains why the main house was built up so high.

On the night the temps dipped so low, we lost power, which meant heat. We rounded up the kids and stayed at the Whiteheads' home. Dave Whitehead had replaced Smelser as publisher. Dave and Tara Whitehead were from Norwich, by the way, though we didn't know each other in Connecticut. Why they had heat, I don't know, but I was grateful. My saltwater aquarium had ice in it.

The Whiteheads had a big Suburban SUV and Dave and I loaded it up with newspapers and went out after one of the major storms and delivered them to subscribers in the hinterlands. You should have seen people's faces when they realized the editor and publisher were bringing their newspapers to them. We had fun doing it. Dave had maybe too much fun, zipping through the snow drifts. There was one near the river that looked like a trap. I told him if he drove into that one, I'd quit. Thankfully, he backed off.

Anyway, for the first time, but not the last, I had been on my own during the move in finding a house to buy before Donna could even see the town, since she was so far along in the pregnancy. I knew she would love it, though, and I was right. It was one of those old red-brick jobs on Second Street whose interior had been gutted and modernized.

The job itself always made sense to me: The newspaper was small enough that I probably couldn't hurt much and it already had one of the worst News 2000 scores in the company. So, if it turned out to be a mistake rewarding the good soldier, there wasn't much of a downside. I guess that's what corporate was thinking.

A little explanation of News 2000 is needed. News 2000 was an evaluation process corporate used, among other things, to decide what kind of job the editor was doing. What they thought was so visionary about the year 2000 I don't know. It was only a few years away. As part of the process, editors from other sites and corporate looked at the newspaper on mandatory submission dates and "wildcard" dates that the newspaper's own editor picked. After the review, the newspaper was "graded" and given a numerical score. Marietta's score was consistently low, which is why, I assumed, it needed a new editor.

It would have helped if the editor-judge had any knowledge of the town or had anything in common with the town. But usually, the judges were from our bigger properties. That part made no sense to me. I guess it assumed all our best talent was at big properties and that's just not true.

On top of that, before the actual judging, the editor was asked to rate where he or she thought the newsroom would score. I dutifully scored my newspaper and said I thought we would improve by 18 points over our previous score. I wrote my explanation and sent it in.

I got a scathing note from News Executive Mark Silverman in reply. Picking me as editor had been a mistake, the note said, because I was obviously out of touch with the reality of my own newspaper. I was predicting that we had improved so much in just a few months. Obviously, I was in over my head. A nice confidence-builder for a young editor it was not.

I saved that note under the glass on my desk and, when the scores came out and we had improved by 22 points, I simply copied it along with the cover sheet of the News 2000 report showing our score, and sent it back to Silverman. He called me on the phone to congratulate me and apologize.

Here is why I felt so strongly that we had improved: When I walked in, there were very few weak links on the small crew that was the Marietta newsroom. We just needed new leadership and new ways of doing things. That was on me, of course. The news team loved the community. They were smart and very talented. Better, I thought several times, than I deserved to find at a small-town newspaper.

We would win runner-up Most Improved Newspaper in the company that year and circulation went up. I guess things like Silverman's note was why News 2000 was so controversial internally and outside our company. I liked the measurement of quality, but we'd carried things too far.

I joined the Rotary Club and got involved in the community, even though it was not "normal" practice at the time. I thought it important that we be seen as trying to help make the community better.

I coached baseball in Marietta as I had in Dale City. It was a way to immerse myself into the community and get to know real people – not that the officials weren't real, but you know what I mean. I coached baseball at every stop except FLORIDA TODAY, where injuries and health issues kept me off the field. I coached baseball before I had kids playing, while my kids played, and then for years after they played.

I made some lasting friendships on the ball fields: bankers, mail carriers, taxi drivers, dry cleaners, people from all walks of life. For a while it seemed that all I did was baseball and newspaper stuff. But it was a great life in Marietta, you know, except a police chief who talked about wanting to hurt me, stray tree branches, and the naked guy. But more on that later.

We set about improving all aspects of the newspaper and that included investigative reporting. We began to focus on what we called reader interaction, which meant we were reaching out to get readers involved with what we were covering, how we were covering it, and – in some cases – helping us to create content.

Domestic violence was a big concern in this small Appalachian town – as it probably is everywhere if we want to be honest – and the readers we spoke with talked about what they called the cycle of learned violent behavior, passed down generation to generation.

As our journalism improved and we began to win contests, we were setting our prize winnings aside. We got help, too, from the Gannett Foundation, and we created something we called the Survivor's Bank. Victims of domestic violence, we learned, stayed in abusive situations primarily for one of two reasons: They were financially tied to their abuser, meaning they were willing to take a beating in exchange for not being forced to move their children further into poverty, or they were really in love with their abuser and felt things would change. Women in love always seem to feel they could change a man; I'm just not sure that's possible.

The key, we felt, was breaking the cycle of violence. That took money, which we could make available to victims. We formed an ad hoc citizens group and secured some money. We took applications and asked that the money be used to secure a safe place to live, to cover expenses while they went back to school or just to tide them over until a new job came along. It was a loan, not a handout, and we expected when their own finances improved for the money to be paid back at whatever pace the victims felt comfortable.

We put together a special section of the paper, written by victims of domestic abuse and other experts. It included some courageous well-known people in the community telling their stories publicly for the first time to their small-town neighbors.

I remember a court officer – a woman – came into court one day with bandages on her head still seeping with blood. We heard of other cases and cover ups of key public officials' abusive behavior.

Our coverage of domestic abuse won major Gannett awards. I was proud of that. And I was proud of the national attention the project brought to the issue of domestic violence and to our little newspaper.

While working on this book, I ran across a research paper on what was being called public journalism at the time. Written by researcher and author Ann Weichelt in 1996, it included our "Stop the Hurting" project, based on an article about The Times' efforts in Presstime magazine. It was a pretty good summary of our project. Weichelt fairly presented the national debate at the time over these kinds of "public journalism" and "reader interaction" projects.

"According to Presstime, two other newspapers have taken up the challenge in 1993. The managing editor of the Marietta Times, Robert C. Gabordi, invites the readers of the newspaper call him with their views. This forum has now been expanded into a radio call-in show. At one reader's suggestion, the paper ran a free 12-page, ad-free tabloid called 'Stop the Hurting.'

"It was written by readers, community leaders, experts and victims and was aimed to stop the epidemic of domestic violence. As a follow-up, the paper sponsored a public forum on the topic. An outgrowth of the meeting was the formation of a 'survivor's bank' that loans money on a short-term basis to victims of violent predicaments."

In a column, I told the story of what motivated me on this issue. It was one of my earliest memories as a kid. I think I was still in a high-chair, and I watched as a man angrily dumped a table of hot food on my mother.

I don't know who the man was, I just don't remember. My parents divorced at a time when that was still a really big deal in this country, especially for Italian Catholics. I was young, not even 3. Despite being born on my father's birthday, we didn't celebrate many birthdays together.

I need to pause here to catch you up on a few things. My mom had never been particularly healthy. She smoked a lot for a long time before quitting late in her life. But she wasn't – to my knowledge – in any immediate danger of major illness when she told me not to go to work on the North Hills project. I thought she was just guilt tripping me when she told me that if I went to North Hills, I would never see her alive again.

In January 1992, I went to North Hills. In February, she had a brain hemorrhage and almost died. She recovered and went home. But in April, it happened again and it was far worse than the first time. On Easter, our family made the decision to disconnect her from life support and she died peacefully. She was 58 years old.

I was angry for a long time that she kept that promise to die. She never met Jessica, who was born later that year, or Alex, our youngest. She wasn't there to celebrate my first senior editor's job or watch any of her own children fully achieve our dreams.

Jessica was born that July in Virginia. We moved to Marietta when she was just weeks old. It wasn't long before we noticed that things were different for her than with our first three. She would learn things and then lose the skills she acquired. Like playing patty-cake with me. Over and over, she would seem to learn and lose skills. She seemed to stare off into space.

The doctors in Marietta told us we were just being nervous new parents, but we knew better. It took 16 months of trying, but when she was 22 months old, at the Pittsburgh Children's Hospital – our fourth hospital in this adventure – in a room that included a social worker and psychologist to help Donna and me cope, we heard what the doctor called the worst possible news. Jessica had Rett syndrome, a neurological disorder that involved a missing or damaged chromosome.

She wasn't going to die from Rett syndrome, but she wouldn't get better, either. I should take a minute or so to educate you about Rett, but I've been doing that with readers ever since the diagnosis, which these days can be accomplished with a simple blood test.

Rett affects its victims in widely different ways. Some can walk. Some can talk. Some have some ability to respond on command. Jessica can do none of these things, though she does know what she likes. "Shake It Off" by Taylor Swift puts a smile on her face almost every time she hears it. She loves going to Disney and can be pretty demanding. I have to stop watching whatever ball game is on TV if she needs a Mickey Mouse fix. She watches black and white versions of "I Love Lucy" and is a big "Flintstones" fan. Oh, she loves her sports, too, and will watch a New York Mets game or almost anything related to Florida State. She grew up at ballfields, after all.

There are clinical trials going on now to develop drugs and other treatments for Retts. I suggest going to Rettsyndrome.org to learn more.

Like all parents, we were expected to deal with this while raising our other children to be "normal" and doing our jobs. Coming home from Pittsburgh, Donna drove because I don't think I could. I'm not sure she should've, either, but that is the story of our life together. She's always been the strong one.

I crawled in the backseat with Jessica and alternated between sleeping and crying. For the first time, I had a dream on that ride home that I would have many times again. God was standing at a light switch turning it on and off while I pleaded on my knees for him to leave the switch on in my little girl's brain.

Much progress has been made on Rett syndrome, but getting a diagnosis took us 16 months of pure hell, overnight stays in hospitals, test after test at hospital to hospital. Despite having what we thought was good insurance and a decent paycheck, we plunged deeply into debt.

One rude doctor in Akron has no idea how close he came to being socked in the nose when we visited to get his diagnosis after weeks of him ignoring our phone calls. It was the first time anyone used the phrase "mentally retarded" with us. When I questioned what he was saying, he turned to me and said, "Well, just look at her. Can't you tell?"

Rett almost always targets girls. Jessica is now in her 20s and she's home with her otherwise empty-nest mom and dad.

I wrote about her diagnosis and the process. The column won first place in the Ohio Associated Press Managing Editors annual contest. I did not enter it into the Gannett contests and I'm not really sure why, but I think I simply didn't want to mix corporate life with my family at the time. That was crazy thinking; the Gannett people were nothing but kind and generous to my family over the years.

The other three children were doing fine, although when we moved to Marietta, our oldest, Rob, had an interesting observation for a 11-year-old. We were walking downtown, and he looked at me and said, "Dad, does anyone live here besides white people?"

Editors from several Ohio newspapers discuss economic development during as part of "The Other Ohio," an early reader interaction or civil/public journalism project. The project was the vision of John Robinson Block and The Times joined him before we enlisted other state newspapers. The photo is courtesy of The Blade of Toledo, which published it on Page 1 Oct. 30, 1994.

I learned that politics were a big part of the editor's job when I was approached by the editor of The Blade of Toledo about joining them in what became known as "The Other Ohio" project. The Marietta Times and The Blade would work together to make a point that the communities outside of the Three Cs mattered, with the three Cs being Cleveland, Columbus and Cincinnati. We drew in other newspapers whose communities felt the same way.

We wanted a share of the economic growth and development attention that the big cities were getting from the governor's office. I think the Times was asked to join because the incomparable Nancy Hollister, Marietta's former mayor, was lieutenant governor. She took notice and I think she agreed with our basic point, though she did so quietly. I'm not sure that we accomplished much other than to send a message. But, given that so much of the population was in one of the Three Cs metro areas, it was a message that could be easily ignored.

By the way, when I visited Marietta in March 2020, I almost immediately bumped into Hollister while having lunch at the Lafayette Hotel downtown. What a pleasant happenstance that was.

Anyway, The Blade was owned by the Block family. They insisted that one of the meetings take place in Marietta. I'll never forget the scene they created when they pulled into the tiny Marietta Times parking lot in their oversized limo.

Politics was ugly back in the early 1990s, but nothing like today. Although his politics and mine were different enough that in today's world we might be considered enemies, I really admired Democrat Ted Strickland, who somehow managed to get himself elected to Congress in 1992 in what had been a staunchly Republican district that included Marietta.

He became something of a sensation when he went to Washington. The Washington Post did a centerpiece on the new congressman who traveled without an entourage and who owned just one suit. Strickland lost a very close election in 1994 to Republican Frank Cremeans, who rode a Republican wave to victory.

I didn't like Cremeans. It wasn't his politics I objected to, but him. He once told me that he was the better candidate to represent family values because he and his wife had children and Strickland and his wife chose not to have children. I don't know why the Stricklands didn't have children. I don't know whether it was a choice they made, but neither did Cremeans. It made me angry he would say something like that.

"Well, then, I would be a better candidate than either one of you," I said. "We have five children."

I remember the exact moment I knew Cremeans would win the election. It was during The Marietta Times-sponsored debate. I forget the question asked by the Gannett News Service reporter, but not Strickland's answer: "We may have to raise some taxes," he said.

Game. Set. Match.

This was the 1994 election, mind you. The year of the Republican wave in Congress. The year of the Contract with America not to raise taxes. No one was going to win while doing anything but ruling out raising taxes.

Cremeans took the audio of that answer and played it over and over and over on radio and TV. I heard it in my sleep. The district was more conservative than Strickland to begin with, and the one-liner was a reminder of that to voters.

After the election, I had lunch with Strickland because I wanted to tell him I thought he was a dumbass for talking about raising taxes so close to an election. But he would have none of that.

His answer was truthful and ethical, he said. If it cost him the election, well, it was the truth. I had to feel good about that, except that we were stuck with Cremeans for two years.

Cremeans would never win another election. Strickland would win back his seat in 1996 in a very tight battle with Cremeans.

His district included portions of Ohio that my new newspaper, The Herald-Dispatch in Huntington, W.Va., covered. I got the Huntington executive editor's job in 1995. Again, I didn't apply for it, but "people" at corporate thought I would be a good fit with Publisher Tom Bookstaver. So, Strickland and I would bump into each other several times and we stayed friendly over the years.

A quick aside on the Huntington job interview. Tom and his wife, Cathy, were picking me up from the Radisson downtown (it is now the Doubletree). I had somehow torn my suit jacket on the hotel door when it caught a snag. I ran downstairs to a men's shop and quickly bought a new one. People my size don't quickly buy clothing, though, and the sleeves were too long. I told the guy at the store my sad story and they quickly shortened the sleeves.

All's good, so far. Tom, Cathy and I went to dinner. Donna didn't join us because she was staying behind at the hotel with Jessica. I decided to bring her back a dessert, I think at Cathy's suggestion. Chocolate brownies with chocolate sauce. When I was getting out of the car, I noticed the dessert had leaked all over my new jacket. Then I noticed it had leaked on Tom's fancy backseat. I figured the job opportunity was screwed if I spoke up. So, I got out quickly, turning my jacket so the stain couldn't be seen, and went upstairs to my room at the hotel.

Several months later, after I had safely landed the job, out of the blue Tom complained that someone had spilled chocolate in his backseat. What a shame, I commiserated. I hope he misses this part if he reads the book.

OK, back to Strickland. He would hold onto the congressional seat until he was elected governor of Ohio in 2006. I was glad I had moved on by the time Strickland and Hollister ran against each other. I was very fond of both.

Sadly, Strickland's administration faced controversy over a sex scandal in the attorney general office and the struggling national economy.

Efforts to fix the nation's health care didn't begin with Obamacare. In the 1990s, Hillary Clinton was leading the charge for health-care reform for her husband's administration. Major changes are always called reform by the politicians, but for me reform implies improving something. I wasn't sure what was being proposed was an improvement and I wondered how the Clinton plan would change things for our Jessica and other children like her. As I've said, her diagnosis and the repetition of tests had nearly broken our finances.

Hillary Clinton was traveling around the country pushing the plan. I wrote an editorial saying if this health-care plan was such a good idea, she ought to come to places like Marietta. Be inclusive of small Midwestern towns, and other places where every day Americans live. I knew she was planning a trip to the Cleveland area, so I invited her to come to Marietta.

She came.

Somehow, someone in the administration must've gotten her the editorial, which appeared on the front page of the tiny, local newspaper, and she read it and thought, hmm, what a good idea.

I remember a pre-event meeting with Mrs. Clinton in the conference room at the Marietta Times and asking her why on earth had she come. Really, why.

Her reaction should not have surprised me, but it did.

"Why, Mr. Editor, you invited me," she said.

There was a lot of logistical stuff to get done. Marietta College had offered its auditorium. And there were tickets to be given out – the place had a seating maximum and we didn't want to have people show up expecting to get in but getting left out. I did worry about "stacking the deck" with Democrats in this small town, but things like that were out of my hands.

One of the first lady's advance team asked if I knew of any Girl Scouts leaders who would be willing to bring a couple of girls to deliver flowers to Mrs. Clinton at the podium, and it turns out I did: My wife, Donna, and a few of the girls, including my daughter, Danielle, who was a Brownie Scout at the time.

What was the impact on the community? For a little while, their national government didn't seem so big and unfeeling, it was there personified in the presence of the first lady. And it happened because their local newspaper thought they deserved an opportunity to be included.

Marietta obviously had a huge impact on our lives and my career. When we left for Huntington, just 100 miles down the Ohio River, I knew I would always carry a part of that place in my heart.

COLUMN: Help my child make a difference

By Bob Gabordi
Executive Editor, Tallahassee Democrat
Published July 17, 2007

Monday was my daughter's birthday. She is 15 years old.

She left the house in the morning with a little tiara on her head – she is her daddy's little princess after all these years.

She was born on my birthday, the best little present you can imagine, the fourth of our five children. Her birth was typical, in the sense that all birth is typically remarkable.

Her first few months of life were typical, again in the same sense that the young lives of all children are typically remarkable. But we began noticing signs that she was not developing the same as our other children.

Her mom and I spent the next 16 months in absolute hell as we tried to get a diagnosis. Four hospitals, tens of thousands of dollars and God only knows how many sleepless hours later, we learned she has something called Rett syndrome.

Then it was all gone

Like many Rett kids, Jessica developed typically for many months, and then lost many of her skills. One day we were playing patty-cake and I heard her say "da-da." Then it was all gone. I dreamed once that I was watching God turn a light switch on and off in her head and I was pleading with Him to leave the light on.

We've since learned that Rett Syndrome is a unique neuron-developmental disorder found almost exclusively in females. It affects all racial and ethnic groups. It is extremely rare and has to do with something called an MeCP2 mutation. It results in a shortage or absence of normal MeCP2 protein, none of which I truly understand.

I do know that when Jessica went to school today, she was in her wheelchair. She has never walked or talked. She cannot feed herself.

I also know she has brought some incredible good into our family and our community. She is a beautiful child who is dearly loved by her brothers and sisters, and her mom and dad.

Because of Jessica, her dad – the newspaper editor – has quietly and sometimes not so quietly brought the needs of children with disabilities to the attention of governors and political leaders in the three states in which she has lived.

She is also why I have gotten involved with Whole Child Leon, an organization that exists simply to help families with children.

I wish there had been something like Whole Child in my community 15 years ago, a place where parents – all parents – of children up to age 6 can fill out a confidential profile so that our community's resources can be directed to help.

Help a child

It's easy to find. Simply go to www.tallymoms.com and click on the Whole Child Leon button.

My daughter and I want to urge you to get involved in our community by helping a child, if not your own then someone else's baby. Tell a parent about Whole Child and about how easy it is to use; once the profile is filled out, help can be on its way.

Trust me. I know how important that is.

Access to the site is available at most social service agencies in town, too. Get involved. It would be the best way to celebrate our special day. Helping another child helps us in so many ways.

Happy birthday, Jessica. I love you.

Bob Gabordi is executive editor of the Tallahassee Democrat and Tallahassee.com. You can leave comments on his blog at Tallahassee.com, or contact him at bgabordi@tallahassee.com or at (850) 599-2177.

OUR OPINION: City must assure public about police department

Phillis needs to show proof

In a report out today from the state Attorney General's Office, Marietta police Chief Roger Phillis accuses Mayor Joe Matthews of having heavy ties in gambling.

This is perhaps the most serious of many apparently unfounded comments made by Phillis to state investigators and others, according to the report. Phillis must be forced to prove his charges against the mayor, or he should resign immediately.

If the chief of police believes the city's highest elected city official has broken laws, or has connections to illegal gambling operations, why hasn't he done something about it?

Phillis allegedly told state investigators that his troubles were politically motivated. The term he uses is "witch hunt."

But further, while the report apparently clears Phillis of criminal wrong-doing, Phillis is alleged to have acknowledged joisingly saying:

► That he intended to retire to his farm and grow marijuana to supplement his pension.

► That he would shoot anyone who came near the farm.

► And that Washington County Sheriff Bob Schlicher was involved in the murder of Ronda Manley.

According to the report, Detective John Winstanley of the Washington County Sheriff's Office said he heard Phillis' make reference to killing his wife by putting her into a "chipper shredder." This was made while the chief was under stress and going through a divorce.

Winstanley said he was not sure if the chief was serious.

The problem is that while Phillis might have been joking, some people took him seriously, and that led to the mayor seeking an investigation.

Phillis says that there is evidence the mayor was out to get him. We think the mayor did what he must do under the circumstances.

According to the Attorney General's Office report, another officer said the chief came into the station carrying an assault weapon. At the time, according to the report, officers were concerned about a rumor the chief "might go over the edge and start shooting people from the court house tower."

Phillis may think it funny to make jokes about growing and selling illegal drugs, about shooting people and about killing his ex-wife. But he is the top police officer in Marietta and carries a gun. There is nothing funny about drugs or murder. Nothing at all.

Schlicher was among those who took Phillis' comments seriously. He

was concerned, according to the state report, for the safety of his deputies should they have to approach the chief.

According to the report, members of Phillis' department accused him of being unpredictable in his behavior. The mayor, according to the report, says the chief is insubordinate and increasingly difficult to work with, that he fears that if pushed too far Phillis might "crack and hurt someone."

In a terse statement attached to the report, Washington County Prosecutor Michael G. Spahr says that it shows no evidence that Phillis committed a felony offense.

But there is ample evidence, if the report is correct, that inside and outside the department, Phillis acted inappropriately. His so-called jokes are more than that. They are disgusting.

The report may not show criminal behavior, but there is ample evidence of behavior unbecoming of a police officer.

His comments to investigators go beyond even any of this. He has, according to the report, accused the mayor of criminal behavior. Now it is

time for the city to call him on the carpet, to demand that he offer evidence to back his claim or resign immediately.

On that, there should be no compromise, no deal, no waiting for Phillis to retire gracefully. He must prove it or go, simple as that.

The report gives the city all the reasons it should need to move quickly to fix a problem that appears to have grown out of control. The city administration owes to residents to offer assurance the police department is being run competently and fairly.

What took so long?

Another question must be asked about a report from the state Attorney General's Office regarding the action's of Marietta Police Chief Roger Phillis: What took so long.

This investigation was opened in July. The last interview occurred in mid-September. It is now mid-November. We repeat: What took so long?

No doubt, the state office which conducted this investigation is overworked. It has eight officers for 88 counties.

Still, it seems shameful that a criminal investigation, in which no charges would be brought, should take two months to write up.

This investigation was no secret — how could it be when investigators interviewed a newspaper editor and reporter? — and that made spend a matter of fairness to all involved.

So what took so long?

Opinion of The Marietta Times published Nov. 17, 1994. The editorial did not address comments Chief Roger Phillis made about me. I addressed that separately in signed columns.

CHAPTER FIVE

ROGER PHILLIS – THE EVEN SCORE?

Marietta Police Chief Roger Phillis was right about one thing. In August 1993, on the anniversary of Ronda Manley's murder, Phillis said if her killer wasn't found quickly, he might hurt someone else.

It took 10 years for police to tie Aubrey Davis to Manley's murder. When he was charged in Manley's death, he was already serving a 20-year sentence in Northwest Correctional Complex located in Tiptonville, Tenn., for aggravated kidnapping and attempted aggravated sexual battery stemming from a 1998 incident in Chattanooga, Tenn. It took a tip from a jailhouse informant to finally resolve the Manley murder.

As Phillis had predicted, Davis had hurt someone again. The second crime occurred six years after Manley was raped and brutally stabbed to death by Davis, her body left in the Oak Grove Cemetery. In 2017, after completion of his sentence in Tennessee, Davis began serving time in Ohio for Manley's murder.

I had been senior editor of the Marietta Times for only a few weeks when Manley, 18, was reported missing. When Davis was finally charged, it was because of a Washington County Sheriff Office's cold-case unit, working with Marietta police, matching DNA evidence to bring her killer to trial. In 2002, Davis, then 48, pleaded guilty to the murder in Washington County in 1992.

It was the Ronda Manley murder more than anything else that put me at odds with Phillis. He wasn't used to a newspaper editor or anyone else standing up to him. He was at odds with a lot of people in those days.

I never believed Phillis understood how the Manley murder impacted people in Marietta. When Davis was finally arrested in 2002, the Parkersburg News & Sentinel quoted Manley's friend and classmate Toni Brown-Crump, who expressed relief so many years later.

"I'm glad to know that her killer is serving time for this regardless of how many years later it is," Brown-Crump told the newspaper. "(Davis) needs to be held responsible for the heartbreak he's caused so many people."

I'll admit we were hard on Phillis. When he told us two years into the investigation that two officers were investigating the killing full time, reporter Cynthia Hoover checked police work records. They showed over a six-month period one officer had averaged eight hours per week on this case. The other officer had averaged three hours per week investigating the killing.

Despite his words, Phillis was not making the Manley case a priority. So, we pushed harder, and he pushed back. As journalists, when words and reality do not equal out, we push for the truth. That is our job. But this was the first time I thought an officer tried to intimidate me. It would not be the last, but it was new and different for me.

Phillis was a career law enforcement officer. He might even have been a good officer, both before he was chief and afterward in Williamstown, W.Va., where he worked until his retirement. But he was not a good chief and not a good person. He was a bully.

He did not take kindly to a newspaper editor and reporter who wouldn't just take his word, and he showed incredibly poor judgment in the things he said.

When the newspaper requested the police records that would show the Manley murder was less of a priority than the chief had been saying, Phillis called the victim's mother. He told her the newspaper's investigation might hurt the police effort to find her daughter's killer, the mother told Hoover. That not only wasn't true, it also created extra stress on a woman whose daughter had been missing for two years. It was just a mean thing to do.

But that was Phillis. He would have conflicts with other people, too. For instance, he warned newly elected Mayor Joseph Matthews, a former firefighter, that he risked getting a parking ticket if he parked in the chief's spot. I think it was Matthew's first day on the job. Strange that he threatened to ticket the boss instead of just helping the new mayor find his own spot.

Washington County Sheriff Bob Schlicher warned me that Phillis was talking about hurting me. I never took the talk too seriously. But the sheriff did, and he promised to keep a watch on me for a while.

I was not the only one Phillis had talked about hurting. At the request of Matthews, the state attorney general's office opened an investigation into Phillis. The mayor said he wanted help investigating "allegations of threats against members of the Washington County Sheriff's Office, the Marietta Police Department and the local news media," the report stated.

The state Bureau of Criminal Identifications and Investigations interviewed me and one of our reporters for their investigation, so it wasn't much of a secret. When the 39-page report came out in November, soon after the election and several months of investigation, there was no evidence that Phillis had committed crimes. It did show Phillis was guilty of incredibly bad taste and judgment.

The report found, among other things:

- Phillis admitted to saying he intended to retire and grow marijuana to supplement his income. But he said that was not serious.
- He accused the mayor of having ties to illegal gambling. He denied having said that and suggested the investigator made that up.
- He said Schlicher had ties to the Manley murder. But he said that was another joke.
- As for me, he said that he would retire some day and "turn into the monster" that I portrayed him as being.
- Detective John Winstanley of the Washington County sheriff's office said he heard Phillis talk about killing his ex-wife by putting her into a wood chipper-shredder. He said he wasn't serious about that, too.

Phillis challenged the veracity of the report and accused the investigator of lying. But other than that, he said, he didn't want to talk about the report with the Times.

"I'm not going to have a long dissertation with you daily on this matter," Phillis told the reporter. Prosecutors said the report did not offer evidence that the chief had committed crimes.

Everything he said was taken out of content and was not said seriously, he said.

I wrote a column off that investigative report that rightly, I think, made light of the "threat" against me. The chief didn't deny saying things about me – he called me "Shorty Gabordi" in the report - but, he said, as he had with other comments, he was only joking.

Good to know, but there it was in black and white for the whole world to see in an official government investigation: I'm short. I decided to have some fun with that as the whole thing seemed ridiculous to me.

I wrote a column confessing to being short, which was now part of an official state record. I said I was going to have to apologize to all the people I had convinced I was tall instead of the actual five-foot-three that I am.

"After two days (of thinking about it), I decided to tell my wife. For 18 years, I had hidden the cruel truth from her," I wrote. "I'd ply her with a little wine and a nice dinner. Flowers and chocolates would be nice, too. …

"She cried, of course. Then she admitted to knowing. Oh, she pretended not to know, but she did. … She pulled out a picture from our honeymoon, when I tried to get on an adult ride at the amusement park. I wasn't up to Mickey's hand. Not tall enough."

Actually, that last part was almost true. We did have that photograph, but I was tall enough, just barely, to get on the ride.

I actually got two columns out of that state report. I think the second one was better than the first. It really was a compilation of reactions to the "Shorty Gabordi" comment in the first column, which drew more reaction than anything I had ever written to that point.

I wrote about how I had fooled everyone into thinking I was tall. My neighbors, I said, were surprised by the revelation. My kids' friends at the middle school were taller than me in back-to-back testing, which they insisted we now do. When I walked in to get a haircut, my local barber announced, "Shorty Gabordi is here," which set the natives off and running.

I got phone calls asking me to join a short-person network (I not so politely declined) and one of my coaching buddies, who also was a teacher, sent home a "special" wisdom-filled note with my kid. It was not pretty.

But if I was having a rough time, imagine what the chief was going through.

Because of another column I wrote drawing attention to it, he was suspended for three-days for a letter he wrote to Municipal Judge Milt Nuzum.

I should probably admit that I was surprised by the tension with the chief. Up until this point, I always had a great relationship with the police. Naturally, there was conflict from time to time, but for the most part, I had good relationships with police.

What other reporter do you know who had the police tell them where and when they were going to do a prostitution and drug raid? That's what happened in New London, when the chief called me in to give me details on a raid at a bar on Bank Street two days before it occurred.

I wrote a story advancing the raid, in other words, the story appeared the morning of the raid that night. That was a lot of fun getting it through the copy desk. Ed Dunn, who we sometimes called Ed Overdone, was furious when he read my copy.

How can I write this and tip off the bad guys? he demanded.

It was a fair question, I said, but Chief Donald Sloan told me I could write it as long as I didn't name the specific bar, which I didn't, saying only that it would be a Bank Street bar. I explained he had called me in specifically because he wanted us to do a story.

"He said he figures the bad guys won't read the paper in the morning, so it would be a good warning for everyone else to stay away," I said.

Ed was a good copy editor, one of the very best. He just had a bit of a temper in those days and I knew I pushed his buttons more than most.

That night, police arrested five people at the bar. Sloan told reporters his team would continue to work undercover through the weekend. Another 21 people were arrested the next night.

In New London, my relationship was with more than the chief. In those days, you had to go into the station and read reports on paper and it helped if you had someone point you in the right direction. I rarely went in without an extra cup of coffee just in case the desk sergeant was thirsty, which he usually was.

I'm certain my relationship building paid dividends, even when I was writing the Showalter stories about how police screwed up that investigation. They knew what was going on and a little coffee helps ease the sting a bit, too.

But there was no relationship building going on in Marietta, not with Phillis as the local police chief. There was no relationship foundation upon which to build. Phillis didn't like journalists or anyone else he couldn't push around.

At some point, Marietta police started parking a car at night across the street from our house on Second Street. Not every night, but many nights. A cruiser would be there when we went to sleep and when we woke up. Was it the same one? Was it there all night? I don't know and never bothered to try to figure it out.

We parked our car on the street, too. It was a minivan, with the flat rear door and window. We had five children now. What else would you drive? Minivans became our staple for many years. Nothing like having a cop outside your front door to keep the bad guys away, or so I thought.

One morning, a tree branch smashed our back window. You know, the flat window. If it just fell from a tree, it would have had to curve magically to end up through the glass. Possible? I guess, but highly unlikely.

I went across the street and knocked on the officer's window.

No, sir, he said. He didn't see or hear anything. Oh, well, these things happen when you live on a beautiful tree-lined street on a windy night.

The officer wasn't around the night a naked man showed up at our back door at 3 a.m. in the middle of the winter, either. The naked guy had no obvious connection to the newspaper, but it just was interesting that all these things were happening. The guy just got drunk and tried to crawl into bed with an ex-girlfriend. She got mad, slapped him around a little and kicked him out, sans clothes. He saw our back-porch light on and, well, the poor guy was cold.

Donna was halfway down the stairs when I shooed her back to the bedroom to get some sweatpants, socks and a sweatshirt. I never let the guy in the house (remember I had five kids to protect) and begged him to just keep the clothes.

I promise I'm not making this stuff up.

Phillis and I left Marietta about the same time. Ironically, we both ended up working in West Virginia. I went to Huntington about 100 miles downriver and Phillis went to Williamstown, the even smaller town right across the Ohio River from Marietta. Oddly, he sent me a beautiful card that featured the poem "The Evened Score."

The poem is magnificent, written by Richard M. "Pek" Gunn, poet laureate of Tennessee. I've never figured why he sent me that card. I guess he knew that the baseball theme would appeal to me and it did. My interpretation of the poem is that the author is telling us not to worry, we all eventually get what is coming to us, the umpires' bad calls even out.

I was particularly taken by this stanza:

> *"But somehow these things will be righted,*
> *We reap what we sow perhaps more,*
> *And the things that today seem benighted,*
> *Tomorrow will even the score."*

I hadn't realized that we were keeping score.

COLUMN: **Short story**

By Robert C. Gabordi
Managing Editor, Marietta Times
Published Nov. 19-20, 1994

So there it was in black and white in an official report on an investigation by a branch of the state attorney general's office.

I am short. This had been uncovered, according to the report, by Marietta police Chief Roger Phillis.

"Tell shorty Gabordi," the report alleged the chief said, "that one of these days I am going to retire and turn into the monster he thinks I am."

The report went on to say that "Gabordi stated that he does not feel threatened by the chief's comment."

Well, not per se, perhaps. But the implications were shocking. I mean, I didn't know anyone had noticed.

I thought I had hid it so well. Now the years of lies had been exposed, It was all a waste.

"Five-seven," I'd say when asked. "Almost five-eight."

Now I was caught. The chief had finally solved a caper. I'm short and he nailed me.

I anxiously read the next day's news reports. The chief was denying saying what he was alleged to have said in the report. He said the official report was filled with lies and rumors.

He denied saying the mayor was involved with gambling. He denied joking about wanting to kill his ex-wife. He denied this and he denied that.

But he never denied that I'm short.

Breaking the news

After two days, I decided I had to tell my wife. For 18 years, I had hidden the cruel truth from her.

I'd ply her with a little wine and a nice dinner. Flowers and chocolate would be nice, too.

"Honey," I began after the candles were lit, "I have to come clean with you. The chief has caught me cold and I have to come clean with you. I'm short. I'm not five-eight. I'm ..." My voice trailed off.

She cried, of course. Then she admitted to knowing.

Oh, she had pretended not to know, but she did. From the first date on. She pulled out a picture from our honeymoon, when I tried to get on an adult ride at an amusement park. I wasn't up to Mickey's hand. Not tall enough.

Perhaps if she had told me then, told me that I'm short, I mean it might have changed my life. The years of sitting down for group pictures, of wearing my pants extra short so my legs looked longer.

I mean it's hard always finding the shortest chair so your feet touch the floor. Sometimes you have to slump so no one notices your legs dangling under the table.

It had been hard, and now it was all a waste.

We told the children, of course. It was all going to come out. It had to now. The document was a public record.

Taking it hard

My oldest son took it the hardest. After all, how will he ever face his friends? He wanted to move out of town and has refused to go to school. He'll recover, I suppose. Kids are strong like that.

My boss was angry. Mainly, he said, I should have come clean with him. After all, we have strong company counseling programs for stuff like this.

I guess I fell victim to the – pardon the expression – *big* lie syndrome. That's where if you tell a big enough lie no one really doubts it. The problem comes when you start to believe your own lie, mistaking it for the truth.

So I'm thankful to Phillis for letting me know I'm short. After reading the report, now I understand that it is the truth that really will set us free. That's a good lesson for him, too.

Robert C. Gabordi now publicly admits to being 5 feet, 3 inches tall. He is managing editor of The Marietta Times

This is one of the columns I wrote that caused a stir in the Tallahassee community, as I alleged that FAMU had been covering up hazing in its band for a long time. The column itself doesn't discuss race, but that didn't stop some from using it to call me racist.

CHAPTER SIX

RACE AND JOURNALISM

It was 1995 and we were brought into the white marble room on the 31st floor of the Gannett tower for a post-conference discussion of our "feelings." We had just attended the National Association of Black Journalists conference at Unity, which brought together several organizations. E.J. Mitchell, an African American editor who I was particularly fond of since he had been assigned to work for me at Gannett New Media as a loaner, asked the question of his white counterparts in the Management Development Program:

"So how did it feel?"

It brought me back to George Washington Carver School in Lexington Park, Md. I had been assigned as a white student to what had been an all-black school. I was in the seventh grade and was among only a handful of white kids at the school. I ran for student council and was elected, then elected treasurer.

The feelings being expressed by my fellow Management Development Program members I had experienced as a child, and, like most children, I was adaptable. It just wasn't a big deal finding myself as a white kid to be surrounded by people of a different race, as the minority.

Years later, I would experience the feeling again while traveling in Pakistan. It was a bigger deal in Pakistan because there was a language barrier, as well, but not that much of a deal there either.

I understood where Mitchell was coming from, though. In every community I served in as editor, race was a factor. Even reporting and editing in big cities like Washington, D.C., working at Gannett News

Service, race relations were an issue in the late 1980s. I was news editor for the south and northeast regions. Lee Ivory was my boss, the managing editor. One day he had to go to Radio Shack, across the street from our office. I said I'd go with him.

Inside the store, I watched as a store employee followed Ivory around. Here he was, dressed in a suit and tie, being followed around the store. I, meanwhile, could have robbed the place blind. I wouldn't forget about this incident and years later, I wrote about it at one of my newspapers. I forget the circumstances that prompted the retelling of this tale, but the incident had a huge impact on my perspective.

Marietta's black population was less than 2 percent of the total, so the problem became one of visibility. There is a saying in journalism that we give voice to the voiceless, but, sometimes, it is our job to make sure the invisible are seen.

It was as if the only population that mattered was white. There is even a marker showing where the first white settlers arrived, although Native Americans had been there for years.

I had preached and trained the staff in diversity, but it became clear, I needed to make a statement. The opportunity arose during the Washington County Fair.

I waited until the last-minute to check a photo page we did from the fair. I knew I wouldn't find any black faces in the photos. I had been to the fair and saw a fair number of minorities there. I called the photographer in and ordered him back to the fair. Do not come back without at least one adorable child's black face having fun at the fair, I ordered. Message sent and received from that point forward.

In Huntington, there were questions of overt discrimination by the police force. Some had accused police of targeting young black males and suggested they were treated more harshly than white males doing the same things. We got involved by writing about it and sponsoring community meetings.

There was an incident that spurred things. It occurred in Riverfront Park where a group of kids were messing around. The black kids were arrested and the white kids were scolded and sent home, some people alleged.

There were additional concerns raised. Police hiring and training on diversity were questioned. When we called a meeting to discuss concerns, there was an overflow crowd, and a line that extended more than a block to try to get into the church where we held the meeting. Tensions were high; the incident at the park was only the match that lit the fire. The anger had been smoldering for some time.

To be honest, we didn't know what to expect when we called the meeting, which was held in a predominately African American church. We were relatively new at this community engagement thing, something most news organizations would get better at in the coming years. We didn't know if 20 people would show up or 200, but, in the end, we had many, many more people than that.

We figured we had plenty of space, even if we had to use the basement and the loudspeaker system, people could at least listen to what was being said. But there was still a line and too many people for the space we had.

We had a sign-up sheet for people who wanted to speak, and a microphone set up in the aisle so that speakers could have their say and sit down. The sign-up sheet was mostly ignored. People lined up and the line went out the door. I had a pretty good opening speech prepared, but made an on-the-spot decision to cut it in half and let people talk.

Most of the talk was about alleged transgressions by police or ideas for solving them. There was overwhelming consensus that more black officers were needed and training on race sensitivity was required.

There were also people who came to talk about jobs in the black community. One of them was a young woman named Marina Mathews. It was about halfway through the evening and I was beginning to get tired. There were a lot of emotions and anger in the room, but Mathews said she had a specific question for me. I stood up.

"I have a journalism degree and I'm a good writer. Why can't I get a job at The Herald-Dispatch?"

In other words, she was saying to put my money where my mouth is. The more this woman talked, the more I wondered what I could possibly say, so I went with the truth, which is always a good thing.

To be honest, I said, I've never heard of you or seen your resume or job application. You have applied, right?

Well, not exactly was the response. She had called, but not gotten much encouragement that we would hire local people, she said.

I made no promises, except that if she called me, I would interview her. I know what it is like trying to get a job at the hometown newspaper, I said.

She called and went through the interview process and, since we happened to have an open position, we hired her. She worked as a reporter for several years. She died after leaving Huntington at a very early age.

Not all the anger that night was directed at the police. Some people wanted to talk about the courts and the justice system in general. I remember one older man standing up and saying it was all very simple: Two people arrested for the same crime, one black and one white, ought to get the same sentence. Simple, right? But that rarely happened, he said.

About this time, I got a phone call from a nameless voice. He described my routine of going to the YMCA to work out, the route I drove to go to work and then return from work. He knew the names of my kids and the schools they attended. Then he made his point: We know about you and suggest you back away while you can. Nothing more specific.

I called the police chief who seemed genuinely concerned. He doubted it was anything more serious than a scare tactic. Someone who wanted to get me just would have gotten me and not put me on guard. He offered protection, but I declined. He doubted it was someone from his department, but admitted he wasn't certain about that.

Sometime after that, I was coming from speaking at a local school when I saw blue flashing lights in my rear-view mirror. I was near a convenience store, so I pulled in. Soon, it was two cruisers, then three, four, then five. I quit counting.

The voice on the speaker instructed me to slowly get out of my car with my hands in plain view. Then I was told to put my hands on the trunk of my car. I don't recall how my license got out of my wallet or my wallet out of my pants, for that matter. But I do recall hearing someone say, "Lieutenant, I think we can have him take his hands off the trunk now. I don't think we need to hold the editor of The Herald-Dispatch for questioning."

Boldly, I turned my head without removing my hands from the trunk and said, "That's executive editor. The title is executive editor."

The way it was explained to me, someone matching my description and driving a car just like mine had just robbed something and was getting away when police saw me and reacted. I didn't believe a word of that but decided the best thing to do was to go public with it and pretend to believe the explanation. Why is simple: I wanted the incident on the record and that the official explanation was mistaken identity. OK, I thought, if it really went down the way they claimed, they were even more incompetent than the public suspected.

It was – of course – an outrage and I could have been indignant about the whole episode. I could have gotten angry at the scene, no doubt that's what my mother would have done. I guess that's what a lot of people would have done.

But it was broad daylight and I was sure by now lots of people were watching. I really didn't want to give them any reason to shoot me. We were within a few blocks of my home. I really didn't think the police were going to shoot me under the circumstances, unless I did something stupid, which I did not.

And for all I knew – even to this day for all I know – I'm not sure if the police were telling the truth. Maybe it really was a case of mistaken identity. Maybe they were that incompetent. Maybe they really suspected a guy with a tie on coming back from speaking to school children and casually driving into the office had taken the time to stop and rob something and then causally drive his car to his day job.

Maybe. You never know.

So, I left it at that and wrote a column, saying if you ever get stopped by police – no matter what – listen to them and follow directions. No further apology was forthcoming.

That the newspaper had pointed out the department's flaws on race and diversity issues and this was just an unfortunate coincidence. Maybe.

Asheville was complicated: It had created zoning in order to implement segregated areas for blacks to live and work, but now was an island of progressive thought in a sea of far-right wingers. In 1995, Virgil Smith became the first African American publisher of a daily general-interest newspaper in North Carolina when he took over the Asheville Citizen-Times. While it seems inconceivable to me that did not happen until the mid-1990s, the reaction internally was even more astonishing.

One newsroom staff member asked him if having a black person as publisher wasn't a little like putting slaves in charge of the plantation. In what is only a testament to Smith's character and desire to be a change agent, the staffer was still employed at the newspaper when I arrived in 2001.

Asheville had a restaurant in town, the Ritz, that was something of a museum, too. It was in an area that had been zoned for black-owned businesses and had apparently been a hotel or bed and breakfast kind of place at one time. It had a room upstairs that baseball great Willie Stargell would stay in when his minor league team was in town to play the Asheville Tourists.

I had a managers' retreat at the Ritz one time. The food was spectacular and very Southern. It was spring and we must not have been paying attention, buried in our discussions or the amazing food, but we looked up and pulled back a window covering to find it had snowed several inches during our meeting.

It has been more than 15 years since I've been there, but if the restaurant is still around, I highly recommend the food. And if you can find someone to talk about the building's history, I recommend that, too.

The segregation era had long since faded away by the time I came to town, but the sentiment had not.

I would get phone calls and emails on occasion that would make me angry. Occasionally, I would respond. At times, the temper I inherited from my mother would show through.

I wrote a column once reacting to complaints about having too many black faces in photographs, especially on the front page. It was odd, I said, that I never got such emails or phone calls when the newspaper's photographs showed only white faces. The column went on to explain that we wanted the newspaper to reflect the diversity of the community, and that young people should be able to pick up a newspaper and see daily life as they know it.

One such email got my goat. It referenced Smith and made derogatory and racial comments about him. I had enough and called the circulation department asking that we cancel the person's subscription.

I then wrote the guy back and told him:

"I'm cancelling your subscription to the newspaper and if you have any trouble getting your money refunded please let me know. I'll pay for it myself. I wouldn't be able to sleep at night thinking it was possible that any money came from you that might end up in my paycheck to buy milk and food for my children."

The guy went ballistic and wrote CEO and board chairman Doug McCorkindale, among others, including every member of the Gannett board.

McCorkindale wrote him back, saying, "I agree with Bob."

Tallahassee was even more complex than Asheville on race and the Tallahassee Democrat had a history of being on the wrong side. The Tallahassee Democrat had backed segregationists 50 years earlier when a cross was burned on the lawn of two young women who attended Florida A&M University and the community had dubbed it the Dixiecrat.

In fact, when I approached Africa Price, who was managing editor of the Jackson (Tenn.) Sun and a Florida A&M University grad, about taking on the same role at the larger Tallahassee Democrat, her first reaction was astonishment.

"What?" she asked. "You want ME to become the managing editor of the Dixiecrat?"

"No," I replied, "I want you to become the managing editor of the Democrat and to promise to never use that term again. It's time for us to create the kind of newspaper that all communities in Tallahassee can own."

She joined me in Tallahassee, but our work was not easy. Tallahassee schools would become minority majority. Even though the community had more white people, more than half of the public school population was black. And the black community did not let me forget, at least not early on, that I had replaced a black man, Mizell Stewart, who was a terrific editor and person. Stewart stayed with Knight Ridder after it sold the Democrat to Gannett, but later would come to Gannett in a corporate role. I had no other transition where the outgoing editor was more gracious or helpful, and the others were all established Gannett properties.

In fact, one of my first meetings with an external group was with an ad hoc black leadership committee in my office. I think it was my first week on the job. The purpose, they told me forthrightly, was to let me know I was being watched, that they would withhold judgment only because of what I had done previously as an editor, but there were expectations that I would be that guy they had heard about in researching my background.

There was a lot of history on race in the community.

In May 1956, the two FAMU students got on a bus and sat in the only available seats, which were in the whites-only section. Wilhemina Jakes and Carrie Patterson paid their 10 cents and sat down. The driver told them to move. They were arrested and, only months after Rosa Parks ignited the boycott of buses in Montgomery, Ala., Tallahassee was faced with a similar situation.

The next night, a cross was burned on the young women's front lawn. The official position of the Tallahassee Democrat at the time was that everyone should calm down. It was, after all, only a small cross, the newspaper opined.

I researched deeper into the incident and the newspaper's history after being invited to speak at a dinner commemorating the 50th anniversary of the boycott. In attendance would be people who lived through the boycott and the children of heroes in the struggle for civil rights. I decided to do what should have been done long before: apologize for our position supporting segregation 50 years earlier. Publisher Pat Dorsey, in his first gig as a publisher after coming up on the finance side, agreed.

In a column about the apology years later, I explained why: "Time doesn't heal all wounds." The wounds in the black community for being pushed aside by their local newspaper 50 years ago were still deep and painful. The apology was a step in the right direction at long last.

Dorsey and I co-signed a column in a special section of the Democrat in May 2006. We said:

"It is inconceivable that a newspaper, an institution that exists freely only because of the Bill of Rights, could be so wrong on civil rights. But we were."

The apology was picked up and written about by other media, including Editor & Publisher magazine, which gave me a chance to explain further.

"(The Democrat) told the black community to calm down and behave and thought that integration was an unreasonable demand," I told E&P. "The failure of the paper was not so much in its reporting, even though it quoted predominantly white people. It was in the editorials and columns."

The night of the dinner I recall saying that we cannot change a culture by running away from our history. I was interrupted several times by applause and as I looked out among the crowd, I could see tears streaming down several faces. Many had waited a long time to hear those words from their hometown newspaper's editor.

That night changed a lot, but it didn't change everything and couldn't erase decades of learned behavior or the fact that, despite anything else, race was never far from some people's minds.

Of course, there were people I had angered, too, in issuing the apology. A freelance reporter who was well-connected with the established white community told me that "old Tallahassee" was very unhappy with me and didn't like me very much.

I said that was just fine with me because I didn't think very highly of old Tallahassee, either.

"Malcolm Johnson must be turning over in his grave," another caller yelled into the phone.

I'd bet he is, I replied. It was the cleverest thing I could think of at the time.

Malcolm Johnson was the longest tenured editor in the newspaper's long history. I was second longest with 10 years. Of course, it helped that he was also general manager. But the truth is he might have been a great editor except for one unforgivable fact: He supported segregation and did nothing to dispel the Dixiecrat image of the Tallahassee newspaper.

Race, it seemed, permeated so many topics. I researched, for example, why almost all obituaries for African Americans were published in the Thursday edition of the Tallahassee Democrat. I came away with a lot of opinions and theories, but the one I think was closest to the truth was this one:

Blacks had a hard time getting off work during the weekdays for things like a funeral, so services were always planned for the weekend. That being the case, Thursdays were a good day for the announcement. It also cut down on the number of days poor folks needed to buy the newspaper, if they knew the services would appear on Thursdays. It was a habit the community just never changed.

Every newcomer to town asked that question, I was told, and it was one of those things that I should just accept and not worry about.

Florida A&M University is in Tallahassee, as is Florida State University. FAMU was founded in 1887 and it is one of the largest historically black colleges and universities in the nation. It was created, at least in part, because Florida's 1885 constitution prohibited black students from attending school with white students.

FAMU's students have been at the forefront of civil rights as well as academic success. The school has much to be proud of, and I've already noted the role Jakes and Patterson played in ending segregation and promoting civil rights.

But my time in Tallahassee saw much upheaval at FAMU. It was marked by administrative woes, troubling state audits of its finances, and a hazing incident that left a young man dead. Its athletic program was likewise troubled during that period.

Florida State, on the other hand, is among the true national programs in sports. The two universities are just not on the same level when it comes to athletics, not in terms of public interest or budget or competitive level. Florida State's athletic program is expected to compete in every sport for conference and national recognition. They are different and bigger.

But when I got to Tallahassee, I was told by my sports team that our policy was equal coverage for both. I changed that almost immediately.

Phones rang. Charges of racism ensued.

Sorry, I said, but coverage of sports programs would not be decided based on race. The truth is FSU probably had more African American athletes than FAMU, simply because it had more sports teams.

FAMU was in the news a lot when I was there, usually for all the wrong reasons. Its finances were always a concern.

Its world renown band, the Marching 100, was suspended for nearly two years after the hazing-related death of drum major Robert Champion. It was discovered that people were marching with the band who weren't even students. It fell on interim president Larry Robinson, who served two stints as interim before he took over on a permanent basis, to implement the kind of changes that allowed the band to return.

Champion's death resulted in charges being brought against 15 people, including some who were charged with felonies.

Despite the fact that a young man died in a hazing incident, there were people who truly believed our coverage of the Marching 100 was racially motivated. Why not a big investigation into the Marching Chiefs, the Florida State marching band? It was a question I heard over and over.

I tried to address the questions logically, saying no one on the Chiefs had died, but trying logic was a mistake. Race is an emotional issue and pointing out that someone had died because of the behavior of members of the FAMU band did nothing to support my argument. Nor did it help to point out that the FAMU band was in fact world renown and with fame comes extra scrutiny. Nothing would stop the critics who were convinced we were being unfair. But we didn't back down from the investigations, either.

During my time in Tallahassee, we covered issues I considered far more important than which sports team got the most coverage, such as why infant mortality rates were many times higher among African Americans than white babies.

There were times when we were critical of black public officials, just as we were critical of white public officials. That included FAMU presidents and the mayor of Tallahassee. Invariably, the defense would include accusations that the newspaper and me personally were racist.

Standing firm in our coverage, regardless of accusation or criticism, after being willing to examine our fairness, is one of the things that journalists must do. It is what sets us apart, that we're willing to take the personal attacks to fight for truth and defend the First Amendment.

Two communities in the same state could not be more different than Tallahassee and Brevard County, the home of FLORIDA TODAY.

Before there was Martin Luther King Jr., there was Harry T. Moore. He and his wife Harriette Moore were at their home in Mims in Brevard County. It was Christmas 1951. Suddenly, a bomb exploded in their home.

Both were badly injured, but weren't taken to Brevard County hospitals, which were for whites only. Harry died in an ambulance on the way to a hospital 30 miles away in Seminole County. Harriette lived nine more days before succumbing to her wounds on Jan. 3.

The murders, despite multiple investigations, including one by Attorney General Charlie Crist, who was running for governor in 2006, have never been solved. Brevard County and much of the rest of the state and nation seem to want to just forget about the Moores.

Crist declared the murders were resolved, but he had found nothing new; evidence, which could not be proven, pointed to four members of the Ku Klux Klan who were previously known to be suspects.

In 1992, FLORIDA TODAY attempted to prick the community's conscience on the Moores and civil rights. Front-page articles and full pages inside told of the community's history and what the couple had accomplished, as well as the price they paid. But it was too little and too late.

In fairness, the TODAY newspaper did not come into existence until 1966, later becoming FLORIDA TODAY. For whatever reason, sadly, the Moore case never resonated with the Florida media. It should have. But it's very clear that Brevard County and the state of Florida didn't want this story to make headlines up North, where tourists came from to fill Florida's beaches, hotels and tax coffers.

Harry was at the forefront of creating the NAACP in Brevard and across Florida. He and his wife had been fired from their teaching jobs and he knew he had become a target of the KKK. He had begun to carry a gun.

The assassination of the Moores reminded me of a story published by the Clarion-Ledger in Jackson, Miss., during and after my time at Gannett News Service. The story was about the murder of civil rights activist Medgar Evers in 1963. The crusading work of investigative reporter Jerry Mitchell helped the state obtain a new trial for Byron De La Beckwith Jr.

Reports by the Clarion-Ledger showed a state agency in Mississippi had illegally helped Beckwith's defense. With new evidence, Beckwith was brought back to trial in 1994 and convicted. He died in 2001 but spent his last years in prison for the murder he committed 31 years earlier.

The difference between the two cases, besides the passage of 12 years, which might be significant since a lot had transpired in civil rights on the national scene in that time period, is that no one wanted the Moores' murders resolved, at least not initially, when evidence is freshest and tracks were unblemished.

I wonder if Beckwith could've been convicted had a politician of influence taken to Twitter and screamed "fake news" or questioned the credibility of the reporter and his news organization instead of being willing to examine the facts.

I thought about this case when FLORIDA TODAY published its podcast series, "Murder of the Space Coast" (more on that in CHAPTER 14) and contrasted how Mississippi responded to how Florida officials refused to even consider a fresh look at the Gary Bennett case, of how the Brevard County state attorney and sheriff criticized the newspaper for looking back into the case instead of re-examining facts themselves.

But if Mississippi was burning back then, as the film would later say, Florida was exploding in the 1950s. A series of bombs were blasting Catholic churches and Jewish synagogues. Everyone seemed to know the KKK was behind the bombings, including the bomb that killed the Moores.

NAACP national executive secretary Walter White came to Florida multiple times. He directly blamed the state government.

"If the governor had acted properly there would never have been this series of bombings and other outrages which have disgraced the lives of people in Florida, both residential and tourists," White said in a national wire service story on Jan. 4, 1952.

Florida Gov. Fuller Warren responded by attacking White, calling him a "hired Harlem hate-monger."

Sadly, Harriette Moore died from her wounds only one day after this exchange. Warren didn't use the term "fake news." That technique had not been invented yet as a method of discrediting reports.

Honestly, as a journalist, I wished the passage of time could have been spanned, that FLORIDA TODAY under my watch could have found a reason to wade back into the Moores' murders.

I would like to say Brevard has overcome its hateful history. But I'm just not sure that is true. During my time as executive editor of FLORIDA TODAY, the one reporter the Brevard County Sheriff's Office refused to work with is a black male and an excellent journalist, Jeff Gallop.

I met with the local sheriff, Wayne Ivey, multiple times to discuss this, and he said it wasn't him, but his team that didn't trust our reporter. He said Gallop sometimes got facts wrong, but as best I can tell, what he got "wrong" mostly was disagreeing with the sheriff's interpretation of the facts.

I sent Gallop to discuss the situation with the deputies in the sheriff's communications office.

He was told he was pushy. He's big and has a big voice. In other words, these deputies were intimidated by our reporter. He was told that when he couldn't get information through one avenue, he tried other ways to get it. In other words, he is a journalist. Gallop came back from the meeting more frustrated than informed. But he continued to report and do an excellent job.

The newspaper cannot force the sheriff or his department to work with or talk to anyone. It's just odd that they singled out Jeff Gallop. Does this mean I think Wayne Ivey, the county sheriff is a racist? All I can do as a journalist is describe the facts and let them speak for themselves.

But what I do know is that he bullied a reporter trying to do his job because his deputies said he was big, boisterous and pushy. Oh, and he's also black. Let's leave it at that.

I was surprised when I was called up on stage with the Brevard area mayors to celebrate the close of the 2019 Health First Mayors' Fitness Challenge. The cities had numerous programs to get people out walking, including a Walk with FLORIDA TODAY that featured me. But this was special because going on these walks was one of the ways I learned to walk again following my stroke in November 2018.

CHAPTER SEVEN

YES, THE MUSTACHE IS PINK

Mark Hohmeister has a wry sense of humor, and when he worked for me at the Tallahassee Democrat, I often couldn't tell if he was just being funny or expressing an opinion on something I was doing or saying. So, when he posted on Facebook support for a suggestion that this book be named "The Pink Mustache," I wasn't really sure if he was praising or mocking me.

"It doesn't get much more local than that," Hohmeister wrote of Leslie Hantman Smith's suggested title. "I somehow can't see Ben Bradley dyeing his mustache pink for a local awareness campaign."

Getting involved in the community is important to me and I believe it ought to be required of every local journalist. We are not like an enemy army of occupation, here only to keep order and report when people step out of line.

Getting involved and helping to build stronger communities is the kind of thing that makes a difference in the life of a community. It really gets to the fundamentals of what I believe is the job of a local editor. There is the editing of a single story or series and that is important. But it is the job of the editor to edit the fabric of the news report, to ensure it is unique and special, reflecting

Yep, the mustache is a hideous shade of pink to draw attention to our Go Pink! reader interaction project of the Tallahassee Democrat.

what is important in that place. I've heard the phrase "great newspaper, wrong community" too many times.

Marshall University played West Virginia University in football for the first time in decades on the day that Princess Diana was killed. Months later, I was at a newspaper conference somewhere out West. I heard other editors poking fun at The Herald-Dispatch because our top story was the football game when most everyone else led with Princess Di. I think we got it right, and they did, too.

Why do I think that? Because we understood our community and knew that it would expect us to understand the emotional and historic importance of that football game. Maybe the other editors knew their communities, too. But they didn't know Huntington.

It is more than that, of course. We saw in Marietta how important reader interaction or public journalism could be with our domestic violence project. If there was any doubt about the level of importance I placed on this it was cemented in Huntington first with our race project and then with West Virginia After Coal. That was supervised by our managing editor, Len LaCara, and it won the national James K. Batten Award for Excellence in Civic Journalism from the Pew Center for Civic Journalism in 2001.

That was at the tail end of my time in Huntington and I was as proud of that award as any we had ever received. It showed what working in partnership with communities and broadcast stations could do, and we used print, video and digital every effectively.

(text continues after the image on the following page)

There are few – if any – organizations in most communities that can pull people together or tear them apart like a news organization.

How do you get to know the community? It takes more than just being born there. You get involved. You engage citizens. You spend as much time away from the office as possible being in the community.

Doing this has opened me up to criticism, I know, but so what? Shortly after I left the Democrat, the new publisher, Skip Foster, was introduced to a meeting of the Tallahassee Tiger Bay Club. This is a club that is made up of politicos, media members, and others who would get together to talk about issues of the day. In his introduction, the speaker said, "and he doesn't give a damn if you go for a walk this weekend."

That was a dig at me, of course, because I did care. I created something called Move.Tallahassee.com that attempted to get people up and moving for their health. The group is still going strong. It really seemed to irk some people that we used my position as executive editor to pull people together to walk and explore the region by foot. I'd put something online and in print and tried to get people to show up for their health, physical and mental. We'd get 50 to 400 people, typically.

It was also their chance to talk to me about whatever was on their minds with one exception: I would not talk politics. This was to avoid private conversations with politicians without a notepad in my hands to write down exactly what they said.

Believe it or not, the walks made some people angry. I'm not sure why, except that they were too busy or too lazy to join us, or just not interested, and worried about who was showing up to try to influence me. Or maybe they worried that I might give special consideration to people who showed up to walk. I don't know, but I thought it petty.

We continued the walking with the editor in Brevard for a few years and we got good turnouts. It was just a tool to get to know the community and each other better. It is just one way but really gets at my belief in what the relationship between the news organization and the community ought to be.

If the haters have their way and news organizations of the type that I'm describing go away, who will be there for the community? I spent my career believing that it was my duty to use my superpowers as the editor of the dominant local news organization for good.

I was determined that we would stand for something, and we would have rules. The most important rule was that whatever we did, we were all in it together.

One of the best examples of that was Go Pink! at the Tallahassee Democrat. Hohmeister was an associate editor on the editorial page and Smith was market development director. We were going all out to bring attention to breast cancer and to get women talking to their medical professionals about their health.

So, we challenged the community to Go Pink! with us. We printed the newspaper on pink paper, painted our building's white pillars pink, lit up the building at night in pink, and even painted our grass pink, which was lovely until it rained. Much of this was Smith's doing. She was very creative. One year, I dyed my mustache pink.

It was hideous, but sure got attention.

Our idea was to get notice, not for ourselves, but to remind women and the men who loved them to talk to their medical professionals about mammograms and other testing for early detection of breast cancer.

There were some who thought we went overboard, but we were definitely all in. We sponsored a 5K that was Go Pink! attire. We got the local hospital, Tallahassee Memorial Healthcare, to bathe its centerpiece building in pink lighting. Local high school and college teams wore pink uniforms. People put up Go Pink! signage in their windows all over town. We raised a lot of money, which we donated to local groups, including Joanna Francis Living Well Foundation.

I met Francis on a youth baseball field. As I've mentioned, coaching baseball was something else I did. I coached my own kids, sure, but coached long before and long after my kids played ball. I felt coaching was something I could do for the community, and I was serious about coaching. I had played at Roger Williams College my freshman year before hurting my shoulder and I knew the game inside and out. I even went to coaching camps and clinics to get better.

It's not that I always had the time. One time in Huntington I changed out of what I called my monkey suit to my coaching clothes in the men's room at the field. I was late and hurrying to get my lineup card to the umpire at home plate. One of the moms called me over to the fence and said in a not so quiet voice, "Hey, coach, I don't know if it is a new style or something, but your pants are on inside out."

See, I told you I know the game inside and out.

I coached for 35 years. Several times, I was selected to coach All-Stars. I coached kids of all ages. One year, I coached my youngest, Alex, in T-Ball while coaching an 18-and-older team. Amazing how with boys of whatever age a lot of the problems back to the same thing.

I was coaching third base when a chubby 5-year-old wanted to whisper something to me.

"See that girl over there?" he asked.

"Yeah, the one playing first base?"

"Yes, sir. I'm in love with her."

"OK," I said. "But what's that got to do with baseball?"

"Next time I hit the ball I'm going to stop and talk to her."

That season, I had to get between a couple of 18-year-olds in my dugout. One, let's call him Thomas, was going after Tim. Both were a fair bit larger than me.

"What's the problem?" I asked.

"You notice how they all want to play left field?" Thomas asked. "Well, it's because my mom is down there sitting, and she has a short skirt on."

"Don't worry about it," I said, "I get to decide who plays where." And I started to walk away.

"OK," I said, while still walking, "so, I'm playing left field."

Soon after we got to Tallahassee, I was leaving the dugout to walk across to the third base coach's box when someone yelled from the stands, "How do we get more Gator news in the paper?"

Of course, that meant the University of Florida Gators, archrivals of the Florida State Seminoles, who are based in Tallahassee.

"You move to Gainesville," I yelled back and cemented my standing with the fans, most of whom applauded their approval.

On another occasion, I was coaching a little kids' All-Star team when a mom poked her head in the dugout. Now this violated one of my primary rules: No parents in the dugout during games.

"But, coach," she protested "I just found out you're the editor and we've been having delivery issues."

Out, out, out of my dugout.

The year I helped coach a 13-year-old advance play Babe Ruth All-Star team, we won the Florida state championship and the Southeastern United States championship without a single loss. As we traveled to the east coast of North Carolina and then West Texas for the World Series, I discovered just how powerful social media could be. I was Tweeting updates, which were being captured on Tallahassee.com. When I got busy with the games, I was sometimes delayed in posting and I really heard it from followers. We took third in the World Series that year, by the way, which was great, but we had higher expectations for that group.

I've always felt the need to be involved in local causes. I thought about it from an academic standpoint and, in fact, got into an argument with Nancy Monaghan once when we were on an elevator in the USA TODAY building long before either of us went to Huntington, me as editor and her as my boss, the publisher.

I'd been in Huntington a couple years before she became publisher. Soon after she arrived, I broached the subject over lunch. "Nancy, I think you should know how deeply involved I am in the community," I said.

Not to worry, she said. She had changed her mind after working as a community newspaper publisher in Chambersburg, Pa.

Good thing. In another chapter, I talk about the work we did in Huntington on police diversity issues, so I'll not repeat it here. But even before I got to Huntington, the newspaper was redefining what community involvement meant, thanks in large part to my predecessor, Randy Hammer. Under his leadership, the newspaper had created something called "Our Jobs. Our Children. Our Future." It created a community response to the loss of 500 manufacturing jobs.

Under me, we continued that and expanded it. We raised the money, for example, to build a library at Geneva Kent Elementary School, which had been named for a former Herald-Dispatch staff member. When Huntington decided to apply for an Enterprise Zone designation, which had the potential to be worth hundreds of millions of dollars in development money, we stepped up and helped by setting up community meetings and offering support in other ways.

We were so involved it made some at corporate nervous. I got a note from Phil Currie, vice president of news, saying so. Be sure you are not sacrificing your watchdog role, he warned, telling me that sometimes I kept him up at night worrying about how far we should take community involvement.

"Phil," I said when we met in person shortly after I got the letter, "I think this enhances our role as watchdogs. Now we know which rocks to peek under and where they are located."

At Asheville, Tallahassee and FLORIDA TODAY we did a number of things to get involved with the community. When planes struck the first of the Twin Towers on Sept. 11, 2001, I was in a basement of a library in Hendersonville, N.C., to help create a task force to look at domestic violence issues. In Tallahassee, I served on Whole Child Leon, Kids Incorporated, and the board of the Early Learning Coalition because I felt a key issue for Florida's capital city was children.

In Tallahassee, we did everything we could related to Florida State and Florida A&M University – and to a lesser extent – Tallahassee Community College. FSU has a wonderful event that was called Seven Days of Opening Nights. I think the name changed because the event grew beyond the seven days. We saw people like Burt Reynolds, an FSU graduate and former Seminole football player, and Willie Nelson because of this event we helped sponsor. The artists would appear on stage for the public, and they provided workshops or lectures or students. It is a very cool event.

One year, I was invited to appear on stage with actor-comedian Martin Short. I had watched him over and over again in the movie "Three Amigos" when my kids were small, and we got a VHS player. As part of his act, Short had me join him on stage for a question-and-answer "interview." If he didn't like the question – or sometimes even if he did – he would whack me with a rolled-up newspaper. I'm not going to lie, it really hurt after a while.

He whacked me one time for saying something funny and he leaned over, smiled and said softly, "That's for being funnier than me. I'll tell the jokes up here."

In Tallahassee, we got involved in a major environmental issue: the health of Wakulla Springs, one of the largest natural springs in the country. It is also where some huge films were shot, including Tarzan and Creature from the Black Lagoon. It's not as if people were sitting around doing nothing beforehand as the pristine springs deteriorated, but our special reports combined with community meetings at the springs made the politicians pay attention and changes were made.

In Brevard County, the big issue was also the environment and we paid more attention than ever to the health of the Indian River Lagoon. The Indian River Lagoon is 156 miles long on the east coast of Florida. It is one of the most biodiverse estuaries in the world. It is impacted by different issues north to south and cleaning it up will take a huge and coordinated effort.

I have no doubt that the passage of a special tax for lagoon cleanup happened in ultra-conservative Brevard County because FLORIDA TODAY led the way. But we also partnered with Keep Brevard Beautiful to roll up our own sleeves and help clean up the lagoon.

Attention on the lagoon and our lawmakers' woeful record in supporting help for the lagoon was the focus of a legislative scorecard grading how they voted; most failed. Only one, Sen. Debbie Mayfield, got it. She said if you looked at the health of the lagoon, how could lawmakers expect to be graded better?

In Brevard and Tallahassee, I started walking programs and helped lead health-related campaigns. In Tallahassee, ironically, I chaired the most successful Heart Walk campaign in county history for the American Heart

Association and the American Stroke Association. The irony is that on Nov. 9, 2018, I suffered a major brain-stem stroke and could've and probably would've died if not for amazing work by the medical professionals at Heath First and EMTs in Brevard. More on that in another chapter.

In Tallahassee, I twice sang on stage as part of fund-raising efforts, and once took second in a dancing with the stars kind of event. I had a torn meniscus the night of the show and considered escaping from the upper floor of the downtown hotel, but the only route that seemed feasible would have been to rappel down the side. So, I was forced to dance with my beautiful dancer instructor. Hey, anything for the cause.

It's not that there have never been conflicts with my journalism and community engagement, which is what journalists always worry about. Twice, I have had issues. In Huntington, I agreed to go onto the board of a nonprofit that helped people with disabilities get equipment to help them be mobile. At my very first meeting, the executive director announced that the treasurer was under investigation because money was missing.

Fortunately, I had prepared for this possibility. I tell everyone that asks me to be involved in their program that I am first and foremost a journalist 24-7. Anything you tell me could end up in a news story. Please exclude me if you have something very sensitive that can't come out. Do that, though, and I'll leave you on my own.

Which is what I did with the mobility group in Huntington. I immediately resigned and went back to my office to tell the other editors what I had learned.

In the other instance, I was on the board of Bridges in Brevard County, which provides services to persons with disabilities and their families. I am – as of the writing of this chapter – chairman of the Bridges board. My daughter, Jessica, attends their day program. I went on the board in the summer of 2018. In early 2019, we received word that an employee had been arrested on charges related to a client in one of our group homes getting pregnant and having a child. This dated back to 2015, not only before I went on the board, but also before we moved to Brevard County.

As board members, we were never apprised that an employee was a suspect until he was arrested. When I found out, I was months away from retiring from FLORIDA TODAY. So, I suspended my membership on the Bridges board. After I retired, I went back on the board.

There are many other things I have been involved with. For instance, I've been an active member of Rotary on occasion. I've been on the United Way boards in Tallahassee and Brevard County. I just think it is important for the editor of a local news organization that focuses on local journalism to understand and be involved with the community. So, I have been.

I've also been involved with some journalism organizations, because I think that's important, too. I was an early member of the Online News Association and a board member and later president of the Florida Society of News Editors. Of course, I also worked with the International Center for Journalists.

I don't know what kinds of things Ben Bradlee did in the greater Washington area. But I think Hohmeister is probably right. I bet he never dyed his mustache pink.

Reprinted courtesy of Gannett Co. Inc.

CHAPTER EIGHT

PRISONERS IN PARADISE

By the time Jim, 49, and Penny Fletcher, 35, were released from their dirty, overcrowded cells in St. Vincent and the Grenadines, jails that resembled medieval dungeons, media worldwide had taken notice of their case. Why not? It had all of the elements of a Hollywood movie: sex, murder, high-stakes politics, drugs and alcohol abuse, and, of course, mystery and drama.

Prosecutors and St. Vincent law enforcement – such as it was – had begun to not only take notice of the media coverage, but also argued that the media had put St. Vincent itself on trial. They took special aim at the Fletchers' hometown newspaper, The Herald-Dispatch of Huntington, W.Va., along with CNN and ABC's Nightline program.

This story unfolded while I was executive editor of The Herald-Dispatch, my second stop as editor of a daily Gannett newspaper. The H-D had a reputation where some great editors had sharpened their skills. I had been in Huntington for only about a year in 1996 when Jim and Penny were arrested on a capital murder charge in the shooting of water taxi driver Jerome "Jolly" Joseph.

It would go on for nine months. Only The Herald-Dispatch had covered the Fletcher's story almost from the beginning until the end, when Eastern Caribbean Judge Dunbar Cenac ordered the charges dismissed.

I admit that I love telling this story, maybe more than I should. After all, someone shot Joseph and the Fletchers lived through what could only be described as pure hell. Still, in a 1998 article looking back at our coverage in the Gannetteer, our company's internal magazine, I called it a "once-in-a-lifetime story."

That was because this was one that you can point to and say unmistakably that had local journalists not been there, had we not been willing to do – and spend – whatever it took to tell it, the outcome would not have been as happy for the Fletchers. It was journalism that mattered.

Specifically, had Mark Truby, our reporter, and The Herald-Dispatch not been there, more than 2,100 miles from home, Jim and Penny Fletcher might very well have hanged. More likely, though, they would have been left to rot and die in their horrible cells.

As it was, in the end, Jim Fletcher's 125 pounds looked skeletal on his 6-foot-1-inch body and, faced with the mere possibility of further delay in their trial, Penny was rushed to the hospital after blacking out for 80 minutes during court proceedings.

No, I'm convinced our reporting was a major factor in why this case even went to trial and why the Fletchers were ultimately freed. That's why this is the story I'd remember most from my career, the one I'm most proud to have been a part of, the kind that would make a whole career of covering chicken dinner banquets worth it.

It proved my belief that there is no such thing as a small journalism outfit, regardless of the number of subscribers or unique online visitors or staff size. Journalists who think their work is small or insignificant, who fail to see the greater good and the bigger picture, do their communities a grave disservice. I pity them for their ignorance.

I cannot imagine the suffering or the anguish of the families – the Fletchers or the Josephs. For a while, it must have seemed that besides their family and friends and one West Virginia newspaper, no one else seemed to care much.

Sure, Bill Clinton, then president of the United States, eventually got involved and presumably asked and received assurances that the Fletchers would be treated fairly. But even that came months after his own State Department told him the couple was not guilty. And St. Vincent Prime Minister James Mitchell seemed to promptly forget that pledge. He knew Clinton placed his trade initiative, then being negotiated with Caribbean nations, above the couple's lives.

Other media outlets, including the Miami Herald, the Seattle Times, the Pittsburgh Post-Gazette, CNN, The Associated Press and, of course, Gannett News Service, eventually picked up The Herald-Dispatch's stories. Some sent reporters to cover the trial. But we were the only one that committed to telling this story regularly and consistently from beginning until end.

"Sending people so far away was a big decision for a newspaper our size and meant spending a lot of money," I said in that 1998 Gannetteer article. Publisher Nancy Monaghan not only backed the decision, she also was pushing us. "She came to me and said, 'You've got to get your arms around this story. It's a big one.'"

I'm not going to say that I never worried about the cost of this story, but I didn't dwell on it. Even in those days, when newspaper companies like Gannett made their stockholders rich and printing newspapers was almost like printing money, we watched the pennies very closely. The cost was always there in the back of my mind.

(text continues after the image on the following page)

Bob Gabordi

The 'Net — a source and resource

As the Fletcher case unfolded, The Herald-Dispatch realized the story had interest and implications beyond the Huntington circulation area. So the newspaper turned to the Internet.

"We needed a Web site — to seek information from other people as well as to give them information," says Bob Gabordi.

In 1995, the Rochester (N.Y.) Democrat and Chronicle launched a special Web site for Ryder Cup golf coverage because its audience extended worldwide. Gabordi remembered and pitched a special site on the Fletcher case to Jack Williams, vice president/business development in the Newspaper Division and head of its on-line development team.

Williams gave the thumbs-up.

Herald-Dispatch Market Development Director Amy Howat and Market Information Specialist Lisa Wallace, who'd posted personal Web pages, volunteered to set up the site. They contacted a local Internet service provider and arranged for the paper's systems department to install a computer in the newsroom with software to build Web pages. The site (www.ramlink.net/herald-dispatch) was up within a week.

"It was a real cooperative effort," says Howat, who got the site listed on Internet search engines Yahoo!, Webcrawler and Lycos and ran house ads in the paper to drive readers to it.

She and Wallace spent only a few extra hours on the project, she says. There were no big glitches. The only challenge: "Getting a PC-based computer in the newsroom to interact with a Mac-based computer which stored photos. Systems figured it out."

The site was "a lead-generator for News as they continued to flush out the story," Howat adds.

The paper received hundreds of e-mails with information from individuals and human rights agencies. The e-mails also gave staffers an idea what typical St. Vincent people were feeling, Gabordi says. "People tended to speak freely because they felt safe on the Internet, whereas they were concerned about using phones in St. Vincent for fear they were bugged."

What price justice?

"Stories like this separate newspapers from other businesses," wrote The Herald-Dispatch's Bob Gabordi in an editorial about the Fletcher murder case.

The paper's decision to follow the case all the way to St. Vincent "made absolutely no sense from the profit-and-loss point of view," he said. "We have invested, to use the financial term, tens of thousands of dollars in this story in travel and legal costs alone. Most businesses need to see an immediate return before risking that kind of cash. But this is what we do, it is what a newspaper does and why we have a First Amendment."

of Force," examined the use of force by police in Cincinnati. Led by reporters John Hopkins and Mark Braykovich and published in June, it was prompted by a controversy over the shooting of a mentally ill black man who was cornered by more than a dozen police in February 1997. The situation had exacerbated tensions between blacks and Cincinnati's predominately white police force.

Hopkins was the reporter who'd covered the shooting; Braykovich is a database expert. The two interviewed police officials, community leaders, witnesses and subjects of police use of force. They reviewed about 1,400 cases involving police use of force and/or injuries to individuals arrested by police during 1995 and 1996. Only once in all those cases did police determine that excessive force was used. Yet, the files of the police's internal investigation unit revealed many questionable cases.

Other findings: Seven of 10 individuals injured in police confrontations or subjected to the use of force by police during the two-year period were African American. Also, many citizens mistrusted police and the independent city agency that investigates allegations of police misconduct.

As a result of the stories, the mayor and council agreed to examine the problem. The independent watchdog agency reorganized and has a new director. An initiative changing the way the police chief is appointed was defeated on the November ballot.

An internal police probe into the February shooting has since cleared officers of wrongdoing. The case was turned over to the U.S. Justice Department, which is still investigating. "There's been no further action on the problem," says Editor Lawrence Beaupre. "Politicians basically have ducked it."

Reprinted courtesy of Gannett Co. Inc.

But I never saw in black and white just how much money our coverage and this story's legal fees cost us. I don't think anyone bothered to pull those numbers together. That's a credit to my Gannett bosses, by the way. No one wanted to bother the editor with what justice cost in this case.

But the marketing department saw it as an opportunity to increase the number of subscribers. They put out what we called brag ads, reminding readers how amazing our coverage was and why they should subscribe. They even gave non-subscribers a chance to order special coverage after the Fletchers' trial. I don't know if it worked, but it was refreshing to see them marketing the value of our content instead of how much the coupons inside were worth.

I was told rather off-handedly that we spent more than $200,000 reporting and defending legally this story. We were prepared to spend a lot more than that had a lawsuit not been dropped relatively quickly. I know that because I was on calls with the multinational legal team.

Oh, the lawsuit. The suit was a story in and of itself. It was filed by St. Vincent Police Commissioner Randolph Toussaint in July 1997 against Truby based on his reporting in April. Toussaint claimed libel and damage to reputation. Shortly after he filed the suit, Toussaint resigned under pressure from other St. Vincent officials.

Toussaint said Truby had damaged his reputation on St. Vincent based on a story published in Huntington. The suit was one of the first filed against a newspaper based on its reporting on the Internet. One big problem with that is the story was not on the Internet. It was 1997 and we had not yet figured out that everything should be on the Internet.

The article in question alleged attempted extortion by Toussaint, who had offered to free the Fletchers for $100,000. Our source was a copy of a letter Truby had obtained. It was written by Arturo Diaz, one of the Fletchers' attorneys and a U.S. citizen from Puerto Rico, to U.S. General Counsel Philip Jones in Barbados.

Diaz was detained and questioned by St. Vincent authorities when he showed up for what was supposed to be the start of the trial on July 7. He was one of two members of the Fletchers' law team who were detained by law enforcement and questioned. In Diaz's case, they briefly took away his passport.

West Virginia Sen. Jay Rockefeller, who would play an important role in the case, was quoted as saying at a minimum, St. Vincent authorities were giving the appearance of trying to intimidate the defense team. It might have been the understatement of the year. Intimidation tactics were standard operating procedure throughout the life of the case.

In our story about the lawsuit, which was written July 19 by Shannon Martz (Truby obviously could not write about his own legal issues), I was quoted while having one of my mother's temper tantrums. I said Toussaint clearly "had other problems, too" with his reputation and that his lawsuit only served to enhance the credibility and determination of our reporting.

"Allegations were made by a responsible attorney to the appropriate U.S. official," I said in the July 19, 1997, story. I called the lawsuit "ludicrous."

Yes, I have no doubt that the courage of The Herald-Dispatch and, in particular Truby and photographer Steve Moses, in standing up to these corrupt officials by doing their jobs as journalists, saved the Fletchers' lives.

An overstatement? Perhaps. Some have said so. The Fletchers had a lot of money and knew a lot of the right people to help. In 1969, Fletcher graduated in the same college class as former Vice President Dan Quayle, from tiny DePauw University in Greencastle, Indiana, with an enrollment of fewer than 2,000 students. Fletcher had other rich and powerful friends, including members of Congress. Before it was over, the family had hired enough lawyers to form a small brigade, including at least one person based in Washington whose task it was to influence opinion.

None of that prevented the Fletchers from spending nine months in that hell hole of a prison, though. All of the family's money and influence didn't help much until The Herald-Dispatch's coverage started finding its way into news outlets around the world. That put pressure on St. Vincent's fragile tourist economy and forced the Clinton administration to get interested.

A lesson I learned in covering this story that I carried with me the rest of my career: When journalists stand up to bullies and demagogues, journalism and truth telling sometimes win.

As an editor, I was blessed by being surrounded by great talent in the Huntington newsroom. Much of it was home grown, products of Marshall University's grand journalism program.

Truby was simply the best reporter with the most potential I had ever worked with. Not quite 30 at the time, Mark was a student at Marshall who we hired even before he got his degree, which he didn't get until years later. He would leave Huntington soon after what became known as the "Prisoners in Paradise" story for USA TODAY and then the Gannett-own Detroit News and then leave that newspaper and daily journalism for Ford Motor Co.

He was smart, courageous and tough. We built a playground once at a Huntington elementary school. Truby was on the jack hammer. That's pretty tough.

I was not surprised to learn he went on to become Ford's chief communications officer and reports directly to the president and CEO of Ford. He left journalism in 2007. We lost a lot of smart, talented journalists in those days, the beginning of the dark times of layoffs and shrinkage for the news business. Gannett sold the Detroit News in 2005 in a three-way, multi-newspaper deal in which Gannett got the Detroit Free Press and the Tallahassee Democrat. That's when I went to Tallahassee from Asheville as the first Gannett editor to become the executive editor of Florida's capital city's newspaper.

I had the impression that the selling of the Detroit News was the final straw for Truby, that he would get out of journalism after that. He sent me a cryptic email right after the sale that led me to think he would go. And he did. Good for Ford. He has had a great career.

Truby would win major journalism awards for his work on the Fletchers' story, which was a finalist for the national Associated Press Managing Editors award for public service reporting. That was announced, coincidentally, during the Fletchers' trial. Truby also won the National Press Club's top award for diplomatic correspondence and the Denver Press Club's national award for police reporting. His talent and potential were nearly unlimited.

Truby was surprised by the attention the story got. When he returned to Huntington from his first trip to St. Vincent, we worked day and night to produce a three-day series.

"The first day was four inside pages – maps, graphics and photos," he recalled recently. "The next two days had inside pages as well. That was before they shrunk the paper. We worked until 2 a.m. for like a week on this.

"When I came back to St. Vincent, people somehow had the copies of the story. Not a printout. It was photocopied and faxed over in pieces and passed around and recopied. People were like, 'You are the guy who did the big story?' They either told me it was amazing or terrible if they were with the prime minister's office."

Truby had great editors and a close-knit team supporting him at The Herald-Dispatch. I think he was closest to Fran Allred, the metro editor, one of the very best the business had to offer, which is a statement about her as a person as much as it is about her as an editor. She raised Mark and a lot of other people in the journalism business, professionally speaking. She taught them about writing, of course, but she also taught them how to work. She worked her way up from the "women's section" to at one point running the place, but she was metro editor when I got to Huntington.

Literally, when I was driving to Huntington from Marietta, I got a call from corporate suggesting I might need to watch her as I settled into my new role to make sure she wasn't a problem. I pulled off the road and listened politely but knew from researching the staff already that she was the glue that held things together. The call made me angry because I knew what they were suggesting, and I knew I wouldn't create that issue right out of the box. I would ignore them. But being right when you decided to ignore corporate "suggestions" is a great risk. You better be right if you wanted a second chance.

I knew quickly that I was right about Allred. She not only made her reporters better, but also everyone around her gained from her wisdom and experience, including – maybe especially – me.

Mickey Johnson was the managing editor and pure Huntington inside and out. I can't remember what strange title they had come up with for Johnson before I got to Huntington, but it was clear he was the No. 2 editor in the room. I decided to name him managing editor to get rid of all pretense, so with the publisher's approval, I did.

Whoops. That was another telephone call from corporate. They agreed with the decision but would have liked the courtesy of being consulted. Managing editors were supposed to be people we think have a future as executive editors. I was sure that Johnson would run his own newsroom.

Johnson left Huntington in 1997 to become executive editor of Gannett newspapers in Ohio and Georgia, managing editor in Pensacola, Fla., and executive editor and general manager in Richmond, Ind. When he retired, he came home to live in Huntington, where he belonged. I was glad he was on the team as long as he stayed, especially through the Fletcher ordeal.

The four of us, plus Monahan and to a somewhat lesser extent James E. Casto, who ran the opinion page, were the decision-makers on the Fletcher coverage, but in reality everyone on staff was somehow involved. My bigger point is that the right group of people were together at the right moment to work on the story about the ordeal the Fletchers endured.

For the Fletchers, of course, it didn't start off as an ordeal. It was a great adventure. They had a 47-foot Wellington cruiser, the Carefree, and they sailed her to Bequia island, one of the Grenadines that comprised St. Vincent, which had been a British colony. The nation's lineage would become critically important to us when we were sued. The ultimate appeal, should that have become necessary, would have been to the Privy Council in London.

To say the Fletchers were the prototypical "ugly Americans" would be an understatement. Jim Fletcher's father, J.R., then 81, who was an elegant and charming man, was only being delicate when he was quoted in The Observer of London saying: "They certainly were not the best representatives of the United States."

They drank too much. They were loud and wild, especially Penny. They used bad language. Several people said they heard her say she was going to "kill a nigger" as retribution for an alleged attack on her at some point during the trip. She denied having said that, but it was the type of attention and comment they attracted.

They had a .22-caliber gun, the same caliber that was used to kill Joseph, the 30-year-old water taxi driver. The gun went missing, as did some of the ammo. They said it was stolen, but there is no evidence that theft had been reported to authorities. It was never found. By the way, it is relevant that while it was the "right" caliber, there was no evidence that the ammunition was a match for the slug that was found in Joseph.

Rumors about the Fletchers abounded, fed, no doubt, by their boisterous, showy lifestyle. Penny's behavior scandalized St. Vincent.

During the trial, the prosecution introduced racy testimony from a former deckhand aboard the Carefree. He said he saw Jerome and Penny embrace in a sexual way. I've never figured out exactly what that meant.

The Fletchers were also extremely generous and, ironically, it was this trait that some say might have been their near fatal flaw. When the local schools could not afford new books, the Fletchers bought them. Instead of gratitude, the politicians were embarrassed, especially Mitchell, the prime minister.

So, when Jolly Joseph turned up dead, the Fletchers were arrested and spent nine months in jail.

Jim Fletcher lost 40 pounds on a diet of tea, bread and rice. Penny Fletcher was hospitalized for an infection she acquired in prison. They sat on hard wooden benches. When they were freed, sitting in chairs with backs was a special treat.

At the beginning, Truby had heard about the Fletchers' story from sources and did some routine initial reporting on it in 1996. Then I heard about it from friends at the YMCA. After those initial reports, we decided we had to go to St. Vincent. I made that decision after a morning locker-room discussion where I was surrounded and pumped for any news we had on the Fletchers.

Truby would make four trips, sometimes with photographer Steve Moses, who complained of having to pay bribes to get permission to shoot photographs. I wished he wasn't so blatant about paying the bribes when he submitted his expense reports, but that was a hint of what was to come. Line items called "government bribes" on expense reports are frowned upon by Gannett accountants. I think I changed his report to say it was for meals, suggesting he was eating well on the company dime.

I'll never forget a frantic phone call from my office. It seemed that our worst fears might be realized. I was headed to Connecticut with my family via car to take care of some family business. The voice on the other end said, "Call Mark. He might be in trouble."

Truby was in St. Vincent and not easy to reach. When I did, he said he had been at the hotel swimming pool when he was approached by a couple of what we think were St. Vincent national police asking questions. I suppose he was easy to pick out. He was wearing his American flag swim trunks, he said. The rumor was they would be back to arrest him.

St. Vincent, like many other countries, has a criminal charge for what they call criminal libel. In the United States, libel is mostly a civil matter. Later in my career, I would see criminal libel arrests used to try to silence reporters on the trail of corrupt politicians in other countries.

My first call was to Gannett super attorney Barbara Wall, who was every journalist's – especially Gannett journalists' – friend. We decided we would call Sen. Rockefeller for help and guidance. The arrest of an American journalist, if that's what St. Vincent had in mind, would be an international incident that no one wanted.

We got through to Rockefeller, somehow. He did whatever senators do in these situations and arranged to have the U.S. counsel in nearby Barbados fly via private plane to St. Vincent and pick up Truby and fly him out.

Truby came back to West Virginia but was not there long. He almost immediately began lobbying to go back to St. Vincent to see the story through to the end. The next week, after the initial danger passed, he went back. It was a tough call, but I felt if we didn't go back, the message would be that American media could be intimidated.

It was important that he be there for other reasons, of course.

This was a local story for us, and we intended to cover it that way. It involved local people. Penny had a daughter by a previous marriage who was friends with my daughter. They weren't best friends but knew each other well enough that she had been to our house and I knew who she was. Huntington, by any standard, is a small town. Everyone is somehow connected, whether by blood or friendship. Word gets around.

In some ways, Bequia island, the largest of the Grenadines, is about as different from West Virginia as you can imagine, literally more than 2,000 miles apart. Both are poor, though, and know what it is like to have people bad mouth you. That might have been another of the Fletchers' almost fatal mistakes, forgetting where they came from.

The Fletcher family had made its money by manufacturing coal mining equipment. Jim had retired early and they were enjoying their life of adventure and leisure. That all changed the night that Joseph was shot.

As best we could tell, Mitchell and St. Vincent's government had no intention of ever letting the case go to trial. It was our opinion that the government wanted to force the family to pay huge bribes or officials would just let the couple die.

The government was that corrupt.

As media and political pressure mounted, the government had no choice but to let the trial begin, and after several delays and tactics aimed at even further delay, it started on July 28. One of the last delaying moves by the prosecution came on July 11 when it sought a gag order on the media. If granted, both internal media and world media would be banned from commenting on the merits of the evidence in the case. Ralph Gonsalves, lead attorney for the Fletchers, argued that such an order would run contrary to the St. Vincent constitutional guarantee of free expression.

Judge Cenac ruled against a gag order and ordered the trial to begin – at long last. He said he believed a jury could be seated – despite the publicity – that would ensure a fair trial.

(text continues after the image on the following page)

For more than 20 years this framed copy of the front page of
the EXTRA produced when the Fletchers were freed hung on
the walls of The Herald-Dispatch until Executive Editor Les
Smith presented it to me. It might've reproduced better if I took
it out of the frame, but I didn't want to risk damaging it.

A couple things I should tell you here:

In a column published the same day as the story on Cenac's ruling, I applauded his lordship's courage in standing up to the prosecution on the request for a gag order. But, I said, it was not so much a victory for the Fletchers, but for the growth of free speech and a free press in the Caribbean region.

"A free press is essential to a free people and a ruling the other way could have had a chilling effect on such liberties, not only in St. Vincent, but throughout the entire Eastern Caribbean judicial region," I wrote.

But I also reported to our readers in that column on something I did that I certainly now regret.

With Truby and Moses in St. Vincent, for about a week I took offline a special Internet site we had built on the Fletcher story. You know already that Truby had been faced with the possibility of being arrested by St. Vincent police, but Moses had been threatened, too, after taking a photograph of a public official in a public place. I knew if they were arrested because of what we posted on the Internet, we'd be hard pressed to cover the story "for our primary readers: people who live in our region" of West Virginia, Ohio and Kentucky.

My thinking on that seems so antiquated now. But that was the start of news being delivered in the digital era and, in truth, I cared more about serving our slice of the world than what the rest of the world could read.

But in a sense, I thought I was protecting that, too. Truby had become the primary source of reporting on this case for the major wire services and other news organizations. I was afraid of losing his voice. I had a lot to learn about digital, but my decision on that was a very poor one.

Just about every day now, our lead story was the Fletcher case. If it wasn't about the prosecution's attempts to delay the trial, it was about the growing concerns over the Fletchers' health or St. Vincent officials' run-ins with the media.

Mitchell suddenly announced he was no longer speaking with American media. The prosecution was complaining about CNN, ABC and The Herald-Dispatch.

But then mercifully the trial began. It opened with the prosecution presenting its case for six days. At the end of that, Gonsalves asked Cenac to dismiss, saying no evidence – directly or indirectly – connected either of the Fletchers with the murder. Cenac agreed and dismissed charges.

After the trial was over, Truby summarized the case against the Fletchers in a column in a Herald-Dispatch special section:

"The evidence against James and Penny Fletcher was razor thin. It was a prosecution constructed with guess upon guess. Supposition upon supposition. Rumor upon rumor.

"The Fletchers went free today and returned to their families after more than nine months in prisons that few of us can comprehend. Their punishment far outweighed the only thing the prosecution proved over the last two weeks – they behaved at times like ugly Americans."

There was still the matter of the lawsuit against us, but that fairly quickly went away, too. We had attorneys in Washington, St. Vincent, the Virgin Islands, and London, where any appeal would eventually be heard, thus the importance of the islands' British lineage. That was part of the agreement between Britain and St. Vincent as the island transitioned from colony to independent nation.

By the way, there were reports that the Fletcher family might have been willing to pay the $100,000 bribe, but I never quite believed that.

We were prepared to defend the suit against Truby, but it did not diminish the threat that should he return to St. Vincent he could still be arrested. I admit we counted on the presence now of major international media outlets and a finally engaged U.S. government to ensure his safety.

He needed to be there for the trial, scheduled for June, although we had little faith that it would actually happen. We weren't even sure that Jim or Penny Fletcher would survive that long.

Truby had to cover the story in St. Vincent because he understood it involved politics at the highest level of government. Initially, this was very confusing. Why wasn't the Clinton administration more involved in ensuring the Fletchers were treated fairly? This had us stymied or at least scratching our heads.

As we understood it, whenever Americans are charged with a capital crime, the U.S. administration investigates through the State Department. That happened in this case, too. But the report was classified as "Secret," meaning we weren't supposed to see it.

We knew what the report said. Sources had told us. But we did not want to go to press with a story of this magnitude based on sources. We had to somehow get that document. Even after all these years, I'm not going to tell you how we got it, but we did. And it said what we had been told it said:

"There is not one scintilla of physical evidence connecting the Fletchers to Jerome Joseph's murder," the State Department report read. "One is led to the conclusion that this is a witch hunt."

The question: Why wasn't the Clinton administration doing more to help, especially after the State Department report? In other words, why would the president keep quiet while two innocent Americans were literally rotting away in jail cells under the worst possible conditions?

I'm still uncomfortable with the answer: politics. Clinton appears to have valued a trade initiative he had under way with Caribbean nations more than these two lives. He was playing a dangerous game of trying to balance the two priorities. For the Fletchers, the timing was just bad.

Clinton did raise the Fletcher situation during a one-day summit of Caribbean nations in May. By then, the Fletchers had languished in prison for months following the State Department report. Now, he spoke privately with Mitchell, who, the administration said, offered assurances that the Fletchers would be afforded due process. Their trial finally was scheduled to begin that summer.

It was not clear, and the administration would not say, if the president raised the issue of how the couple was being treated. But Mitchell was quoted by media outlets as saying they were being treated the same as anyone else accused of capital murder in St. Vincent.

By May, major U.S. media outlets and others were interested in the case. Some were now covering the story with their own teams in St. Vincent. Truby was no longer the lone wolf hanging out by the pool. I felt some comfort in the numbers.

When the trial finally started, it was quickly over. Again, with the world now watching and after nine months of living in literal hell, Jim and Penny Fletcher were free.

By now, all of Huntington was rallying around the local couple. We decided to publish an Extra edition of the newspaper that afternoon. I called corporate to let them know what we were doing. I was advised not to do it.

"This is not a football game so it will be a hard sell," I was told. But no one said we couldn't. So, of course, we did. The publisher backed the decision and we shared the risk. We would print 5,000 copies of the 12-page Extra.

We got the word out via the Internet and local radio. Then the most amazing thing happened:

Jim and Penny's family and friends – those who were not already on planes to greet them in Key Largo, Fla., where Jim's parents had a home – came to the newspaper building to celebrate and to buy copies of the Extra. They were carrying signs, placard style, saying, "Thank You, Herald-Dispatch."

I looked at the crowd in front of the building from my office on the third floor. I went down to be with them as they posed for photos. I'll never forget Penny's daughter's hug or the tears when she said, "Thank you for my mother's life."

It was the same reaction I got from Jim Fletcher when we finally met months later. Sticking out his hand, he said, "I need to thank you for my life and my wife's life."

As for the reaction from corporate, well, I happily called them back to let them know that we had sold out the Extra.

"Well, thank goodness for local autonomy," came the response from Vice President/News Phil Currie.

Yeah, I thought, remember that when the bills hit the budget.

I would be less than fair to not point out that no one from corporate ever mentioned the cost of our coverage in a negative way. It was a grand example of the power of local journalism and serves as an illustration of why it still needs to be protected and nourished, not just from despots but also from anyone who wishes to control messages the public receives.

Gonsalves, the Fletchers' lead attorney in St. Vincent, was brilliant. If that name sounds familiar to you it is because he was elected prime minister of St. Vincent and the Grenadines in 2001, and he has been prime minister ever since.

I met him during his visit to Huntington, shortly after the Fletchers were released. The publicity the case brought was not good for tourism in St. Vincent, a staple of the national economy. That hurt Mitchell's standing with the public.

I also suspect Gonsalves' party, the Unity Labour Party, would have won anyway in 2001, but the glare of the media spotlight on the corruption of the Mitchell government sealed Mitchell's fate. His party lost not because of the Fletcher case, but because the Fletcher case illustrated all that was wrong with his government: inept and corrupt, a deadly combination.

Gonsalves was well educated and much beloved by the public. He wore his nickname, Comrade Ralph, with pleasure. He told me so at dinner that night he came to Huntington.

It was a matter of happenstance, to some degree: The Fletchers were not the first wealthy foreigners from whom the government had tried to extort money.

Plus, with the end of the cold war, the United States would not panic to see Mitchell's conservative party out of power. But even that wasn't enough; it took a brave little newspaper and its courageous journalists willing to stand up and do their jobs to make history.

I do so love this story.

COLUMN: **Acting blurs roles in the Fletcher case**

By Robert C. Gabordi
Executive Editor, The Herald-Dispatch
Published August 1997

The other day in court, James Fletcher wondered aloud about how his hometown would greet him and Penny upon their return. I've thought about the same thing and, when I've asked, I've pretty much gotten the same answer: acceptance, but not open arms.

What has been hard about covering this story is that neither protagonist is very sympathetic. That makes the story less compelling and harder to tell.

That is not to say they are bad people. But neither does getting locked up in a virtual dungeon make them heroes, either. What has happened to James and Penny Fletcher is wrong and tragic. They might be victims, but they are hardly sympathetic in that role. Their admitted behavior, here and in St. Vincent, is a disqualifier.

This story certainly has its heroes, but they have played supporting roles in the script. The real heroes are the Fletcher family members. Without their love and support, their insistence that justice be swift and fair, who knows what would have become of James and Penny.

Sally Duncan, James Fletcher's sister, is the first who comes to mind. She has refused to accept her brother's fate. Nor has she tried to turn him into more than what he is: someone she loves who has made a series of bad decisions, but who doesn't deserve what has happened. And he certainly does not deserve to hang for a crime that, based on the evidence, he did not commit.

The Fletcher daughters are heroes in my book, too, most prominently Julie, who gave the story a public and sympathetic face. For a 14-year-old to face down the media and track down a president, as she did, is an amazing story in and of itself.

James and Penny aren't even the most tragic of this story's victims. That roles goes to the family of Jerome "Jolly" Joseph, especially his mother, Mary. Her eyes, as pictured on our front-page last week, told a story of a mother's pain and frustration. This family has been helpless as events roared out of control, as the focus was lost on who actually killed her son.

What has gone wrong for authorities in St. Vincent is that they misunderstood the willpower and character of a West Virginia family. They could not have expected the reaction here to the arrest of this couple.

Now St. Vincent authorities are trying to look the part of the victims. Prime Minister Sir James "Son" Mitchell is very familiar with the U.S. media. He travels often to the United States to conduct business and meet with St. Vincent expatriates living here.

He paints himself the victim of a smear campaign and tells the St. Vincent people to be careful, and not to trust the media. He claims he was ambushed during a CNN interview, the same message a Bequia newspaper the St. Vincent people. That newspaper is nothing more than a pro-government public relations piece.

Mitchell was ambushed by the truth, with which he knowingly and purposefully played fast and loose. He is now under intense political pressure from his own people about his handling of the Fletcher case. He makes a poor victim, in any case.

The trouble with all this is there has been too much acting, too much theater, with real lives disrupted and lost.

Robert C. Gabordi is executive editor of The Herald-Dispatch. He can be reached at (304) 526-2787. The Editor's Hotline is (304) 526-2710. His email address is bgabordi@huntingt.gannett.com.

CHAPTER NINE

IT'S NOT CENSORSHIP – IT'S EDITING

The Fletcher story would not be the only time I made national news in Huntington, though this time I wasn't crazy about the circumstances. It came at a time that President Clinton was on TV talking about – and trying to redefine – what having sex means.

In February 1998, Garry Trudeau, the cartooning genius who created and draws Doonesbury, was also tackling the topic of presidential sex.

Clinton had, under oath, denied having sex with Monica Lewinsky, a White House intern, who would claim they had sexual relations at least nine times. The president would try to claim he had not lied under oath because – among other things – oral sex had been performed on him not by him.

To tackle the topic in the dialogue bubbles of a comic strip, Trudeau used the term aural sex, pronounced very much like oral sex, but involving totally different body parts. As I understood it – which is a very big caveat – aural sex describes a pleasurable voice's impact on the listener.

Other panels in the series tackling presidential sex dealt with Lewinsky's semen-streaked blue dress.

Doonesbury was carried by 1,400 U.S. newspapers. Many called to complain. Six of us decided not to run the strip as long as the topic was presidential sex.

I called and asked Trudeau's syndicate, Universal Press, to deliver substitute strips. Universal said no, that Trudeau's instructions were to take it or leave it. I decided that as editor I alone would decide what was published in my newspaper: I declined it and I canceled the strip.

You should know how I hated spending time on the comics page. It was always a no-win situation.

Once in Huntington, after months of hearing complaints about how old and out of touch some of our strips had become, I did a survey to find out which strips people disliked the most. There were two that stood out. I wrote columns about it.

We ran potential replacement strips and asked people which they liked best. We publicized the change numerous times and finally, thinking we had consensus, made the switch.

We lost somewhere around 400 subscribers. So, we brought back the old strips and kept the new ones, too. Moving them to a different page. You would think the whole experience would have taught me a lesson about messing around with comics. That is, don't do it.

But I wasn't backing down to Trudeau or his syndicate by giving up my authority as editor to decide what gets into print and what doesn't, despite Doonsbury's popularity. That's when The Associated Press and others wrote about me and the handful of others who made the same decision.

"We didn't run it because I thought the language was offensive and inappropriate for the comics page," I said in the AP story.

Some accused us of censoring Trudeau. I said I thought that was unfair. I call it editing. I was simply applying the same rules to his copy that I applied to my own staff. And while such topics and language might be appropriate – or at least useful and necessary – in news stories, a page aimed at young readers and children could do without the grown-up talk.

If this was censorship, I argued, what about the hundreds, maybe thousands, of cartoonists I decide not to publish every day? Are they being censored or just not hired? I have a contract with Universal, I said. I give them money and they deliver a product that I want to publish. Editors make decisions every day about what they do and don't publish, for lots of different reasons.

I stood my ground even as other media poked fun at me and my decision in this case.

A group of Marshall University professors decided to stage a protest rally at the newspaper building. They carried signs protesting the "censoring" of Trudeau. It was blustery cold with light showers on the day of the protest. Good for the handful of people who showed up to voice their First Amendment rights. I looked out my window and saw them marching back and forth. I decided to go down and offer them hot chocolate or coffee and invite them upstairs to talk when they had finished their protest.

They came up and we chatted. They offered their point of view and I offered mine. I also expressed respect for how they exercised their First Amendment rights to peaceful assembly and to speak out in protest. It was a good conversation.

Then I got support from the most unlikely of sources: Trudeau himself. He wrote a letter to me that we published. He said he should have offered an alternative for editors who did not want to have a sex discussion on the comics page. He said he understood my point of view and he agreed that it was not censorship. His letter effectively ended the controversy in Huntington, at least, over sex in the comics. I renewed our contract with Trudeau and vowed to always carry Doonesbury because, whether we agreed on issues, Trudeau got it in terms of decision making by editors, at least by me.

It would not be the last time I decided not to publish a Trudeau comic strip, though. In 2012, while I was executive editor of the Tallahassee Democrat, the issue was whether government should force women who were considering an abortion to have a sonogram, regardless of the medical necessity. In a column and blog, I called that "dumb and an intrusion by government." I just didn't want to publish it on the comics page.

I detailed to readers my decision to run different Trudeau strips that week, which he offered, as he promised to do. I also made links available to the strips I was not publishing in print.

"Deciding what content to use in which sections of the newspaper … is the job of the editor and we take that seriously," I wrote in a column to readers at the time. "We don't turn that over to reporters and we certainly don't leave that to vendors, such as Trudeau. No one gets a blank check on our pages. If you consider that censorship, so be it. But I don't."

Editing a newspaper – and now an online news site – must be one of the most fun jobs in the world. But I hated messing with the comics. I dreaded every time I felt I needed to weigh-in on an issue with a strip. But that didn't mean I would turn away from it, even if it meant facing down an icon like Garry Trudeau.

HIGH SCHOOL FOOTBALL SCOREBOARD			
LINCOLN 44	RICKARDS 21	MOSLEY 38	FLORIDA HIGH 42
LEON 27	WAKULLA 22	CHILES 17	BLOUNTSTOWN 0

Sports / 1b

FOOTBALL MONEYMAKERS
HBCU classics offer economic boosts similar to smaller college bowl games

Business & Growth / 6A

Promoting democracy since 1905

TALLAHASSEE DEMOCRAT

Saturday, September 27, 2008 • Tallahassee.com • 75 Cents

Chief calls for CI reform

ELLIOTT MCCASKILL / Special to the Democrat

PHIL SEARS / Democrat

"(TPD) utilized our established protocols to ensure the safety of Rachel.... Unfortunately, Rachel chose to ignore precautions.... The choice ultimately led to her murder."
May 9

"We were placing most of the blame on Rachel Hoffman. I regret that now. It made us look like we weren't taking responsibility for what happened."
Friday

Jones changes position on Hoffman, takes responsibility

By Jennifer Portman
DEMOCRAT SENIOR WRITER

The Hoffman family has a new ally in its effort to see a Rachel's Law passed: Tallahassee Police Chief Dennis Jones.

Jones said Friday that he wants to work with state lawmakers and on a national level to help improve the way police use confidential informants.

"We need to do a better job with this," Jones said. "My responsibility is not just to the Tallahassee Police Department but it is for the process

as a whole."

Hoffman's family has already talked with state Sen. Mike Fasano about possible legislation — a Rachel's Law — that would include more careful screening and provide protections for confidential informants.

The family's attorney, Lance Block, welcomed the chief's efforts toward confidential-informant reform.

"His active participa-

tion in that would be welcome," Block said.

This week Hoffman's father, Irv Hoffman, said: "A Rachel's Law is very important to make sure a person is suitable, is represented by a lawyer and has some guarantees."

Confidential informants are an essential tool in law enforcement, Jones said, but the system as it exists now can have too much latitude. Informants, he said, need to have training and officers need to take department policies and procedures seriously.

"I don't want any other

police chief to go through this without being fully informed," he said. "This cost a young lady her life."

■ Contact Senior Writer Jennifer Portman at (850) 599-2154 or jportman@tallahassee.com

Obama, McCain spar in round 1

John McCain and Barack Obama clashed over Iraq, Iran and world affairs in the first of three critical debates Friday, and they also sparred over the economy.

McCain repeatedly suggested that Obama was naive. Obama repeatedly challenged McCain's judgment on policies held supported.

Each man got off at least one zinger:

"John mentioned me being wildly liberal. Mostly that's just me opposing George Bush's wrong-headed policies," Obama said at one point.

"I'm afraid Senator Obama doesn't understand the difference between a tactic and a strategy," McCain said at another.

Read more, Page 9A.

FUTURE DEBATES
■ Oct. 2, 9 p.m. EDT. Vice presidential debate on all topics moderated by PBS's Gwen Ifill
■ Oct. 7, 9 p.m. EDT. Presidential debate on all topics in town-hall setting moderated by NBC's Tom Brokaw
■ Oct. 15, 9 p.m. EDT. Presidential debate on domestic issues moderated by Bob Schieffer of CBS.

Breaking news on your phone
For breaking news alerts, text TallNews to 44636 or go to Tallahassee.com/text.

TPD: We shouldn't have blamed Rachel Hoffman

By Jennifer Portman
DEMOCRAT SENIOR WRITER

Tallahassee Police Chief Dennis Jones admits the department was wrong to have initially said Rachel Hoffman got herself killed when the confidential informant was shot in a disastrous May 7 drug bust.

"We were placing most of the blame on Rachel Hoffman. I regret that now," Jones said Friday. "It made us look like we weren't taking responsibility for what happened."

Speaking a day after the release of harsh internal-affairs reports, Jones said he suspected early on that there was more to the story than simply Hoffman's refusal to obey instructions by following two suspected drug dealers to an unauthorized location. But that's what officers initially told him, he said, and that's what he told the public.

"I think we were too quick to relate what we knew at the time," he said.

Within a few days, however, he began to look into the incident and read the officers' first reports. He realized the department had made mistakes, too.

"That's when I said, 'Whoa, wait a minute, guys. This isn't the way we were supposed to be doing it,'" he said.

Hoffman's family lawyer, Lance Block, said the chief's comments are a step in the right direction.

"It's been obvious for five months now that Rachel Hoffman was the victim of negligence by the Tallahassee Police Department, which directly led to her death," Block said. "So, Chief Jones' comments are clearly appropriate."

Jones ordered an internal-affairs investigation three days after Hoffman's body was found May 9. That investigation found 21 individual violations of nine separate policies.

Please see HOFFMAN, 2A

TALLAHASSEE.COM
■ Full videos of recent and past news conferences about the Rachel Hoffman case.
■ TPD internal-affairs investigation.
■ Florida Attorney General's review of TPD's handling of the case and of the agency's confidential-informant procedures.
■ TPD special investigation into the case.
■ Interactive online project and past stories about the case.
■ Follow the case on our Facebook group: "Rachel Hoffman case: Uncovering the truth."

INSIDE
■ Rachel Hoffman's lawyer requests that the FDLE release its investigative report, 2A.

COMING SUNDAY
■ Read more about why only one TPD investigator was fired.
■ Read TPD Chief Dennis Jones' op-ed piece on the Hoffman tragedy.

Wives of Obama, Biden visit Tallahassee

What: Youth-outreach rally featuring Michelle Obama and Jill Biden.
When: Gates open at 10 a.m.; program begins at 11 a.m. today.
Where: In front of Lee Hall at Florida A&M University.

TALLAHASSEE.COM
■ See live video and live story updates starting at 11 a.m.
■ See a photo gallery after the event.
■ View a video synopsis after the event.
■ See a full story and photos from the event in Sunday's Tallahassee Democrat.

CHAPTER TEN

RACHEL HOFFMAN

It has been 12 years since Rachel Hoffman was murdered at the hands of two thugs while working as a confidential informant for Tallahassee police. Her mother, Margie Weiss, has watched as Hoffman's dear friends have "moved on and grown up" to become parents and pursue their life's ambitions. While she is filled with joy when she talks about her daughter's friends, clearly life has become an on-going, two-front battle for Weiss: Her efforts on behalf of confidential informants and overcoming her grief at the loss of her kindred soul, her daughter, Rachel Morningtar Hoffman.

She has continued to push for legislation to better regulate when police use confidential informants. Florida passed Rachel's Law, which provided some structure and guidance where none had existed. But nationally, not much headway has been made.

"We're the only ones to really get something started, but that was 12 years ago. It's so imperative to reveal the magnitude of this clandestine lawlessness that permeates our society," she said in a text message.

Some background: Hoffman, a senior at Florida State, was stopped by Tallahassee police for speeding while driving a white Volvo. They found a small amount of pot in her car. She was put in a drug diversion program for nonviolent offenders, commonly called drug court, which required regular drug testing. She missed a test and spent three days in jail.

So, a year later, when police responded to neighbors complaining about the odor coming from her apartment, she was scared and desperate to avoid more jail time. Police searched her apartment and they found more drugs: five ounces of pot and some Ecstasy and Valium pills.

They threatened to charge her with maintaining a drug house and possession with intent to sell. This time, she could face serious jail time and federal charges. Five ounces of pot is not an insignificant amount.

Rachel Hoffman was 23, a Florida State University graduate, and naïve when police convinced her to work with them on a drug and gun sting operation. Photo courtesy of Margie Weiss.

Police offered her a way out if she were to become a confidential informant. She took it. Despite promises by her police handlers that they would protect her, Hoffman was brutally murdered by the two men police asked her to set up.

This is a story the Tallahassee Democrat pushed and pushed because we had reasons to believe from the start that police were not telling the truth. It might have been one of the most-covered crime stories in the more than century-long history of the newspaper. Lead reporter Jennifer Portman wrote more than 100 articles, and it was an all-hands-on-deck kind of story. Even sports writer Corey Clark, who covered Florida State major sports, jumped in to contribute.

But unlike what The Herald-Dispatch faced with the "Prisoners in Paradise" story, we weren't out there alone, at least not for long. Statewide media soon got involved, then national TV programs like "Dateline" and "20/20" joined in. Social media, for the first time that I could remember, played a significant role in shaping our coverage on a major story.

This was a story in which local journalists made a difference, but it also changed in important ways how some journalists went about their business. More on that later. First, some background and updates on what is in some ways an ongoing story.

In addition to wanting to get better protection for others used by police as confidential informants, Weiss's other battlefront – maybe affront is the better word in this case – is the notion that somehow dealing with her daughter's "transition to spirit" – as she puts it – would get easier with time.

"(I'm) battling the get-easier-LIE-with-time by keeping reminders of Rachel everywhere. ..." she wrote in her text message to me.

Beside a barrage of text messages, I've spoken with Weiss on the phone a couple of times, too. I told her I've thought about Rachel's story a lot over the years. It stands out for several reasons, including how we used social media, which was innovative at the time.

But mostly it stands out because it made me angry. A lot of things get me angry, but stories rarely set me off. As a professional journalist, it was not my place to get angry in analyzing the facts. I've always had the ability to separate the facts from my emotions.

But this story did get under my skin and made me angry in ways I don't recall feeling about any other story in my 41 years as a journalist. Maybe it was because Tallahassee police had lied about what happened to Rachel.

Police just looked into our cameras and told us Rachel had not followed directions. They tried to blame her for their mistakes – mistakes that cost her life.

Maybe it was because I had children her age and felt her parents' pain and anguish. Maybe I reacted as a parent and not a newspaper editor. Maybe I reacted as a newspaper editor and a parent, I don't know.

Maybe it was because Hoffman was such a kid, 23 years old and a college graduate, sure. But she was also naïve and trusting.

Rachel Hoffman. Photo provide by Margie Weiss

Maybe my anger was fed by the outpouring of love from her friends and Florida State students. Young adults reacted to this story in ways I had not seen before, many wondering out loud if this could happen to her, why couldn't it happen to the dozens of people they knew just like her.

I think it was all of those things, frankly, but I know what set me off first were the lies. The attempts to blame her certainly bothered me, but how the dead girl's parents, Weiss and Irv Hoffman, were treated pushed me over the edge.

To this day, Weiss says, Officer Ryan Pender, Hoffman's main controller and the person she thought was her friend (she labeled him "Pooh Bear" on her phone contacts), has never even told Weiss he was sorry Hoffman was killed.

On May 9, two days after Hoffman was murdered, Tallahassee police Chief Dennis Jones, speaking at a press conference to talk about the drug bust gone bad, gave his explanation for why Hoffman was killed. "Unfortunately, Rachel chose to ignore precaution. ... The choice ultimately led to her death," he said.

A little more than four months later, confronted with the truth, he would change his tune.

"We were placing most of the blame on Rachel Hoffman. I regret that now."

Tallahassee police spokesman Officer David McCranie placed more than "most of the blame" on Hoffman. He put all of the blame. He simply lied when he said, "And the investigator of the case, the investigator in charge, communicated with her on the phone and told her 'Do not leave,' pleaded with her not to leave. ..."

We later learned that communication had broken down, that the technology failed. There was no pleading.

"So, we pleaded with her not to leave. She was able to leave before we could stop her and decided to meet them on her own," he continued.

A lot had changed in that four-month period between statements by the police chief. Lance Block, attorney for Weiss and Irv Hoffman, put the city of Tallahassee on official notice of his clients' intention to file a wrongful death lawsuit. In a letter dated June 30 to City Attorney Jim English, Block disputed Tallahassee police's claim that Hoffman had violated protocols. He pointed out that although police said over and over that she had, TPD had never cited specific protocols.

"Quite frankly, it makes no sense that Rachel Hoffman would have knowingly disregarded TPD instructions," Block wrote. "Her quest for leniency was conditioned on her cooperation, not insubordination. Her safety, her very life was totally in the hands of the TPD."

Instead of failing to follow instructions, Hoffman had gone exactly where they had agreed to go when she met with police "but no one from TPD showed."

Further, he argued, the communications technology failed and "TPD has failed to provide any explanation as to why it did not immediately race to the Gardner Road location to rescue Rachel Hoffman."

An internal affairs investigation and a grand jury would back Block's point of view. Several Tallahassee officers were disciplined, including Jones.

Jones' comments and change of heart were reported on the front page of the Tallahassee Democrat. He would also announce his support for efforts to change how police use confidential informants.

The truth, and police always knew this, is Hoffman didn't choose to ignore precautions. Her killers changed the plan and electronic communication with her police controllers failed. Police had to know that when they faced our cameras and said she had failed to follow directions.

With a drug-enforcement helicopter overhead, and police supposedly keeping her vehicle in sight at all times, police lost track of her, plain and simple.

The drug dealers, a pair of tough-guy criminals, probably could sense something was wrong with this set up. Hoffman had no history of buying cocaine and she didn't know anything about guns or have a reason to buy one. They simply shot her five times, took the $13,000 in cash law enforcement had supplied her, and left her body in the woods two hours away in Taylor County, not to be found for two days. Police only said that she was missing.

Her mother said that all that she knew was that Hoffman had told her she was working on something dangerous with police. Weiss pressed her more information, but Hoffman wouldn't discuss it. Weiss told her to back out. Hoffman told Weiss that she couldn't and that her mother just didn't understand. She was right about that. Weiss didn't understand. Hoffman felt trapped. She had to go through with what police demanded or face what she could not fathom: going to prison for a long time.

"She said, 'You have no idea how much trouble I would get in if I told anyone.'" Weiss said.

She was killed by the men police wanted her to get with the gun police wanted her to buy. Her bullet-riddled body was tossed into a ditch. Police had promised to protect her, and she believed them.

Then, almost as soon as Hoffman's body was found, police began blaming her to cover up their own mistakes. No wonder I was angry.

I was not alone. Her friends and other Florida State students took to social media to vent and tell what they knew. It was one of the first major stories I was involved with that showed the power of social media to be used as a tool by journalists working in what came to be known as legacy-media outlets. It literally changed my notion of how you report and deliver a story in the digital era.

It was a strategy coordinated by our digital editor, Julia Luscher Thompson, who explained what we did in Harvard University's Nieman Reports magazine.

"Facebook groups about Hoffman had already been created by her friends," Thompson explained. "So, we used those groups as our starting point by inviting their members to join our new Facebook group, which we dedicated to keeping people updated with developments in the case and as a place for discussion about media coverage of it. ... As we found out, some might not have known about the story if not for our newspaper using these social media tools."

Margie Weiss and her daughter Rachel Hoffman.
Photo provided by Margie Weiss.

I got a Facebook message from Hoffman's boyfriend shortly after we expanded our reporting on Facebook.

"I want to thank you personally for all you have done. … I honestly don't think all the facts that are out so far would be available if it weren't for you and your staff. Thank you for looking at the big picture: A young woman was murdered while working for (the) Tallahassee Police Department. As opposed to, she was just a drug dealer (so) she deserved to die."

We relied on Hoffman's friends on social media as much as they counted on us. With TPD trying to cut off information about the case, tips on social media became gold. The strategy employed Twitter, YouTube and text messages, in addition to Facebook, Thompson explained.

It seems so commonplace now, but in 2008, when we used a special Twitter account, Facebook pages and a dedicated online page for the Hoffman case, it won lots of attention nationally in journalism circles and – more important – among younger readers.

There was serious backlash against the newspaper by some who labeled us – and me in particular – as anti-police (again). But we pushed forward.

Portman summarized it best in the Nieman article.

"That we were tenacious and tried to reach out to all kinds of readers however we could, gave this story and this issue the heightened importance it deserved," she said. "We didn't let it go away, even if, at times, it would have been easier to do so."

Meanwhile, the Tallahassee Democrat pounded the story daily in print and on Tallahassee.com online, with editorials, columns, and news stories that questioned the official police line. Editorially, we demanded outside review. State's Attorney Willie Meggs, who said he had not been informed that Hoffman was being used as a confidential informant, agreed and empowered a grand jury. Its report was a scathing rebuke of the Tallahassee Police Department.

Drug court was a national movement that started in Florida. It was aimed at nonviolent, first-time offenders and provided for court-supervised education, treatment, and sanctions. It had a high rate of success in keeping participants from returning to the judicial system.

It failed in Hoffman's case, but Hoffman should not have been used as a confidential informant for a lot of reasons, the drug-court program being one of them. What made her a candidate for the drug-diversion program made her an awful candidate to be a confidential informant. Here was this nonviolent soul, young and naive, and she was given $13,000 in cash by law enforcement authorities and told to buy Ecstasy pills, cocaine and a gun from two guys, Deneilo Bradshaw and Andrea Green. Bradshaw was the very definition of criminal.

He probably stole the gun. Just two days before Hoffman was murdered, police records indicated a .25-caliber handgun was reported stolen from a car at the car wash that had employed Bradshaw. He was the prime suspect, according to Block's letter putting the city on notice about the wrongful death lawsuit.

Hoffman didn't know these men but had gotten their contacts from a student. Among the untruthful statements by TPD was a statement by police that she had a previous relationship with the men.

The night her daughter was murdered, Weiss got a phone call from police.

"It was 2 or 3 a.m., I'm not sure," she said. "Police said, 'Rachel is missing,'" Weiss recalled, trying to remember the time. "They said don't come up." Weiss said. She explained that she doesn't remember the exact words, but she did recall that police were trying to assure her they would handle things.

Hoffman not only resembled her mother in looks, but also in temperament and personality. They were close – Weiss says they had a "special connection." She did what most mothers would do: She hopped in her car and came to Tallahassee, despite being told to stay home. She alerted Rachel's father, and drove to the police station.

Weiss saw the report on TV news of Rachel's body being found two days later.

For months after that police mischaracterized what had really happened.

The tragedy of what happened to Hoffman – first when police botched the confidential sting operation and then lied about it – and the Tallahassee Democrat's efforts to reveal the truth, warrant the attention this case has gotten. Thanks to Rachel Hoffman's parents, it resulted in new Florida legislation called Rachel's Law.

After their opening statements blaming Hoffman, police declined to say more or release investigation reports, saying it was an ongoing case.

But no amount of stonewalling could hide the fact that police messed this up from the beginning. A grand jury did not hold back in criticizing the Tallahassee Police Department's handling of the case.

We were determined to cover the story fully and to get the truth, not just what the government wanted us to know, but the whole story. When a judge issued a gag order to seal pretrial evidence from public disclosure, that just made us more determined. I felt the public had a right to know the details of how their police department had performed. Social media and Hoffman's friends and family helped provide information we couldn't get elsewhere.

They all agreed that Hoffman just wasn't right for this confidential informant's role. She didn't "look" the part of a hardened criminal who would meet a couple of tough guys in the woods carrying $13,000 in cash. The bottom line is she just didn't fit the role she was asked to play by police. It was bound to go wrong and it did, tragically so.

Portman and other Democrat staffers mined social media for tips and leads.

"Her friends were checking in with our website all the time," Portman said in the Neiman article. "The morning she went missing, the first place her boyfriend checked was Tallahassee.com."

Portman is an example of why local journalism and local journalists should always matter. The Democrat got instantly better when she agreed to come work with us shortly after I became editor. She is now news director at the Democrat, meaning she is the No. 2 editor. She is headstrong and passionate about what she does. Her work on the Hoffman story was not just a matter of what she wrote, but she also made what others on the team wrote better.

She more recently was credited with keeping alive a story about the murder of Mike Williams, who went missing in December 2000. It was initially ruled an accidental death, with authorities believing he fell out of his boat while duck hunting. But the missing Tallahassee man's mother, Cheryl Williams, didn't believe that and Portman's tenacity forced attention on the story.

Williams' wife and his best friend and insurance agent, who married each other after Williams disappeared, were charged with Williams' killing in 2018, 12 years after Portman first started reporting on the case.

"For investigators, her continued accurate and detailed coverage (of Williams' disappearance) helped keep the public interest, along with the investigation, moving forward at a time when other journalists had moved on," said Mark Perez, the Florida Department of Law Enforcement's special agent in charge in Tallahassee. "Over the years, the questionable disappearance of Mr. Williams could have dimmed in the memory of the public but for Ms. Portman's steadfast reporting and dedication to helping law enforcement and the Williams family find closure. I will always be grateful for her professionalism and assistance on this case."

That is the type of reporter Portman was, and the type of journalist she still is.

Back to the Hoffman case. A column I wrote that published in print July 15, 2008, following great reporting by our team said:

"Hoffman just did not seem to get the gravity of the situation."

She thought the police had become her friends. They called her a "hippie" because she would have fit with the peace, love and dope crowd in the 1970s. Life was just one big happy game to this group.

"I didn't know Hoffman, of course," I wrote, "but the more I learn of her, the more the term 'hippie' seems to fit – all of it."

I didn't know Rachel Hoffman, but I knew many like her when I was a college student. Their world was rainbows and flowers and people nicknamed "Pooh Bear." It seems ironic that we are now legalizing marijuana use in America, the buying and selling of which got Hoffman in trouble with the law.

Very early on, almost as soon as police finished a press conference to announce Hoffman died because she failed to follow directions from police, we knew they were lying. Someone in the newsroom voiced that. Their version was she had willingly disobeyed her directives not to leave the Forest Meadows Park where the deal was supposed to go down.

An investigation by the state Attorney General's Office and an internal investigation by Tallahassee police said otherwise. A Leon County grand jury said the department had been negligent in Hoffman's death.

Mostly, the police's original version of what happened just made no sense. That's where social media came into play.

Reading Hoffman's social media pages now is a heart-rending experience. To this day, 12 years after her murder, many of the same people who poured out their hearts in 2008 are still posting Facebook messages to Hoffman. Rainbows, flowers, and Hoffman's signature purple hats are all over her page.

Activity occurs throughout the year. Her friends post remembrances whenever they see something that reminds them of Hoffman, they talk to her, as if she is reading their posts still today. Activity particularly picks up in December, around her birthday, and in May, around the anniversary of night she was murdered.

We threw every reporter, every senior editor, every resource we could at this story, not just because Hoffman should never have been placed in a position to be murdered, but because the nagging feeling that police had not told the truth and a cover-up was in the works.

It might have worked, too, had the Democrat not been so strong in its pursuit of the truth and had police not picked the wrong parents to cross.

Early on, I wondered if Weiss or Irv Hoffman got any sleep at all. They were relentless.

Hoffman's parents took the position that Rachel was a young woman who made some mistakes, but none for which she deserved to die. And no one deserved to die like this.

I found myself on the opposite side of the police again. Eventually a statewide police organization, which essentially is a union, pulled its contract from the Tallahassee Democrat's commercial printing operation to punish us. They released a video saying that I was anti-police.

Brevard County Sheriff Wayne Ivey would bring up that "anti-police" message years later while meeting with me at FLORIDA TODAY. I've never been anti-police. But I am opposed to public officials lying and trying to hide the truth.

Ryan Pender – the officer Hoffman called Pooh Bear – was singled out for the harshest punishment, unfairly I think, and he was fired. He fought it and got his job back.

This was a failure at the senior management level and several supervisors were reprimanded and suspended without pay. Jones and a deputy chief were reprimanded.

Eventually, the city apologized publicly and settled a wrongful death lawsuit brought by Hoffman's parents, paying out $2.6 million.

Irv Hoffman and Weiss were not through. That's not the type of people they are. They became big supporters of legislation that became known as Rachel's Law that would try to provide protections for future confidential informants.

The law, passed in 2009, would not dramatically change how most departments operated in using confidential informants. But Hoffman's death and Rachel's Law would bring consistency to the rules across the state.

But for Weiss, the fight for change in how police departments interact with citizens goes on, as she seeks a more uniform process.

"I believe there is so much more to uncover (in) this clandestine undercover world," she said. "Make law enforcement safer with civilian welfare taken seriously. And be the real protectors rather than scalawags and deceiving murderers."

She can't help but continue.

"As long as I breathe, I promise to continue this fight to strengthen and nationalize the (Rachel's) law."

It is not just my opinion that local journalists were able to make a difference in the outcomes in this case. Nothing, of course, can change what happened to her daughter, but Weiss credits the Tallahassee Democrat with making sure the truth came out.

"It was through the Tallahassee Democrat that TPD was held accountable, and that we were able to get Rachel's Law passed," Weiss said. "Someone asked me how we were able to get a law passed and that's what I told them."

There were also the once young friends of Hoffman, who poured out their hearts in the days following her murder and continue to do so.

I read every one of their Facebook posts on Rachel's page. Through their words, you could watch them being forced to grow up when faced with a friend's violent death.

"I now realize that this world we live in doesn't play by rules our parents once taught us to believe," Joe Dallas Millado posted to her page on May 12, 2008, just days after Hoffman's murder. "That good always wins, and that questions always have answers. Life isn't fair. ..."

COLUMN: **We've seen a deadly side of our city**

By Bob Gabordi
Executive Editor, Tallahassee Democrat
Published May 16, 2008

Anyone who thinks the battle on our streets between law enforcement and criminals is just like on TV is lost in one of those not-really-reality programs. That's especially so when illegal drugs and guns are involved.

Just like in a war, I'm sure, things happen nightly that good citizens can barely imagine – and many may not want to think about. Every so often, reality jumps up and slaps us in the face. And we are feeling such a sting right now.

If we're going to get the drugs out of our schools and neighborhoods, and if we're going to keep guns out of the hands of criminals, we ought to understand the reality is ugly. This time it cost a young woman her life. In the process, it took some people suspected of dealing drugs off our streets.

Law-enforcement officers work in a world many of us cannot comprehend. The same streets and parks that look so innocent at 6 p.m., when we take our evening walk or play with our childrend, change after dark.

Rachel Hoffman was last seen alive at Forestmeadows Park while attempting to assist police by buying drugs and a gun from two men. Her body was found in Taylor County, and two men are suspected of her murder. It's not clear what went wrong, except that police appear to blame Hoffman by saying she did not follow their established procedures.

Forestmeadows Park has picnic tables and biking trails and tennis courts. The athletic center is located there, along with a pool. It's one of the city's many marvelous parks.

By day. Apparently, it's something different at night.

It's not clear why Hoffman was helping police in this drug and gun deal, only that she had a record and was sentenced to probation and ordered to attend a drug rehabilitation program. At 23 years old, she was a graduate of Florida State University.

The whispers in the community are that police like to pick people like Hoffman in such drug purchases: She's educated, and she's known to them. It's clear how she could help police.

The whispers say police target college students with drug issues for such deals.

Oddly, State Attorney Willie Meggs was not informed of the deal involving Hoffman. Nor was Hoffman's own attorney, Johnny Devine.

So no one other than Tallahassee police knows what police told Hoffman she had to gain. It doesn't explain why they asked her to try to buy a gun.

We'll be asking all these questions and we'll continue to seek answers on many more. We're trying to understand what happened, and we're trying to provide answers to residents who need to know and understand, too. They need to know – and have a right to know – what happens on our streets and in our parks at night.

This is real life, where people like Rachel Hoffman really die.

Bob Gabordi is executive editor of the Tallahassee Democrat and Tallahassee.com. Contact him at bgabordi@tallahassee.com or (850) 599-2177.

daily deal classifieds

CLASS PICTURE OF ASHEVILLE
High School '47 and '48. $25 each.
274-3186.

See This Ad In Today's Classifieds!

Georgia Southern beats ASU, 36-20

Western Carolina comeback
falls short against Wofford

Sports, C1

West African music, dance brought to life

Asheville-based Ballet Warraba
to hold workshops, performances

Living, E1

Cloudy, a few showers
High 64, low 52

WEATHER, A16

ASHEVILLE
CITIZEN-TIMES

VOICE OF THE MOUNTAINS • CITIZEN-TIMES.com

SUNDAY,
October 20, 2002

FINAL

$1.50

Catherine Uritis
Kindergarten
Carolina Day School

The Citizen-Times
recognizes the artistic
talents of local
children by publishing
their drawings of
weather events.
How to submit, B3

Sniper shooting possible in Va.

A2 Police are looking into
the shooting of a man in a
parking lot at a restaurant
in Ashland, Va., for links to
the D.C.-area sniper.

Giants lead series

C1 The San Francisco
Giants defeated the
Anaheim Angels 4-3 in the
World Series opener.

Mountain scene

The last of LEAF

The fall Lake Eden
Arts Festival finishes up
today with performances
by John Whelan and his
band (pictured), blue-
grass group IIIrd Tyme
Out and many more. Call
686-8932.

A drop in the Bucket

The fifth annual Apple
Harvest Fall Festival and
the first fall Lake Festival
are finishing today at the
Rusty Bucket Outdoor
Market, U.S. 64 in Hen-
dersonville. Call 685-3923.

Cheers

Finish the weekend
with Wine Along the
Walk, an afternoon wine
tasting with tasty treats
from 3 to 6 p.m. at the historic Manor Grounds. 265
Charlotte St. Tickets are
$25 at the door. Call 225-
0866.

CITIZEN-TIMES.com

News poll

We asked our readers if
they participate in river
sports. They said:

Yes	32
No	144

What do you think?
If the election for North
Carolina U.S. Senate
seat were held today,
who would you vote for?

Log on to
CITIZEN-TIMES.com
and take part in our poll.

BOWLES	6 •	BRANTMYER	47.2
DOLE/ERISKINE	116-55.	BOWLES	84
BILL A, NO. 22	NATL. WOMEN	90.2
LOTTERY NO.	28	GREEN JACKS	844.7
FORUM	#22-22	FOUR ESTATE	70.8
DANCE	E1-E2	SPORTS	C1-38

©2002 A GANNETT NEWSPAPER
VOL. 133 NO. 293 100 pages

Rita Larkin/STAFF PHOTOGRAPHER

Actor Robert Redford talks to the Citizen-Times from his trailer during a break in filming of "The Clearing."

Actor Redford falls in love with mountains, people while filming

Engaging screen star weighs in on environment, politics

A t some point in his life,
Robert Redford crossed
over from being simply an
international film superstar to a
living legend, something reserved for a handful of people in
any era. His appeal crosses
boundaries of generations and
genders.

He is one of very few people
recognizable by both my 19-
year-old daughter and 72-year-
old father, both thought meeting
him would be "cool" or "neat" or
whatever their generation's
proper term to express that they
were impressed.

It was.

For weeks, people have been
calling the newspaper to say
Redford had been spotted in
town, at this location or that,
while he was here to film his latest movie, "The Clearing." I've
imagined us such calls, even suggesting to one caller that she call
columnist Susan Reinbardt,
Scener or later, I suggested, Susan would write something
about why people meet with
such silliness upon spotting another human being eating dinner.

ROBERT C. GABORDI
executive editor

Redford tries — as much as
can be reasonably tried by someone who has been cast with Natalie Wood, Jane Fonda, Barbara
Streisand, Paul Newman, Brad
Pitt, Demi Moore, Dustin Hoffman, Faye Dunaway, Meryl Streep
and Michelle Pfeiffer, to name a
few — to maintain some privacy.
That's not even counting his work
as a director or producer.

So why, I wondered with
more than idle curiosity the other night, did I have a message to
call Redford, saying that he
wanted to talk to me?

Inside

■ Read Gabordi's interview
with Redford. **Page A9**

CITIZEN-TIMES.com
Web Extra

Hear Redford in his own words.
Visit **CITIZEN-TIMES.com** and
click on Web Extra.

Before dialing the number left
on my voice mail, I walked
around the newsroom asking:
What have we done to bother
the man? Rarely do the famous
call a newspaper editor, other
than to complain about some
perceived mistreatment. I wont-
ed to know what I faced on the
other end of the telephone line.

With the bloodcounters normally reserved for 8-year-olds
(say, "I'm qualified for and I know I
could get," but they involve evening
shifts that end after the city bus system stops running. "There's no
need for me to even apply."

Please see REDFORD on A8

U.S. Senate race turns on voters' wallets

Taxes, budget, Social Security, trade
among areas where Bowles, Dole differ

By Mark Barrett
STAFF WRITER

ASHEVILLE — Pocketbook issues
are a key dividing point in this
year's race for the U.S. Senate between Democrat Erskine Bowles
and Republican Elizabeth Dole —
and a significant focus for voters.

With more stock market indexes
falling 30 percent or 40 percent or
more over the past couple of years,
the unemployment rate up substan-
tially and the federal government in
the red again, there are plenty of
dollars-and-cents issues to talk
about. And, for Dole and Bowles,
there's plenty to disagree about.

Dole wants to invest some Social
Security taxes in individual accounts. Bowles doesn't. Bowles
would consider allowing some recently enacted tax cuts to expire if
needed to shore up the federal
budget. Dole wouldn't. Dole favored
legislation to make it easier for the
president to negotiate foreign trade
agreements. Bowles doesn't.

Like it or not, the federal government can have a big impact on
whether ordinary Americans have a
few George Washingtons keeping
each other company in their wallet
or a lot of Andrew Jacksons and
Benjamin Franklins.

Favorite Kochet, for example,
thinks a little additional government spending on public trans-
portation would help him get and
keep a job. Kochet, who lives in the
Kenilworth section of Asheville, has
a vision problem that prevents him
from driving at night.

He says jobs advertised that he

Ewart Ball/STAFF PHOTOGRAPHER

Bill Trometer says government
regulations and free trade agreements that have hurt local manu-
facturers have a big impact on his
business, Asheville Thermoform
Plastics. Trometer operates a ma-
chine that makes rows of small
pockets in sheets of plastic used
in packaging.

In the coming weeks

As the election nears in 18
days, the Citizen-
Times will publish
a series of stories
on where the can-
didates stand on major issues in
the U.S. Senate race.

TODAY: What the candidates say
about the nation's economy and
what their roles would be in making it stronger.

Oct. 27: Despite strong interest in
Western North Carolina, Bowles
and Dole haven't made the state's
environment at the top of their
campaign agendas.

Nov. 3: The two major U.S. Senate
candidates support a U.S. invasion of Iraq even if America has
little international support.

Election 2002 ✓

plastic-shaping firm on Swannanoa
River Road, "I probably spend at
least half my time filling out monthly reports."

"It's a nightmare. We're not big
enough to have office people in
here," he says of his six-worker

Please see SENATE on A10

Wilson recalls 60 years with Grahams

By Rebekkah Melcher Logan
STAFF WRITER

Not all of the people attending the Metroplex Mission with
Rev. Billy Graham are there hoping to get their first glimpse of
the 83-year-old adviser to U.S.
presidents and countless other
world leaders. Many of them are
returning to Texas Stadium having been at the facility's inaugu-
ral event in 1971. Then too, it was
all about spirit and sports — a
call to Christians rather than
Cowboy football fans. The Rev.
Billy Graham christened the stadium and forged lasting bonds
with hundreds of area churches
and their members.

The foundation of Graham's
evangelical efforts are built on
generational relationships that
often begin with the very young
and encourage people to follow
him into his ministry or to es-
tablish individual ministries of
their own. These relationships
allow Graham's evangelical arms
to reach thousands more people
— some who follow him without
actually moving into contact
with him and some who are
guided by his faith without being directly exposed to his message.

On this, the penultimate day
of the Metroplex Mission, special

Please see GRAHAMS on A10

Graham ministers to youthful crowd

By Dale Neal
STAFF WRITER

IRVING, Texas — Leah Lundberg, 19, edged closer to the
stage at Texas Stadium to get a
good snapshot of her favorite
group, Jars of Clay.

"I just want to go up there
and mosh," said Lundberg, but
the California student had other responsibilities as a Metroplex Mission volunteer.

"We're helping with the
youth ministries," said Lundberg,
the teen who rode in buses
with a busload of classmates
from the Joshua School in Lake
Home, Calif., just to be a part of
Billy Graham's mission to
north Texas.

Graham broke attendance
records Saturday at Texas Stadium for the Concert for the
Next Generation, a night of
energetic Christian rock and
rap, and then to hear Graham
at the end of the evening.

The teens jammed up and
down to deTalk's hair-driving
remake of "Jesus Is Just All
Right With Me" and "Our God
is an Awesome God."

Kirk Franklin encouraged
the crowd to "lose your Holy
Ghost mind," working the
teens into frenzy.

When Graham finally took
his turn on stage, the crowd
roared as if he were a rock star.
Then they grew quiet to hear
his message how they could be
all right with Jesus.

Jesus could fill the empti-
ness, the sense of not belonging that many teens experience, Graham said just as it did
for him when he was only 17
years old.

"It's a wonderful thing to
spend your life and know Jesus
is in your heart," the 83-year-
old evangelist told a crowd,
most of whom were young
enough to be his grandchildren.

With Saturday's Concert for
the Next Generation and into the
parking lots, organizers were
more than pleased with the ex-
timated 82,000 who attended
the third night of the mission.
And with more young people
in attendance, the Graham
team looked for a higher per-
centage of commitments to
Christ at the evangelist's trade-
mark invitation.

Bowles, Dole debate negative political ads, Social Security

By Scott Mooneyham
ASSOCIATED PRESS

GREENVILLE, N.C. — Elizabeth
Dole and Erskine Bowles attacked
each other for negative advertising
and their stances on Social Security
Saturday night in the U.S. Senate
candidates' second debate.

Dole, the Republi-
can former Cabinet
secretary and Red
Cross chief, took a
much more aggres-
sive tone than in the
first debate between
the two, saying
Bowles initiated the
mudslinging that has
marked their televi-
sion ads.

She directly questioned the Democratic former White House chief
of staff throughout the debate.

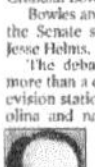

"I, for one, very much hoped I
could change the tone of politics
when I entered this race," Dole said.

Bowles, though, accused Dole of
attacking his wife in a TV commercial which questioned plant closings by a textile company run by

Elizabeth
Dole

Erskine
Bowles

Crandall Bowles.

Bowles and Dole are running for
the Senate seat being vacated by
Jesse Helms.

The debate, broadcast live by
seven public television stations
across North Car-
olina and nationally by C-SPAN,
was held at East Car-
olina University be-
fore more than 100
people.

On Social Security,
Bowles said he be-
lieves the plan to
partially privatize
the system could
potentially bankrupt the system
and jeopardize federal surplus-
es. Dole called it an irresponsible,
"do-nothing" approach.

But he said her proposal, which
would allow younger workers to invest some of their withholdings,
would make the system insolvent
quicker.

"If you are going to take money
out of the Social Security trust fund,
that money is no longer there to pay
the benefits," he said.

CHAPTER ELEVEN

REDFORD, WILLIE, AMY, THE PRESIDENTS, ET AL

As a journalist, I often had the chance to talk with – and in some cases, actually meet and interview, some fascinating people: a few presidents, a few actors, sports figures, and so on. Here's a few impressions of people over the years:

Robert Redford

I always had strict policies against unnecessarily bothering famous people – or people in general – just because we could. There were enough times when what they did, whatever that was, caused us to do what we did, which was report on it. We had to call them at home, interrupt their dinner, track them down on the job, whatever. I just wanted it to be unavoidable when we had to interrupt.

So, when I found the phone message on my desk saying Robert Redford called, I naturally assumed we had violated my rule and that someone from the Redford entourage had called to complain.

Redford – for those poor young folks who spend too much time playing with their phones – is one of the most beloved actors of his generation. He was 65 in 2002 when he came to Asheville, N.C., to film scenes in the movie "The Clearing."

For weeks I had been getting phone calls from people to report Redford sightings at restaurants and so on hoping we'd do a story – I don't know – maybe on his favorite places to eat, I guess so more people could have the chance to bust in on the man's meal. I referred them to our very talented features columnist, Susan Reinhardt.

So, I walked around the newsroom when I got the pink phone message sheet asking if anyone knew anything I needed to know before returning the call. No one knew anything, giving me that "not me" look I knew only too well as the father of five.

I returned the call, somewhat sheepishly, still not sure if I was being pranked.

Of course, I didn't expect Redford to pick up. I got his publicist, Joan Eisenburg, who assured me that Redford just wanted to talk.

"He read your column," she said. "He liked it."

I try not to blather in situations like this. I try to act all cool and professional. But this was Redford, someone who my 19-year-old daughter and 72-year-old father both not only knew, but also would think it was cool that he liked my column.

"No fucking kidding," I blurted out. Cool, Bob. Way to go.

Eisenburg just laughed, thankfully. She said he wanted to meet me and hoped I would write a column about it, and that he wanted to say thank you to the people of Asheville and talk about mutual concerns over the environment.

Sure, I said, regaining my composure. I suggested we meet at the newspaper building, thinking I could score coolness points with three generations of female employees, but Eisenburg just laughed at that, too. No, I would have to come to the set, and we could meet in his trailer. I could bring along a photographer, if I wished, she said.

Sure, I said. And we set a time for later that afternoon.

Twenty-something Rita Larkin was on the copy desk. She had started as a photographer. We were pressed for time. I asked her if she could come with me to shoot photos but didn't tell her of what just yet. Sure, she said.

"Good," I explained, "But you can't say anything to anyone until we leave the building."

She got her equipment and we left. I explained what we were doing on the car ride over.

When we got to the set, which was off in the woods behind a church in Weaverville, we were ushered to a waiting area where dozens of people were gathered. I recognized a couple of Buncombe County deputies and talked to them while we waited for someone to get us.

"Are you real cops (guarding the place) or extras in the movie," I asked.

They were both, was the reply.

We soon did the interview and Redford was everything I thought he would be. Of course, he is a world-class actor, so for all I knew it could all be a put on.

We joked about him calling me up for an interview. I told him I thought I was being pranked.

"Yeah, sorry about that," Redford said, sounding contrite. "You should have asked if (Paul) Newman was on hold."

Redford, who was very much a gentleman, but also very into politics, wanted to talk about drilling for oil and its impact on the environment. He wanted to talk about the newspaper's push to get Elizabeth Dole, who was running for U.S. Senate, to join our debate so we could assess her position on environmental issues. He wanted to take a swipe at President George W. Bush and the Tennessee Valley Authority for its pollution of the air in the bowl formed by the mountains surrounding Asheville.

Before we finished, he gave me his personal phone number in Utah where he lived some of the time. I appreciated that, but of course never called it.

Larkin shot a bunch of photos. We used one, which wound up on the front page along with the start of my column. I don't know what happened to the rest of the photos.

Mobile phones were still fairly new technology in 2002, but I had one. On the way back to the office, Larkin asked to use it. Sure, I said, but the network was spotty at best. She dialed a number and then asked for her mom. I think the call was to Atlanta. I knew it was long distance and we'd be charged extra.

"Mom," she screamed (and I do mean screamed). "I just came from an interview with Robert fucking Redford."

I could hear the screaming from the other end.

"Mom," I said out loud, "so did I."

Bill Clinton

Honestly, I've never been a Bill Clinton fan. Not when he showed indifference to the fate of a Huntington couple imprisoned in St. Vincent, not when he lied about his sexual relationship with intern Monica Lewinski, not when Secret Service prevented me from going to my hotel room at an American Society of Newspaper Editors conference because he was in his room somewhere on my floor, and not when he came to Huntington in 1996 to launch his campaign for re-election.

He was much too slick for my tastes, though I loved his ability to joke and laugh and appear to genuinely enjoy being himself. And he was, after all, president of the United States.

So, when he decided to "kickoff" his railroad trip to Chicago for the Democratic convention in Huntington, I was excited. And I can tell you exactly where I was when I found out about it. I was in my car about to go through a drive through car wash. My mobile phone rang. That was exciting news at the time. It never rang unless it was the office because nobody had that number. Like I said, it was 1996, and mobile phones had been around for a while, but they were expensive and rarely used, not like today when it is the first and last thing most people touch every day.

When I answered the phone, Sen. Jay Rockefeller was on the other end, only I didn't believe him.

"No, it's not," I said.

"Yes, it is," came the reply. "Your office gave me the number."

I'll have to talk to them about that, I thought, but didn't say it.

Rockefeller might have been the richest man I had ever met. He certainly felt most guilty about being rich of anyone I knew. I asked him once why he spent so lavishly on a re-election campaign in which he would win more than 80 percent of the vote, and he explained because he could. In fact, he said, every day he could spend as much as he wanted and then go to bed and wake up with more money than he had the day before. So, why not? he reasoned.

On this day, he wanted to tell me that I'd be getting a phone call shortly at my office from the president's campaign staff and/or security team. They wanted to brief me on plans for a visit by the president.

This was going to be a big deal. It would take place at the CSX building, where there would be a ceremony featuring some of the state's leading Democrats and a public rally. CSX is a large freight railroad company, one of the biggest in the United States, and has a big presence in Huntington. We had meetings with the security team, which laid out how things would work. We offered to host whatever media needed help, giving them desk space and Internet hook ups at The Herald-Dispatch office, which was a two-block walk from the rally.

We were very accommodating, of course. The security folks asked what we needed in return. I said I wanted two things:

- Jim Tweel of Jim's Steak & Spaghetti restaurant is next to The Herald-Dispatch building. Over the years, Tweel hosted and fed people like President John F. Kennedy and Muhammad Ali. If the president couldn't come to Jim's, maybe Jim could bring Clinton takeout. They would check and get approval. It was a matter of civic pride that the president should interact with Jim Tweel. I'm sure the significance of the iconic Jim Tweel in the community was brought to Clinton's attention by more important people than me, but nonetheless it was on my wish list and it happened.
- The second request was more personal. My publisher, Tom Bookstaver, despite his reputation in the company as being very budget and finance focused, was really a nice man. The truth be told, he was pretty nice during budget time, too. He asked me to see if he could present the president with a copy of that morning's newspaper, and so I made that request. It, too, was approved.

Charlotte Pritt, the Democratic Party's nominee for governor and a former teacher, was tapped to lead the Pledge of Allegiance at the start of the event. Pritt had been a member of the West Virginia House and Senate in her career. She was young, smart, and it was a heavily Democratic state at the time.

I guess she just got nervous and botched the words. The guy filming for C-SPAN looked over at me. I shrugged.

"That's the way we say it around here," I said and turned away.

Pritt, of course, lost the race and she never won another major race. She ran unsuccessfully for governor in 2016 as a candidate for the Mountain State Party. It is a shame that happened. I'm sure Pritt had recited the Pledge perfectly hundreds of times before, but it's not the kind of thing you can mess up when the TV lights are on.

I was also impressed with just how tall Jay Rockefeller was when the senator stood next to the president. Clinton is no small change at 6-foot-2, but Rockefeller is a giant (you know, at least by Shorty Gabordi standards) at 6-foot-7. Man, those are big guys.

As long as we're here, let's take a little side trip down the 1996 politics of West Virginia road.

Pritt was beaten in the general election by the Republican nominee Cecil Underwood, who had been the youngest West Virginia governor when he was elected at 34 years old in 1956. When he defeated Pritt in 1996, he was the oldest person elected governor in the state.

I should have liked Underwood for a lot of reasons, but – despite his age – he didn't seem to have much vision for how things could be different. The state was stuck between the proverbial rock and hard place on coal: It was great for the economy, horrible for the environment, and some of us thought the longer West Virginia held onto coal as the savior the deeper the trough it was creating for the economy.

Underwood lived in my neighborhood in Huntington, and he was certainly elegant and well spoken.

In the primary, he defeated Jon McBride, a former astronaut who I would encounter years later as editor of FLORIDA TODAY at a space-related event, and David McKinley, who I don't remember.

McBride joked about it when we bumped into each other in Florida, but he said he remembered me from West Virginia. He should have. The Herald-Dispatch endorsed him over Underwood, our hometown candidate in the primary election.

We ended up endorsing Underwood in the general election, but I think he never forgave me for the slight in the primary. He came to my office to complain about it – he said to try to understand it – but I declined to engage on our "motives" beyond trying to make the right decision for the state. I think that only made him angry.

Rosalynn Carter

In his book, "Confessions of an S.O.B." (1989), Al Neuharth describes the process of recruiting Rosalynn Carter to the Gannett Board of Directors. She served from 1983 to 1997, when she retired at age 70. I had at least two brief encounters with her during that time.

The first was the result of an assignment sometime around 1985 or 1986, I simply don't remember. I was assigned – I think by USA TODAY, but it might have been Gannett News Service – to write an update on Amy Carter, who was attending Brown University at the time. That wouldn't be so simple.

First, the Carters tried hard to see that Amy had as "normal" a life as humanly possible, which proved not at all humanly possible, given she was the first child to live at the White House since the Kennedy children. Her treehouse was famous for hosting sleepovers with her friends, and she attended District of Columbia public schools.

Of course, Secret Service agents were assigned to guard her no matter where she went, but that's a different, but interesting story.

My job was to track her down and write about her life as a college student at Brown, where she would struggle academically, probably because she got caught up in so many causes which took time away from studying.

I had no idea how to contact her and I didn't think I would find her just walking near the Brown campus, where I had lived briefly following college. But I knew the Gannett board was getting ready to meet at a downtown hotel.

I wrote a note to Mrs. Carter, clipped it to a business card and talked a security guard into letting me place the note on her seat for the board meeting. I said I would wait outside the room and if she didn't mind, I needed help for a story.

Still, I was shocked when she came and found me on a break. She said Amy would be gone for the weekend, but if I called her right away I might have a chance of reaching her. I did, but that's not the rest of the story.

Amy took my call but begged off saying she didn't have time for an interview; she would talk to me next week if I could wait. She had an exam to study for and she was going to a friend's house for the weekend, and she had a choice to make, talk to me or study. I suggested she should study.

Fine, she said, and thanked me for understanding. She also said she'd appreciate it if I didn't put it in my story that she was leaving for the weekend to stay at a friend's house, because she wasn't sure her father knew.

"Don't worry, he won't hear it from me," I said.

I wondered aloud for the next several days if she really thought I was going to call the former president with that kind of news? Or that I would put it in my story?

Amy would eventually be dismissed from Brown for academic issues, but I can say with 100 percent honesty that I advised her to study rather than talk to me.

My second encounter with Mrs. Carter cemented my view that whatever her politics, I admired her greatly. I was selected to be in the first Gannett Management Development Program for newsroom leaders. It had been an 18-month program with training sessions held in northern Virginia and the District, as well as at FLORIDA TODAY, in Nashville, and elsewhere. It was close to graduation and plans were for a big dinner.

Every program member was assigned to a board member for the dinner, I guess with the idea that we might hit it off, get some extra mentoring and so forth. I was assigned to Mrs. Carter. We talked a few times leading up to the dinner. She impressed me as charming, soft spoken, and strong willed.

But the night of the dinner, she called with bad news. She wasn't going to make it; she was asked at the last minute to fill in speaking at some event at some embassy. My memory is the Romanian Embassy, but that could be wrong. She would do her best to get there late, but didn't want to embarrass me, she said.

I said something like I didn't think that was possible and wished her luck. The phone almost immediately rang back.

She would try to get there, she said. Save her a place.

The event took only minutes at the embassy. I came away that night with a single lasting impression of the transformation that occurs in this remarkable woman. High energy. You could feel the passion.

I've never met anyone like her in my life, not then or now.

Willie Mays

Say, hey, Willie!

I've been a New York Mets fan for as far back as I can remember. They came into the National League when I was 6 years old in 1962. That year, my step-grandfather took me to a Phillies-Mets game in Philadelphia. He was a big Phillies fan and assumed I would be, too, living in south Jersey. And I might have been, ironically, had he not taken me to that game.

The Mets were getting clobbered. That stands out in my memory. And nearly everyone in the stands was laughing at them, making fun of them, and rooting against them. I was offended and instantly became a Mets fan. Been a Mets fan ever since.

Oh, it's easy to follow teams with satellite TV and high-speed Internet. But over the years, in the small towns I've been in, well, it was a challenge. I found a spot from which I could pick up radio broadcasts of Mets games, for example in Marietta, Ohio. It was on my roof.

I would go out an upstairs window and connect my radio antenna to a wire that ran to the chimney and listen to the Mets games, which faded in and out. Ralph Kiner was mainly on TV by then, but Bob Murphy was still on radio, along with a young Gary Cohen. It was Murphy, Kiner and the colorful Lindsey Nelson doing both radio and TV in my youth.

I grew up listening to those voices and climbing out onto the roof in Marietta was not only a matter of getting the games of the team I loved, but also listening for Murphy's happy recap and Kiner's Corner after the games. Their voices coming in over the radio were one of the happiest parts of my childhood. You could count on them to be there, night after night, 162 games per year. We didn't have a TV when I was a kid. It was not a political statement. We just couldn't afford one.

So, you would see why 1969 was special in my life, when the Amazin' Mets stunned baseball and won the World Series. And you can see why 1973, when I was a high school junior, was almost as special, when the Mets won the National League pennant and returned to the Series, which they ultimately lost.

But longtime Giant and baseball legend Willie Mays was finishing out his Hall of Fame career as a Met that year. Willie – the Say Hey

Kid – seemed to play the game as he lived his life. If he ever had a bad day, you wouldn't have known it.

Of course, he did have problems. Baseball players didn't make millions per season back then and guys like Willie Mays and Mickey Mantle enjoyed more fame than money.

At some point, Mays and Gannett hooked up to make commercials endorsing USA TODAY, which is why Mays was at the Gannett meeting where I met him. Tom Curley, who was my editor for a year in Norwich after Gannett bought the newspaper, and I had stayed relatively close friends. He was publisher of USA TODAY.

I could see Curley at a distance sitting at a bar with someone who – even at a distance – looked familiar. I honestly wasn't close enough to know who it was. But Tom saw me and began motioning me over. His companion now had his back to me as I walked up.

"Bob," Curley began, "allow me to introduce Willie Mays."

I was stunned as Mays turned around with a hand stretched out to greet me.

"Willie," I stammered, "thanks for 1973."

"Ah, a Mets fan," the great one said with his big smile. "That was a fun year. It was great being back in New York."

He had started his career with the New York Giants and moved to San Francisco with the team in the 1950s. The orange in the Mets' colors was taken from the Giants' orange. The blue was from the then Brooklyn Dodgers, who moved to Los Angeles and became all Hollywood.

Then I did something I had never done before and have rarely done since. I asked another human being for an autograph. Willie seemed delighted. All that was around was a Gannett napkin, so he signed that.

I gave it to my brother Lou, since he was a Giants fan growing up.

BUZZ ALDRIN

OK, so by the time I met the second man to walk on the moon, he was 86 and I'm pretty sure he didn't know or care who I was. It was a thrill for me, nonetheless. The truth is he had much more meaningful relationships with people on our space team at FLORIDA TODAY, which is kind of how it should be.

Donna and I attended the first three annual fund-raising galas for his foundation, ShareSpace, a nonprofit that was created to try to rekindle young people's interest in space. They believe that can be done through science, technology, engineering, arts and math (STEAM).

At these events, Col. Aldrin was a delight. He told stories from the moon landing and the heroics involved – and the luck – without appearing boastful or particularly fortunate. My favorite story was about the very real fear at the time that the layer of dust on the moon was much deeper than we now know it to be. There was a fear that they would sink deeply into the dust.

"That's why I thought it was a good idea to let Neil (Armstrong) go first," Aldrin told the audience.

Of course, the lunar module would have already sunk into the dust if that had been the case, but it was funny anyway, especially under the circumstances.

Aldrin was sitting on stage, his Presidential Medal of Freedom appropriately on his chest, with the lunar module in the background and he bantered with John Travolta, telling stories from the moon landing.

He also told the story of how a felt-tipped pen saved the mission and the lives of Aldrin and Armstrong. They were sitting in the lunar module when Aldrin noticed something out of place on the floor, he said. It turned out to be a circuit breaker for the engine arm. Without it, they had no way to fire the engine to meet up with Michael Collins, who stayed behind in the Columbia spacecraft.

Ground control in Houston had no solutions, either. Aldrin realized that the felt marker he carried might work. It did. He stuck the pen in the hole where the breaker was supposed to be and the engine fired. You know the rest of the story. They returned safely to heroes' welcomes around the world.

It was nice getting to meet Travolta at the event, too. Like everyone else there, we had our picture taken with Aldrin and Travolta, who was exceedingly polite and very deferential to Aldrin, which was as it should have been.

The next year, George Takei was the guest in the role played by Travolta, but the following year, there was no special guest and no Buzz Aldrin, owing, no doubt, to a family dispute that spilled over into the media and the courts.

OTHERS

I attended events with most of the U.S. presidents of my adult life. Carter, I've mentioned earlier.

Ronald Reagan spoke at one the Washington dinners I attended, but I can't recall which one. For the record, Reagan was probably my favorite of the bunch. I think he genuinely understood that he was president for all Americans, regardless of party affiliation or philosophy. He was an amazing communicator, even if his administration once classified ketchup as a vegetable for school lunch purposes.

I don't think I was ever in the same room with George H.W. Bush, but I wish I could have sat down with him for an interview. Fascinating man. Baseball player at Yale. He was captain of the team and played in two College World Series. World War II veteran – a Navy pilot who completed 128 carrier landings. I think we would have found a lot to talk about.

SPORTS PEOPLE

I've met a lot of sports stars because of my work, but as big of a fan as I am, I've never really been enamored by them – except Willie Mays.

In Huntington, I got to know future NFL quarterback Chad Pennington well enough. He was a journalism major at Marshall and worked a little for The Herald-Dispatch. Once he was drafted in the first round, though, everything changed. I had to work through his agent for everything and his agent wanted $1,000 a week for Pennington to continue to write a column for us. That, of course, was out of the question. That was more than some of our veteran columnists were getting and Pennington was still learning journalism.

Some people thought wide receiver Randy Moss was an ass in college, but I liked him and saw huge potential, not only as a football player (everyone saw that) but also as a person. He would have to grow up – mature, if you will – under the bright lights of the NFL, but the Randy Moss I saw at Marshall would show up at a men's basketball game and purposefully move to the lower seats so little kids could come get autographs or talk to him.

I saw stuff on the field, too, like Moss walking away when opponents would abuse him on sideline plays. That's not stuff I think he handled well his first year at Marshall, but he adjusted to it in his second year in college. Unquestionably, Moss was the best college football player I ever saw, although Jameis Winston had the greatest single season the year he won the Heisman while quarterbacking Florida State.

Byron Leftwich was the funniest and most courageous. Maybe that's the wrong word. Maybe determined is a better descriptor. After we left Huntington for Asheville, Donna and I went to watch Marshall at the GMAC Bowl in Mobile, Ala., as fans. At a public parade in Mobile, I felt someone gently pushing me in the back as we watched a marching band go by.

"Excuse me, sir, but I can't see over you," a voice politely said.

It was Leftwich. I turned only to see this huge man, all 6-foot-5 of him, smiling like he was getting away with something. We bumped into him again when we decided to have a quiet night out, we thought, away from the football crowd at a movie theater across town.

Donna and I were literally the only people there to see the film, "Vanilla Sky." Then in came the entire Marshall football team. Coach Bobby Pruett sat down next to me, saying "Hi, Jeff." He could never remember my name and decided Jeff would work. By the way, the film was new that year (2001) and we had no idea what it was about, either before seeing it or afterward. It was horrible.

Bowden, Dawson and Ruffin

Pruett instantly became my second-favorite football coach when we moved to Tallahassee, where Bobby Bowden ruled the Seminoles. He lived in our development, although about a mile away.

When I got to Tallahassee, I knew football would be a strong community interest, which was fine with me. I asked our Florida State reporter, Steve Ellis, if I might meet Bowden. He said he would check. Bowden thought it a good idea.

I knew how busy he was and thought I was lucky he agreed to see me at all. I wished only a few minutes to get to know him. I thought I'd be pushing it to get 15 minutes when he greeted me at his office door.

More than an hour and 20 minutes later, I reluctantly had to excuse myself. Never in my wildest imagination did I think I would be in there that long, that he would allow me that much time, but it turns out we had mutual friends in Huntington. Red Dawson, who would become more famous by the film "We Are Marshall," among them. Eddie and Betty Barrett, my neighbors in Huntington, were others. Eddie, a former Marshall athletic director, had tried to hire Bowden to coach Marshall and he almost took the job. That would have made him the coach that awful night in 1970 when the team plane crashed, killing all 75 aboard.

Dawson was a Marshall assistant coach, who, at the last minute, did not fly back with the team from East Carolina that night. The plane crashed just short of the runway at Tri-State Airport near Huntington. Dawson played college football at FSU in the early 1960s and Bowden was his position coach. Dawson became a Hall of Famer at FSU and played for the old Boston Patriots in the American Football League before its merger with the NFL.

To me, at first, Dawson was just some guy I met at the YMCA and then saw at church. Newspaper editors usually don't have many friends, and I didn't. But Dawson was somebody I liked, and we were close enough that he invited me to his home to watch football. Then he decided to run for sheriff, and we could no longer be friends. I told him the newspaper was not going to endorse him because we felt the other guy was more qualified, and that sealed it. He lost the race, but things were never the same between us. Years later, even when he was visiting Bowden in Tallahassee, we rarely got together. I guess that's part of the price of being a journalist.

There's a scene in the "We Are Marshall" film where Dawson visits West Virginia University just before the 1971 season. Bowden was the head coach at WVU. It was right after the crash and Marshall wanted to simplify its offense by running a veer formation that WVU was using.

Marshall was using mostly transfers and freshmen after getting NCAA approval to suspend the rule against freshmen playing varsity. During the visit, Dawson discovered that Bowden had green crosses symbolizing the Marshall tragedy on the backs of all WVU helmets. It made me cry.

I also cried when Nate Ruffin died. Dawson and Ruffin are forever linked by the fact that both were a part of that 1970 Marshall football team. Ruffin was the player – a co-captain – in the film who was injured and didn't make the East Carolina trip. But that's not how I knew him. Ruffin had been human resources director at The Herald-Dispatch before my time in Huntington and went on to become a Gannett executive. Somehow, we became friends along the way.

When he was in town, I would invite him to The Herald-Dispatch sky box at the Marshall stadium for games. One time, late in my tenure in Huntington, Ruffin and Dawson ended up in our box. I don't recall the details of how that happened, but Ruffin turned to us and gave us the news of his impending death. There was no way around it, he said. The docs were certain. After a long struggle with leukemia, the end was near.

"I wonder sometimes why God spared me from the plane crash only to have this horrible disease," Ruffin said as we all fought back tears.

When he died in October 2001, he was a vice president at the Freedom Forum, a foundation to support a free press and free speech. He was just 51. He was finally reunited with his teammates, buried next to several of them at Springhill Cemetery in Huntington.

Buster Posey

FSU head baseball coach, Mike Martin – called Eleven by most because that was his longtime uniform number – is also a very special man. He retired in 2019. He is both kind and tough and he always donated balls and used bats to the local leagues and teams. He coached a lot of players who went on to play Major League Baseball. Few accomplished or had the character of Buster Posey.

Posey, a Gold Glove catcher for the San Francisco Giants, is one the few I've met in sports who was as much a gentleman as he was an athlete. Pennington is another. I was introduced to Posey at an FSU team picnic by Brian Henry, son of the Democrat's sports editor, Jim Henry. Brian was a pitcher on the FSU team and played professionally. He wrote a column for us while he was in the minor leagues.

I swear to this day if Posey met an older man or woman, it would be yes sir or no sir, yes ma'am or no ma'am. Rookie of the Year, MVP, World Series champion three times over, sure, but what impressed me about Posey was how he and Henry took the time at the picnic to walk around with my son, then a middle schooler and aspiring baseball player, and introduce him around. Posey is just a nice young man.

Column: **Actor Redford falls in love with mountains, people while filming**

By Robert C. Gabordi
Executive Editor, Asheville Citizen-Times
Published Oct. 20, 2002

At some point in his life, Robert Redford crossed over from being simply an international film superstar to a living legend, something reserved for a handful of people in any era. His appeal crosses boundaries of generations and genders.

He is one of very few people recognizable by both my 19-year-old daughter and 72-year-old father. Both thought meeting him would be "cool" or "neat" or whatever their generation's proper term to express that they were impressed.

It was.

For weeks, people have been calling the newspaper to say Redford had been spotted in town, at this location or that, while he was here to film his latest movie, "The Clearing." I've laughed at such calls, even suggesting to one caller that she call columnist Susan Reinhardt. Sooner or later, I suggested, Susan would write something about why people react with such silliness upon spotting another human being eating dinner.

Redford tries – as much as can be reasonably tried by someone who has been cast with Natalie Wood, Jane Fonda, Barbara Streisand, Paul Newman, Brad Pitt, Demi Moore, Dustin Hoffman, Faye Dunaway, Meryl Streep and Michelle Pfeiffer, to name a few – to maintain some privacy. That's not even counting his work as a director or producer.

So why, I wondered with more than idle curiosity the other night, did I have a message to call Redford, saying that he wanted to talk to me?

Before dialing the number left on my voice mail, I walked around the newsroom asking: What have we done to bother the man? Rarely do the famous call a newspaper editor, other than to complain about some perceived mistreatment. I wanted to know what I faced on the other end of the telephone line.

With the blamelessness normally reserved for 8-year-olds falsely accused of messing with dad's TV remote, editors gave me a lot of turned up plans and shakes of the head.

"Nope, nothing, came the responses. "Not me."

Turns out Redford hadn't called to complain, but to compliment. He wanted to say thank you to the people of Asheville for their kindnesses and respect shown toward him, said his publicist, Joan Eisenberg. He would be leaving soon and wondered if I had the time to talk.

Undoubtedly, he would want to weigh in on other issues, too, she said, such as the fuss the newspaper is raising over the lack of true debates between Elizabeth Dole and Erskine Bowles.

"He read your column," she said. "he liked it."

I said something like – loosely translated and cleaned up to meet my own standards about what can be said in a family newspaper – "No kidding?"

Maybe we could meet at the newspaper building, she suggested. I encouraged that, saying it would appeal to three generations of women employees. Eisenberg laughed, saying no doubt it would. Told later of my comment, Redford gave that Redford smile – the sly grin I recalled from "The Sting."

Later, as we were talking, it became obvious that Redford is a man who is comfortable with being Redford. God bless him. Too few people feel that way about themselves.

For timing reasons, the conversation instead was held in a trailer at a church in Weaverville, where the film is being shot. In it, Redford plays a businessman who is kidnapped. There were lots of people dressed as FBI agents and Buncombe County deputies running around the area. They were "extras," I guessed.

"Are you real cops or actors?" I asked a group while waiting for Redford.

"A little of both today," replied one who I recognized as a Buncombe deputy.

As a journalist, I've interviewed a lot of famous people, some presidents, and a few sports starts, once even Bob Hope. The difference was I had sought them out with a purpose in mind. Except for a question or two about Michelle Pfeiffer or Jane Fond (pre-Hanoi), I wasn't sure what I might ask Redford – and I was hoping the conversation wouldn't go there.

While waiting for Redford, I decided to let the man talk, to ask as few questions as necessary to keep the conversation moving. Instead of an interview, I thought we'd just talk. That's what happened.

He was dressed in nylon sweat pants and a T-shirt, hardly the image of a rugged outdoors man or a Hollywood sex symbol. This is one of the biggest names of my generation (the 1970s) of movie-going. What's this all about? I wondered.

He really did want to say thanks to Asheville, and he began before the microphone and recorder were set up. He talked right away about how much he enjoyed his stay here. Too often, he said, Hollywood people come into a community to work, do what they do and just leave. He tries at least to write a letter to the local newspaper editor before leaving. This time, having read a column I wrote, he called.

Redford is someone who likes a good political fray. The discussion that should occur, he believes, is good for democracy and America. As much as anything, I suspect, the steep differences on the issues between Dole and Bowles and the lack of genuine debate, drew him out. I suspect he thinks this campaign is not just about North Carolina, but also about America, where it is headed and what it will become.

Besides his film career, Redford is about the environment and conservation. While here, he was drawn to the Blue Ridge Parkway and its natural beauty. He has watched developers tear some of that down in the West, in Utah, where he has a home, and elsewhere.

We agreed that these are the types of issues that need to be debated in the U.S. Senate race in North Carolina, and why one such debate ought to occur in Western North Carolina. It is why we have pressed Dole to accept our invitation to such a debate. Bowles did.

As the conversation continued, one word kept coming to mind: grounded. Redford is an actor who takes his craft seriously, never having been content to simply play the handsome, blue-eyed, blond man, avoiding roles that would merely typecast him as such.

Now 65, he is still able to play the leading man opposite Hollywood's most beautiful women. He is literary and intelligent, outspoken and determined to give back to his profession and to help create discussion on issues he thinks are important.

He actively worked to prevent oil drilling, for instance, in the Arctic region. He has campaign for candidates who share his beliefs. He is well aware of who Robert Redford is and jokes easily about himself. If who he is causes people to listen to what he believes is common sense public policy on issues that impact the future of the nation and the planet, so be it.

Listening to him talk, I reminded myself that this is a great actor, asking if I would know where the man ends and the actor begins.

I think I saw the difference, the line of demarcation, and I know I saw the man. Not a bad way to spend a rainy afternoon.

Robert C. Gabordi is executive editor of the Citizen-Times. His telephone number is (828) 232-5954. His email address is Bgabordi@CITIZEN-TIMES.com.

Catholic schoolgirls were an unexpected sighting at the Wagah gate closing exhibition that features some of the best trained soldiers in the Indian and Pakistani armies. They cheered for the home Pakistan team as fans do at American college football games.

I was touched – as were my colleagues – by the sweetness of the children we encountered on our trip to Pakistan. A 12-year-old boy rushed to meet any Americans because America is where his father lives. A 13-year-old Afghan refugee attending a private school funded by a non-profit agency talks about her aspiration to travel to America to fulfill her dream to become a medical doctor. A little girl with the face of a princess plays on the beach in Karachi. Two Afghan refugee boys gather anything of value and throw the rest in smoldering fires.

Note to readers: These photos were gathered during my first trip to Pakistan in 2012 with the International Center for Journalists. I was one of 10 members of an American delegation of journalists on the trip.

CHAPTER TWELVE

WORLD TRAVELER AND HOST

Sometimes I shake my head and wonder how this happened. I'm the type of guy who doesn't like to go out for a cup of tea by myself. I would rather skip lunch than sit alone. Traveling anywhere ties my stomach in knots.

So, how did I ever get roped into traveling by myself to places all around the world?

I guess I felt obligated as a journalist to stand up for free speech and this is how I did it.

Many Americans truly do not understand how we are looked upon by the rest of the world, especially people who have spent their whole lives trying to win freedom, something we take for granted. That saying about America being a shining beacon of hope in a stormy night is a very real thing.

This was brought home to me by a little girl living in an Afghan refugee camp in Karachi, Pakistan. She attended a school provided by The Citizens Foundation, a nonprofit organization. You could see the garbage burning across the creek from the school in the camp that was her home. Barefoot little children tried to walk through the fires and smoke to recover items of trash coming downstream that they could turn into money.

It was during my first trip to Pakistan in 2012 and I was traveling in a group from the United States, part of an International Center for Journalists exchange program. All of us represented media outlets that had hosted Pakistani journalists in the United States. Asked by someone what America means to her, the 13-year-old didn't pause even for a breath.

"America is my dream," she said.

She wants to be a medical doctor and doesn't think that can happen for her in Pakistan. So, she dreams of coming to America to study and then returning to take care of her people.

I realized that I was in deep in the effort to attain peace through journalism when I was on a plane headed to Turkey and then to Armenia in 2011. A year later, it would be the first of three trips to Pakistan.

On the Turkey trip, I traveled alone. Totally alone.

During my last trip to Pakistan, while teaching at the Center for Excellence, I spoke to the Karachi Press Club and was presented with a beautiful sash.

I hosted more than two dozen foreign journalists in Asheville, Tallahassee, and at FLORIDA TODAY. These were total strangers who I invited into my newspaper and home, some to stay with my family, most through the ICFJ, but not all of them.

It started after the breakup of the former Soviet Union as its former Republics struggled to come to grips with what freedom and democracy would look like in their country. I was in Asheville and I was approached by the ICFJ about hosting journalists from Ukraine and Georgia.

I know it sounds corny, but I thought about what Gen. Douglas MacArthur said about a free press being the enemy of an authoritarian dictator, which is why he helped create a free press in post-war Japan. Helping this program in its mission to strengthen free press worldwide seemed patriotic, a duty as a journalist.

I believed if we could get to know each other better, it could help create better understanding among the people of our countries. I have no doubt that we had some impact in Pakistan.

When I was in Asheville, ICFJ helped us get to Indonesia and Sudan to document the work of Franklin Graham's Samaritan's Purse organization, which was based in nearby Boone, N.C. We sent reporter Rebeccah Cantley (now Rebeccah Lutz) and photographer Steve Dixon to Indonesia after the January 2005 tsunami and ICFJ helped foot the bill.

They went to Meulaboh, the city closest to the epicenter of the 9.1 earthquake that caused the tsunami that took nearly a quarter million lives. Areas they wanted to reach were blocked not only by destruction from the storm, but also a raging civil war. Somehow, they were given passage by combatants on both sides. For many Indonesians in remote locations, we guessed, Lutz might have been the first blonde woman they had ever seen.

I reported on their trip in columns in the Citizen-Times. For me, it was the start of a relationship with ICFJ that would last the rest of my career and beyond.

Jessica Gabordi shows off her new friend, Ibrahim Kasita of Uganda, at her school, Gretchen Everhart Trainable Center, in Tallahassee May 2, 2013.

In Tallahassee, we hosted journalists from Africa, South America, Asia, and the Middle East. Independently, I hosted others from Europe and South America.

The first person to visit Tallahassee was Mark Oloo, a Kenyan, who was overwhelmed by the wealth he found in America. Our staff pooled money and purchased a laptop for him to take back to Kenya. He literally cried at the generosity, which, he said, would allow him to get work as a freelancer and feed his family. Native journalists could not make enough to survive without their own equipment, he said.

Particularly poignant was a trip he took to Florida A&M University, an HBCU, for a football game. The experience left him with a lot of questions about U.S. history and how so many black people ended up in America, which he would clearly love to do.

His education on U.S. history and even his own country's history was lacking. He was shocked to learn that the black people he met in America were descendants of slaves. Mark left with a stash of money from donations, too, which, he said, would help him pay for additional schooling. From time to time for a while we would send him additional money.

More journalists followed Oloo to Tallahassee.

I hosted Mehmet Fatih Oztarsu from Turkey and Ofelya Kamavosyan from Armenia. If you are not familiar with the history of their countries, I suggest you read about it. There is much to it, including Turkey's long denial of a genocide that wiped out its population of Christian Armenians near the beginning of the 20th century.

At times it was illegal in Turkey to even talk about it. It is still a very sensitive subject.

The ICFJ paired a Turk and an Armenian to work on a project while they were in the United States, then to present their findings at a conference in Ankara before going to Yerevan, the two national capitals.

If any pair of journalists had a chance to make this project successful it was these two. Both are outstanding people, kind and gentle in their dealings with me and my family. Mehmet might have been the only Turkish journalist living in and reporting from Yerevan.

But they disliked and distrusted each other. I had no clue how intensely until we were in Ankara in front of the people from the U.S. Embassy – the U.S. State Department had helped sponsor the program – and others, including some ethnic Kurds. We wore headsets to hear translations of what was being said in our native language.

Their project was to investigate what had happened to Christian crosses embedded into the stone and concrete foundations of Apostolic churches. Over the years, they had disappeared.

Despite having worked together with the assignment to make a joint presentation, they presented different conclusions. A big argument broke out and accusations and finger pointing followed. I stood up and gave a short talk about how what had just happened showed the need for diversity of thought in our journalism, that they had proved how two intelligent people from different backgrounds could look at the same information and draw vastly different conclusions. That is why, I argued, diversity in news organizations is so important to truth telling.

The trip was a huge success in many ways, including a simple tourism perspective. In Ankara, we visited the Ankara Castle, a fortification from the medieval period. When we went to Armenia, we visited the Holocaust Museum. We also took a bus ride to ancient ruins and got caught on a narrow, winding mountain road surrounded by oxen.

I am still friends with both Mehmet and Ofelya, and I value both of them very much.

But we also met with high-level government officials and other journalists from both countries. This came at a time when Turkey was being considered for membership in the European Union and its government had applied a full-court press. Everywhere you looked, someone was writing an opinion piece touting democracy in Turkey under the leadership of Prime Minister Recep Tayyip Erdogan. Our delegation of American journalists met with several high-ranking Turkish government officials.

I challenged one minister who we met with about an opinion guest column in The New York Times, suggesting Turkey was a shining light for democracy in the Islamic world.

"If that is true," I asked, "why are there 26 journalists in prisons for what they have said and written?"

The response was infuriating. He said the number was only 22, not 26, and that Turkey is not America and that these people are terrorists, not really journalists. The answer should have been a clear signal that

Turkish democracy, which has since crumbled and Erdogan's government has raided and closed unfriendly news operations, was a sham.

I had a similar experience in Pakistan when we met with the information minister. She said she wondered why Pakistan's image suffers in American media when Pakistani soldiers are fighting side-by-side with Americans in the war on terrorism.

Well, I said, Pakistan had yet to adequately explain how Osama bin Laden had eluded capture for so many years after Sept. 11, 2001. U.S. forces killed the mastermind of terrorism attacks on the United States in 2011 near the Pakistani capital and its military training academy.

Interestingly, when state-run Associated Press of Pakistan (APP) reported on my response, they said I had complimented her on Pakistan's commitment to democracy, which is not at all what I said. The APP is not affiliated with The Associated Press.

I had one more "event" on that first trip to Pakistan, when I declined an invitation for our group to have dinner at the home of Azhar Abbas, one of the leading journalists in the country and the brother of a major general in the Pakistani army's secret service, their version of the United States' CIA. Earlier in the day, Abbas had insulted Gannett, my employer, and I was in no mood to eat with him, so I stayed at the hotel while the rest of the group went to his home.

Guards were with us everywhere we went, and some had to be left at the hotel to protect me. It was Italian night at the hotel. I went back into the kitchen to explain to the chef how to make homemade pasta. The guards came with me, of course. We had a grand time.

As an aside, I met with Abbas on a subsequent trip in 2016 over dinner. I believe we mended differences and I invited him to join me the next day for a class I was teaching at the Center for Excellence in Journalism, which he did.

On the first trip to Pakistan in 2012, we met with groups of journalists at different media outlets in Islamabad, Lahore and Karachi. I recall one most poignant conversation that included a journalist using a crutch, his head still wrapped from a beating he endured for a story he wrote. It was hard to know who the enemy to a free press was in Pakistan; such a beating could have come at the behest of a government official, the military, or the Taliban.

We wondered at their courage and asked if they could ever really consider themselves free as long as Pakistan ranked among the most dangerous places to practice journalism in the world.

"We are as free as our courage allows us to be," came the response.

We also met with students at the Lahore University of Management Science (LUMS), perhaps Pakistan's best-known university. Questions came up, as they always do when traveling abroad, about America's reliance on its military might in making foreign policy.

The student who voiced this was speaking, no doubt, for many others in the political science class. I stood to answer, explaining that as a journalist in the United States, I neither speak for our government nor would I try to alibi policy. But as a journalist dealing with truth telling, I felt obligated to clarify some things.

In a blog post that published daily back in Tallahassee, I wrote about the experience.

"The question is based on a premise, I said, that is simply not true," I wrote, "and truth-telling is my job. America is also the most generous and giving nation in the history of the world, giving from a national treasury that is overspending its budget and from private donations of time and money of its citizens."

There was time to be tourists, too. In Pakistan, we traveled to the countryside near Islamabad and ancient ruins of civilizations that had controlled the region. On these fields, I saw a boy with a tattered book bag start towards us. I started towards him, as well, signaling it was OK to approach. But our guards intercepted him and checked his bag. They said he just wanted to talk and spoke some English. I learned he was 12 and that his father lived in America and, like many Pakistanis who lived in the West, sent home money to support his family. The boy just wanted to meet Americans to feel closer to his father.

My friend Nancy San Martin of the Miami Herald and I were struck by the faces of the children. Someday, we said, we would come back to Pakistan to write about the children, the faces so beautiful and pure in a land that had been ravaged by poverty and war.

We visited Wagah, a border town in the Punjab province of Pakistan and the site of a famous and colorful military ceremony practiced between Indian and Pakistani elite soldiers. It has all the atmosphere of a major sporting event, music, chanting from the crowds seated in bleachers on their "side" of the gate. It ends with a lowering of the two national flags.

On the night that we visited, I was struck by the sight of what appeared to be uniformed Catholic school girls, escorted by nuns, cheering wildly for the Pakistani soldiers. I don't know what I expected in the Muslim Republic of Pakistan, but that was not it.

I was invited by ICFJ back the next year for an alumni summit of Pakistani journalists who had taken part in the program. There were a few Americans sprinkled in. I ended up on a panel to discuss the government's decision to ban YouTube because it refused to remove a blasphemous video insulting Mohammed.

I traveled alone on that trip and it was relatively uneventful. I was acutely aware that I stood out in the crowd I found myself in at the airport when my driver dropped me off and pointed to a sign, where I found myself in a very long line. A man in a uniform soon came up to me and said, "You are an American, yes?"

Yes, I replied.

"Do you have $20?"

Yes, I replied.

"Come with me."

We were out of the line and passed the customs people in no time. The man took my boarding information and $20 more to the ticket counter. Again, no waiting. I had my passes.

He again asked for $20 more, and I again – now somewhat happily – gave it to him. He brought me to a room to wait, where there was food and tea and television sets and promised to come get me when it was time to board. He did and walked me to my seat on the plane.

I don't know who he was and how much of that money he used to pay for my entrance in the waiting room or was shared with others to get me through so easily, but I've always considered it among the best $60 I've ever spent.

I returned to Pakistan one more time in 2016, this time to teach at the new Center for Excellence in Journalism at the International Business Academy in Karachi. I spent a week lecturing in a classroom and a week traveling and speaking at various media outlets and agencies. Again, I was guarded everywhere I went.

The topic was modern news management, but most of the discussion was on digital and new technologies and how to incorporate that into traditional news organizations. Two of my friends from previous visits – including one person I had hosted – were in the class.

One night, we went to dinner at an amazing restaurant overlooking the Indian Ocean. We sat outside on a deck, taking in the evening breeze off the ocean. It was a beautiful night. That's where Abbas and I were joined by the incredible Kamal Siddiqi, director of CEJ and also one of the leading journalists in Pakistan. I think Siddiqi had set up the seating so Abbas and I would be forced to talk.

He told me that some members of the board of advisors to CEJ might join us. It could be that Abbas would be one of them. Of course, he did, and we sat across from each other for dinner. We talked about the curriculum for the next day and he mentioned how he might stop by to listen, if I was OK with that. I told him to give me a time and I'd make space on the agenda. I envisioned a three-way conversation with me, Abbas and Siddiqi discussing the future of journalism in the U.S. and Pakistan, editing leadership and standing up for press freedom, and that's the way it went.

As the conversation went longer, I became more in awe of these two men. Courage and bravery under fire? They had lived through it time after time.

I stay in touch with my Pakistani friends. I have met some of their families. I've been invited to weddings and celebrated birthdays and the birth of children. I've no doubt that programs like this one bring Americans closer to people around the world, dispel some of the strange ideas we have about each other, and make it harder to dislike each other. I'm sorry the Pakistan program has ended at ICFJ.

"I've come to the conclusion that your family is a lot like my family," one program participant said after living with us for two weeks.

"I love Americans," another said. "It's just that sometimes I hate your government."

Well, that makes us more alike than you know, I said.

CHAPTER THIRTEEN

INNOVATION AND TRANSITION

For much of the latter part of my career, change began to matter almost as much as the journalism. Almost.

I felt the message coming from the public was clear: We had to do things differently to keep their attention. But for many of my colleagues, change was always bad. Any change. I thought it was ironic that the same journalists who would push others for change, be it societal change or otherwise, couldn't see that we had to change to protect our journalism. We all knew it was critical, but we didn't move fast enough.

The transition to digital and the resulting shrinkage of our industry was couched in terms like "transformation" and "innovation." But the truth is we waited too long, we fought against market forces too long. I'm not sure the news industry leadership totally gets what is happening still, but they are starting to.

We had plenty of warning. Economists and business leaders outside our industry told us what was happening back in the 1990s, but we were still rolling in cash so nobody wanted to listen then.

I was in the audience when Intel's Andy Grove warned the American Society of Newspaper Editors in 1999 that we were racing toward a "strategic inflection point," and that we were about three years away. Most of us scratched our heads and wondered what the hell is a strategic inflection point.

We sure found out.

It is the point when disruptive forces in the marketplace force you to either change how you operate or die. I was sitting with a senior executive of Gannett and said I sure hope someone was listening.

Three years earlier, we decided to cover a big Marshall football game on Herald-Dispatch.com with what would be called a live blog today. It escaped notice or concern by the NCAA, which would eventually try to regulate such things. It did not escape notice by Gannett.

Months later, while I was in Rosslyn, where the company and USA TODAY were then located, I was called into a vice president's office and asked to explain my decision to – without authorization – "give away" valuable content on the Internet. How did I justify charging some people for the content in the newspaper while using valuable resources to give the same content away to nonsubscribers?

It was a very good question and I wanted to wax poetic about how we had to change if we were going to survive, but there was the nagging issue of how to make money from the move to digital. I had been at it for longer than most, having spent time at Gannett New Media, the company's first venture into what we called electronic publishing.

Drawing on all that knowledge, I came up with the best answer I could: I don't know.

It is why in my 50s I enrolled in Northeastern University and got an MBA specializing in marketing. I was working full-time as executive editor of the *Tallahassee Democrat*. I wanted to try to figure out – how you monetize, to use the buzzword – digital journalism. In 2011, I graduated and thought I had an idea for how we could make money: have people pay for it, just as they would for any other "product."

I put together a marketing plan for how the *Democrat* could make money from our coverage of one of the best college sports programs in the country. Several of my Northeastern classmates contributed. I submitted it to my publisher and sent a copy to corporate.

Soon, I was invited to corporate for a discussion. That's all that was said: a discussion. It was just our digital editor Bjorn Morton and me since publisher Pat Dorsey was unavailable. We learned people from our newspapers in Greenville, South Carolina, and St. George, Utah, were also invited. We had been picked to gauge our interest in turning our free websites into paid-content sites, using different models for experiment purposes.

Obviously, I thought, I had gotten someone's attention with my plan. Just as obvious: They rejected almost all of it. The paid-content plan we unveiled in Tallahassee had almost nothing in common with what I had come up with.

Still, I was beside myself with excitement and enthusiasm. It was a plan, however flawed, for moving forward, a business plan to support our journalism and protect our journalists. No matter what, we had to make it work and to some extent, we did, at least for a while.

Let me try to explain what we were going through at that time. In 2005, when I became executive editor of the Tallahassee Democrat, we had multiple job openings. We needed to hire 22 people in my first couple of years. We tore down a wall that had separated the newsroom from a production shop that was no longer needed for production. That eventually became space for our capital news team, which theoretically would be six people now: the three from the Democrat and three more from Gannett News Service.

Another room became a modern training/conference room, complete with the latest technology, including a Smart Board. It was in that room that we would digitally "broadcast" – or live stream - our election night coverage: news and analysis unlike anything anyone else was doing, including local TV.

We produced a "video special" during a Florida State basketball game using Apple technology on iPhones. We were able to cut away to reporters getting in-game fan reactions, reporters working game coverage, and analysis back at the office. The model was our election coverage, but we wanted to see if it had sports applications.

Then 2008 happened and we began tearing down the team we had just built. This was the year that the recession really started to impact our budget and Andy Grove's prediction of a strategic inflection point began to show up.

Obviously, I had fired people for cause before. It still bothered me no matter how much they deserved it. But now I was being asked to lay off people who had done nothing wrong, nothing to deserve it, and it hurt. The night before I had to do that I went to church and prayed for strength and wisdom. After the layoffs were finished, I prayed I'd never have to do that again. I did, several more times.

So, I was ready to try anything, and paid content made sense to me.

I went on a campaign to rally support for what we were doing, at least to create better understanding. The initial plan allowed customers to subscribe or sample for $2 per day. Otherwise, it was a hard wall. We would later roll out a meter system across Gannett, where a viewer could get a certain number of clicks for free each month.

That was the idea of a hard wall: The only way to get our content, in theory, was to pay for it.

But we did not follow the Intel model Grove had described at the ASNE meeting. Faced with disruptive technology and new challengers, Intel got out of the business of manufacturing RAM chips and focused on making microprocessors. You might not understand the technology any better than I do, but everyone wanted a computer in the 1990s with Intel inside, whatever it was.

We did not tear down our print operations in favor of investing in digital. Instead, we created business models that tried to protect print for as long as we could while we built digital operations. From the consumer's standpoint, if you bought print, you got digital. But not the other way around. It was very confusing.

The expectation was for journalists to cover news for all platforms. We were told we had to do more with less, but that only goes so far.

It was like trying to change the oil in your car while driving down the highway at 70 mph. Worse, instead of projecting the image of creating a spanking-new product, you know, one with Intel inside, we became in the public's mind a dying industry, trying desperately to survive a few more years.

With every round of layoffs, the image felt more real. It's complicated: It takes fewer people to produce a digital news operation than print, but it doesn't take fewer journalists to cover a community the way it should be covered. Digital attracts fewer dollars than print, so how do you pay for the journalism? Oh, back to that question again.

Editors tried to focus on journalism. And we largely did. Great work was – and is still – being produced. It just looks and sounds different than it used to and there is less of it. We're still great when it comes to covering the big stories, but it is the day-to-day of life in America that is getting shortchanged.

When I got to FLORIDA TODAY on Florida's Space Coast, it had a well-earned reputation for innovation in its coverage. It had, as I understand it, Gannett's first website. FLORIDA TODAY was created by Al Neuharth and was the forerunner – not the offspring – of USA TODAY.

We decided we were going to make innovation and a return to our roots in investigative reporting keys in our structure. We held a retreat. I hate that word because it sounds like what you do just before you surrender, but we had a strategic planning meeting (that even sounds better) on the beach. We invited a diverse group of non-journalist young adults to join us and keep us in check.

The question: How do young adults spend time with media and consuming information? That would give us direction on how we produce information. I kept hearing the word "podcast" throughout the day. It was everywhere.

It was also clear that the group at least understood and welcomed the watchdog role the media plays in society.

Not every journalist gets into the business to play a watchdog role on government or institutions. Not everyone wants to give voice to the voiceless or help the afflicted in their struggles against the rich and powerful. Some just want to help people understand what is going on around us.

It reminds me of the time a woman called me when I was executive editor of the Tallahassee Democrat. She was angry. She screamed obscenities because she missed her favorite singer who was in town for a concert. This, she said, in no uncertain terms, was my fault.

"But," I protested, "the show was the front cover of our weekly entertainment section, Limelight."

Maybe so, she said, but she canceled us because the price went up when we added news online. Thus, it was my fault she missed the concert. It was hard to argue with that kind of logic.

OK, back to our planning meeting. At the end of the day I turned to our news director/managing editor Mara Bellaby, who is a brilliant journalist, and said I wanted us to do a podcast series. And I wanted it to be investigative journalism. It had to be both entertaining and follow our guidelines for what constitutes good and ethical journalism.

From that point on it was up to Bellaby to create the journalism. Our goal was to take a legitimate journalism project and do it primarily as a podcast. The result was our award-winning series, "Murder on the Space Coast," with John Torres as the lead reporter and narrator, and Rob Landers as the producer.

It was really good journalism. Torres is brilliant and creative. He even wrote the music for the program. Landers pulled together all the pieces. Bellaby was the lead editor and read and listened to every word before it published. It has been going for multiple seasons and has had a million listens. (More on "Murder on the Space Coast" in Chapter 14.)

It was not the first of its type – the cold-case murder mystery – but it certainly was one of the first tackled by a traditional news organization as a piece of journalism. It also showed how powerful journalism can be when various platforms are used, meaning it was created as a podcast, but adapted for print and video.

One day Gannett put out a call for ideas for innovative ways to do journalism. Bellaby and Emre Kelly of our space team came up with the idea of an augmented reality rocket launch app. It won and we got to work with Gannett's new development team of former Electronic Arts employees.

It took months to do, and much of that time I really was in way over my head. The team traveled from northern Virginia to watch an actual SpaceX rocket launch, to hear and record the sounds. There was a back-and-forth on a lot of issues and details, but there was agreement that we could create an app that simulates an actual rocket launch, that uses the coordinates of where the rocket should be at the precise second it should be there.

There was a lot of testing and failure. The app was imperfect even after it went public. But 321 Launch was a success on a lot of fronts.

Audience, for instance. We set a goal of 10,000 downloads of the app within six months. We blew past that mark within weeks. Quickly, we surpassed 100,000, despite ongoing technical issues that had to be overcome.

More important, the app was nothing more than a way to get people who would not normally do so to look at our space journalism. We showed it early on to a group from Buzz Aldrin's foundation, ShareSpace, that included Andrew Aldrin, the son of the second man to walk on the moon; Christina Korp, executive vice president; and Jim Christensen, executive director. They were collectively impressed and offered development tips for what was next.

With the 50th anniversary of Neil Armstrong and Buzz Aldrin first walking on the moon fast approaching, I wanted to use augmented reality to recreate the launch of Apollo 13, the moon landing, and the successful return of the three-man crew – Michael Collins being the third person, although he stayed in the orbiting command ship during the landing on the moon.

We did some augmented reality during the lunar landing anniversary coverage, and we produced a full-length documentary video on the local people behind the Apollo program.

It is important to understand that – again, initially at least – the audience attracted to the 321 Launch app was decidedly younger than our typical consumer. More than 40 percent of the audience we reached was 30 and younger, and that was a win for our team.

Regardless of anything else, we had proved that we could attract a younger audience to our journalism and that technology mattered. The problem was – and remains – that we needed to figure out how we're going to make money from the new technology. And, yes, we're back to that question.

More than a quarter century after I was called into the corporate vice president's office to discuss what I was thinking, we were going live with news and sports without a business plan. It was clear to me that we had not made much progress in figuring out the how-to of building the kind of revenue that would support our journalism.

I have no doubt that we have greatly increased our revenue from digital, video and all our experiments. These are the things that can save journalism. I only question if will it do so in time to protect communities and save the country?

COLUMN

321 LAUNCH, a new AR rocket launch app, is ready for historic blastoff from Space Coast

By Bob Gabordi
Executive Editor, FLORIDA TODAY
Published March 26, 2018

Chances are you know augmented reality, even if you don't know you know it.

If you've ever watched an NFL football game on TV or used a GPS with live photo imaging overlaid by a road map, you've seen augmented reality. But until now, AR has never been used like what you are about to see from us.

USA TODAY and FLORIDA TODAY are preparing to release the first-of-its-kind rocket launch app using AR technology. Release in the App Store is scheduled for noon to 4 p.m. Thursday, March 29, and after 2 p.m. that day in Google Play, just ahead of the April 2 SpaceX launch. The app will be available as a free download in the App Store and Google Play — meaning it's compatible for iPhone and Android.

What sets this app apart from anything else is the interactivity of the app and the ability of the user to take action.

What's augmented reality? I really like the simple, plain language explanation of AR that I found on the website of Philadelphia's Franklin Institute. AR is what made the Pokemon Go app so popular. It's what allows you to use an app to try on a new dress without leaving home. It's used for industrial design and in training workers. Neurosurgeons use AR in working on 3D models of the brain.

Our app, called 321 LAUNCH, works in sync with actual launches, such as the April 2 SpaceX launch, at Cape Canaveral Air Force Station, to give users a close-up view of a real launch and landing. It integrates live video and real-time updates and analysis from FLORIDA TODAY's space team — James Dean and Emre Kelly — as well as links to space news and launch schedules. Additional rockets will be added.

Visit usatoday.com/321launch for more and to follow the app's development.

How it came to be

The app is the result of months of development and testing by the USA TODAY NETWORK's Emerging Technologies team and FLORIDA TODAY.

"Rocket launches are perfect for AR," said Annette Ney Meade, innovation director at the USA TODAY NETWORK's Innovation Lab, who coordinated the project.

"Even if you are lucky enough to watch a live launch in person, you will still never get very close to the rocket. This experience lets you get as close as you like to an exact model of the rocket at the very moment that the actual rocket lifts off for space," she said.

Download it, share your experiences with friends and relatives, and brag about it on your social networks. We think it is going to create a whole new way of looking at America's space program, and we are just at the starting gate for what the app can accomplish.

"For those of us who live on the Space Coast, 321 LAUNCH gives us a new perspective," said FLORIDA TODAY's news director, Mara Bellaby, who envisioned the app and led our team's effort. "It's one thing to walk out into your backyard or head over to the beach for a launch — and that's always going to be amazing. But now you can also experience the excitement of a 3D rocket right in front of you that's in perfect sync with the real one as it prepares for liftoff and blasts into the sky."

We hope Space Coast residents will share in our excitement and tell their friends, relatives and potential visitors about 321 LAUNCH. Let them know that they can now watch the launch with you in real time. And it's a new way for snowbirds to take part of the Space Coast with them when they are away.

Fun things the app can do

Part of what makes the experience so real is that it is, well, real. Veteran journalists who regularly direct coverage and report on space were involved in every step of the development of the app.

"321 LAUNCH brings a rocket launch to you. Literally, you can launch a rocket from anywhere," Bellaby said.

And she is not fooling.

I've launched AR rockets from my office, my kitchen, the bottom of my pool and from the observation deck at Exploration Tower at Port Canaveral because I thought it would be so cool to launch a rocket with the VAB in the background. And it was. So cool. Over the weekend, I launched a rocket at the Melbourne Air & Space Show and then went to Vero Beach and launched a rocket at Historic Dodgertown.

But I don't want you to get the wrong impression. While the app definitely has an undeniable cool factor, it's not a game or a toy. It is meant to be a fun way to experience a rocket launch and to enhance our space coverage. We hope it also gives people another reason to get excited about America's space efforts.

Members of the Emerging Technologies team visited the Space Coast to capture the feel and sound of a launch, but they came away with much more.

"I'll never forget our first visit to KSC to gather information that would guide the creation of our app," said Ray Soto, director of Emerging Technologies. "My team and I left inspired by the rich history and passion of the Space Coast. AR technology lets us bring the thrill of a launch into your own home for an unforgettable experience. You aren't just watching, you're there!"

Are you ready for this AR app?

The app gives you two choices: a "live mission" function for use during actual launches and a "launch simulation" function that allows students and teachers to learn about launches by building and launching 3D rockets.

If you try the 'launch simulation,' you can launch a rocket on demand," Bellaby said. "Space reporter Emre Kelly talks you through the process so not only is it fun – but you'll learn something, too. When it blasts off, you'll hear the roar and see the fire. It's almost like being there. We hope the whole experience encourages more people to pay attention to what's happening at KSC and the Cape."

And it is just a start. We have plans not only to add other rockets, but also to integrate additional technology and features.

It only makes sense that this amazing augmented reality rocket app was launched here, on America's Space Coast.

Gabordi is executive editor at *FLORIDA TODAY*. His direct dial number is 321-242-3607 and cell phone is 850-591-2229. He is *@bgabordi* on Twitter and */bgabordi* on Facebook. You can also find him on LinkedIn. His email address is bgabordi@ floridatoday.com.

Support local journalism: Sign up for a digital subscription to get breaking news, in-depth coverage and all the local news from FLORIDA TODAY. Go to floridatoday.com/digitalunlimited to sign up.

SEPTEMBER 18, 2016   SERVING BREVARD COUNTY SINCE 1966   FLORIDATODAY.COM

sunday

FLORIDA TODAY
PART OF THE USA TODAY NETWORK

MURDER ON THE SPACE COAST

WHAT ABOUT OTHER SUSPECTS? APPARENTLY THEY WERE IGNORED

DOG-HANDLER'S CLAIMS: PURE MALARKEY

EVIDENCE TO THE CONTRARY? SHRUGGED OFF OR REINTERPRETED

Did he do it?

REPORTED AND WRITTEN BY JOHN A. TORRES FLORIDA TODAY

Gary Bennett knows little of life beyond the menacing rows of razor wire that have surrounded his cage for decades. After 33 years, the memories of fishing from a dock or taking a swim or drinking a cold beer are fading.

For the last six weeks, Bennett's story — his arrest and conviction for the 1983 murder of Helen Nardi — has been the subject of FLORIDA TODAY's investigative podcast "Murder on the Space Coast." The podcast was inspired by a simple question: Was the right person arrested, prosecuted and convicted?

As we dug into this case it became apparent that — at the very least — Bennett never received a fair trial. The state made up evidence against him, and the courts turned down his numerous appeals.

Police apparently ignored other possible suspects and violated Bennett's rights by denying his request for an attorney during a 12-hour interrogation. Evidence that seemed to point to Bennett's innocence was shrugged off — or reinterpreted.

The jury that convicted Bennett heard testimony from a dog handler whose abilities were already being questioned and whose involvement in cases across the country led to dozens of convictions being thrown out. The dog handler claimed his dog could do the impossible in linking a murderer to the crime scene or weapon. It was pure malarkey, but the jury was told it was science.

The case against Bennett bore remarkable similarities to three other Brevard cases where the convicted were later found innocent and freed after decades in prison: Juan Ramos, Wilton Dedge and William Dillon.

The dog handler. Jailhouse snitches who conveniently appeared and promised to testify about alleged confessions in exchange for breaks. The replacement of competent public defenders with state-appointed attorneys who offered up pitiful defenses.

"That's what they did to us," said Dillon, who was exonerated for a murder he did not commit. "They took young kids that were easy to do, easy to throw away and they just took us and threw us away and now society won't try and correct the problem."

Read the story

Let us take you back to a hot July afternoon in 1983, to a brutal murder that left a woman with 26 stab wounds and a neighbor who quickly became the suspect. **Page 25A**

John A. Torres on what angers him most about the Gary Bennett case. **Page 29A**

Listen to the podcast

Listen to all six episodes – plus a bonus episode – of "Murder on the Space Coast," watch video from Bennett's prison interview, see photographs from the crime scene, find court documents and follow a timeline of the case.

More online at floridatoday.com/murder

COLLEGE FOOTBALL

CARDS MAKE IT 'NOLE CONTEST
No. 10 Louisville stuns No. 2-ranked
Florida State 63-20. **SPORTS, 1C**

An insider's tour through Florida
hidden treasures
Florida is so much more than beaches and theme parks. If you're a subscriber, you'll find a special section in your newspaper today. Hidden Treasures, highlighting some of our lesser known treasures on land and at sea. Whether you are entertaining visitors who have escaped the winter weather or are just looking for ideas for that staycation that doesn't break the budget, you can explore and enjoy our tropical paradise in a whole new way.

INSIDE TODAY FOR SUBSCRIBERS ONLY

2016
FLORIDA TODAY'S
BEST
OF BREVARD
WINNER

WHO COLLECTED THE MOST VOTES?
From Air Conditioning to Waterfront Dining,
find out who is tops. **Pages 16-17A**

Plenty of sun,
feeling warmer
H: 87   L: 78
Details » 34A

Autos	Section D
Help	33A

Lottery	2A
Horoscopes	33A

Opinion	22-23A
Obituaries	26A

Space Notebook	6A
SportsTalk	3C

© 2016 FLORIDA TODAY | Vol. 51, No. 186 | To subscribe: 321-242-3966 | For home delivery pricing see page 2A

CHAPTER FOURTEEN

"MURDER ON THE SPACE COAST"

I'm going to be frank: I wasn't going to add this chapter. Our podcast series, "Murder on the Space Coast," is complicated and hard to explain. Season one deals with the Gary Bennett case. He is a wholly unsympathetic character until you consider he has spent 36 years in prison for a crime he probably didn't commit, one that the state could not get a conviction on until it made up evidence.

But then I watched the biographical film "Crown Heights" on Netflix. It was a reminder that justice and doing the right thing are the most important things our legal system is supposed to guarantee to Americans. Legal fairness is what we grow up believing is the least we can expect.

No system is perfect, but mistakes need to be corrected and wrongful convictions – those based on lies – need to be overturned.

That's what happened in the film, which is based on the life of Colin Warner, who was wrongfully convicted in 1982 of second-degree manslaughter. It is not what has happened for Bennett. And it is very clear no one who can change things for Bennett cares.

Brevard County Sheriff Wayne Ivey and State Attorney Phil Archer had that chance to be heroes. All they had to do was to decide to be on the side of justice and fairness. But as we were producing our first investigative podcast at FLORIDA TODAY, "Murder on the Space Coast," neither was willing to step up.

Let's not sugar-coat this: Bennett has hardly been a model prisoner. In March 2020, the Florida Commission on Offender Review looked at his prison record and added four years to his eligibility for parole. He is not eligible for parole now until April 13, 2041, according to a FLORIDA TODAY story.

It's that behavior that makes Bennett so unsympathetic. Prison is a tough place. Bennett will tell you he has done what he has needed to do to survive it.

The commission did not look at what got him into prison to begin with, the lies and deceit of the prosecutor and made-up evidence that led to his conviction. This commission ignored an initial review from its agency that had recommended releasing Bennett in 2021.

John Torres, the FLORIDA TODAY columnist who has been the reporter on "Murder on the Space Coast," wrote this after the commission added years to Bennett's parole date:

"I'm not sure how the parole commission expects a prisoner who says they are innocent to behave. Should Bennett never question authority? Should he admit to and profess remorse for a crime he says he did not commit?

Reporter John Torres, Editor Mara Bellaby and Producer Rob Landers show off hardware for winning first place in 2017 in the annual EPPY awards by Editor & Publisher magazine for Best Podcast for sites with 1 million or more monthly unique visitors for Murder on the Space Coast season 2.

The FLORIDA TODAY series focused on the initial investigation and conviction. It was rock-solid reporting by Torres. Every word was reviewed by Mara Bellaby, Torres' direct editor and who succeeded me as editor of FLORIDA TODAY, and me. Our attorney reviewed advance copies of the podcast. We took every precaution to get it right.

The first season of the podcast showed that the former prosecutor, Dean Moxley, who later became a judge, used the testimony of a man, John Preston, who claimed his dog had almost supernatural powers to tie Bennett to the scene of the crime. Preston claimed the dog could identify Bennett's scent on the murder weapon.

Preston was later shown to be a fraud and Arizona voided the convictions of all cases involving Preston and his magical dog.

But when even the testimony of Preston might not be enough to convict Bennett, Moxley came up with a jailhouse informant who claimed Bennett, who had told everyone else in the world he was innocent and has maintained that stance ever since, told him he had committed the murder.

Eventually, the podcast expanded beyond Bennett and took a deep dive into what passed for justice in Brevard County during the 1980s. It showed that the same prosecutor had used the same fraudulent dog handler multiple times in the same pattern of getting convictions. In some of the cases, DNA evidence showed the men convicted using Moxley's standard playbook were not guilty. But DNA evidence did not exist in Bennett's case.

Ivey, in a meeting at my office, told me that he and his department did not think very highly of the series. Understandable on some level. After all, Bennett was tried and convicted – well before Ivey's time as sheriff – of murdering his neighbor Helen Nardi. It was a horribly gruesome crime scene. Bennett's behavior in prison won't win him many law enforcement friends, either.

Archer just refused to address it.

We thought this case was relevant more than 30 years after the murder for two reasons:

No one was ever held accountable for the travesties that occurred, the ruining of young men's lives with made-up evidence, and the continued imprisonment of Bennett with some of the bad actors still exercising power and influence in the county.

And no one – especially not the people we elected to do so – really cared about the injustices that were done, at least not enough to say so publicly.

Let's go over this again: At least three people eventually were let out of jail when the evidence became so overwhelming that local judicial officials had no real choice. But not Bennett. Ironically, because he was convicted on lies and not physical evidence, there was no physical evidence to disprove his guilt.

But what bothered me most, what still sticks, is the complete indifference to the truth our elected officials have shown. Instead of being heroic defenders of justice, they chose to attack FLORIDA TODAY and its decision to report via podcasting.

Archer, by the way, was re-elected in 2020 without opposition. So, as I said, no one cares about Bennett and what happened to him.

Podcasting was chosen for reporting this story for several reasons.

One reason was that we were looking for a story that lent itself to experimenting with podcasting. We had access to a lot of audio from our files and from investigatory files. Obviously, you need audio for a podcast, otherwise it is little different than a reporter reading a script.

But quantity of audio, while important, is one thing. More important is having quality audio that helps tell the story and provides details. What we had was very good at helping us fill in gaps. We also were able to get new audio from people in the community who lived through the Bennett investigation and trial and other experts.

Another reason we decided to create a podcast with this story is that we wanted to reach people who we couldn't get to with print alone. We thought a podcast would reach younger people who had all but abandoned print.

We also thought "Murder on the Space Coast" would reach beyond our normal print circulation area and could have a national audience.

On that, we were right. Information we got from distribution sources such as SoundCloud.com showed more than a million listens.

So far there have been five seasons of "Murder on the Space Coast" and it has been a journalistic success, winning an annual EPPY, an international award from Editor & Publisher magazine.

The riff with Ivey over FLORIDA TODAY's investigative reporting grew over time and additional stories. After I retired, he began to follow the Trump routine with disparaging "unfriendly" media, saying he didn't consider FLORIDA TODAY a credible news source. He warned one reporter who asked a question Ivey didn't like to never question his authority.

He went on radio to talk about the newspaper's lack of support for President Trump, although that had no relevance to any of the issues we covered and, in fact, the newspaper had made no endorsement in Trump's presidential campaign.

Over time, Ivey quit inviting FLORIDA TODAY to press conferences, even those called to relay vital information about the coronavirus pandemic.

The newspaper's relationship with Archer was broken over these podcasts, to the point that he considered it the enemy, and that's a shame. Archer had won a lot of respect while he worked jointly with FLORIDA TODAY to propose a new state law that would make it easier for Florida to prosecute violations of ethics laws. Somehow, FLORIDA TODAY went from partner to enemy over something one of his predecessors had done.

Why?

Podcasting brought the story home in powerful new ways and reached people newspapers had trouble otherwise attracting. But it wasn't the only way we told this story. We also held community meetings where witnesses, sources and family members were on stage with Torres. That moved it from being simply a story to something far more real and powerful.

We charged people a fee to get into these events to defray our costs, which included rental of the space and food and drink. Some found that objectionable, as if journalism is supposed to be free. That is easy for people whose salaries and other expenses are paid by taxpayers to say.

Journalism is not inexpensive. Bills have to be paid. It is just the way the world outside of government works.

Besides, we had rented the space and had to pay for the food. But I'll never apologize for assigning a monetary value to our work. Being ashamed of that is what has kept the salaries of reporters and editors so low over the years.

The simple fact is absent known lies and testimony of criminals who gained from lying there was only one piece of actual evidence the state had against Bennett: the presence of a single palm print in Nardi's trailer, a place he freely admitted to having been while helping his neighbor bring in bags of groceries.

In a column I wrote in January 2017 to preview additional seasons of "Murder on the Space Coast," citing Torres' work, I said:

"Listeners to season one demanded more. After all, justice has never been done for Gary Bennett – nor for the other victims of a justice system that made deals with the devil – quite literally – and made up evidence that put innocent young men in prison for decades."

The question is, as it always has been, why?

"Murder on the Space Coast" has generated millions of listens. Torres, the FLORIDA TODAY reporter, did an interview recently with Erin Moriarty for the TV show "48 Hours."

"Murder on the Space Coast" was done differently than just words on paper or even digitized words on a computer screen. We picked the Bennett story for its first season, our first podcast, because we hoped that the drama of audio might engage a new generation to care enough about justice to get involved. No doubt older audiences cared, but not enough to do anything. We hoped this would be different. So far it hasn't been.

Part of what we were hoping to accomplish in doing "Murder on the Space Coast" was to see if good journalism can be done in a podcast. Mission accomplished. Torres has been brilliant, as has Rob Landers, the series producer.

Torres has been promoting the podcast and its next season and his new book, "Paradise Rolling: A Terry Payne Deadline Mystery," which is available on Amazon. I'm sure the book is great, and I'm definitely going to get a copy and read it. Torres is a marvelous reporter and writer and I wish him nothing but gobs of success.

But Bennett is still in jail with ever fading hope of getting a fair shake. And it's hard for me to feel good about that.

Let's backtrack a little. FLORIDA TODAY decided to pour a lot of its dwindling resources into podcasting. Torres worked on this more or less full time. Landers was asked to devote hours that he didn't have to produce the podcast. Bellaby read and re-read every word, as did I. We both listened to every podcast before it was released. She also fact checked to make sure we stayed true to our journalistic principles and steered clear of entertaining for entertainment sake. I'm sure we drove Torres and Landers half-crazy with rewrites and tweaks.

At first, I thought the podcast sounded too much like a newspaper columnist talking and did not take enough advantage of the medium. I'm a huge fan of old-time radio shows, especially detective shows like "Yours Truly, Johnny Dollar" featuring Bob Bailey. I wanted more storytelling and dialogue, and less narration.

Because we were asking for 30 valuable minutes of time per episode, there needed to be an element of entertainment, balanced by solid journalism. In other words, the journalism needed to be well told. If we were going to capture the attention of busy young moms and dads while they were in the doctor's office waiting room, or sitting on a beach chair before the soccer game or driving to work, we had to take advantage of all the medium had to offer.

All of us worked to ensure the journalism was the highest quality, but Bellaby – who had reported from places like Moscow and Ukraine – kept an especially close eye on that.

I felt strongly that we needed to keep each episode to 30 minutes, no more and preferably less. There was no limit to the number of episodes we could do, but I felt we needed digestible pieces for the listener, especially since this series contained breathtaking developments and, at times, gruesome details.

Many others in the newsroom were involved – Rachael Thomas and Jennifer Sangalang had big roles in social media. Thomas had a critical speaking role on the first piece, as did Landers.

We were new to this podcasting business, which means our audiences in Brevard County were new to it, too, at least many of them. We published in print and online guides to how to get our podcasts and how to listen.

We taught – literally – many on the Space Coast how to subscribe to the podcast series via one of the major podcast providers. We told them it was easy to do and free. We asked them to show their support by subscribing to FLORIDA TODAY, at least the digital version. That seems like a fair ask, given the amount of work that goes into our journalism.

The podcasts represent one piece of the future for news organizations, which use voice, video, augmented and virtual reality, and text in powerful presentations.

But we also have to create better ways to pay for our journalism – for the technology and equipment, the reporters and editors. Or it all will just go away.

Florida Today Executive Editor Bob Gabordi to retire March 1

John McCarthy FLORIDA TODAY
USA TODAY NETWORK – FLORIDA

Bob Gabordi, the executive editor of FLORIDA TODAY, will retire March 1.

Gabordi, 62, who is also the chief news executive of Treasure Coast Newspapers, told FLORIDA TODAY staffers of his plans in a newsroom meeting on Jan. 22.

"Forty years is a long time to do anything, and I still love it," he told his colleagues. "But there are so many more things I want to do."

FLORIDA TODAY News Director Mara Bellaby will become editor immediately following Gabordi's retirement.

Gabordi is ending a journalism career that started at the Cranston Herald in Rhode Island in 1978.

Most of Gabordi's career has been with Gannett, the nation's largest newspaper publisher and parent of FLORIDA TODAY and USA TODAY.

Since joining Gannett, Gabordi has held a variety of reporting and editing roles in Connecticut, Ohio, West Virginia, North Carolina, Florida and at Gannett headquarters in suburban Washington, D.C. He is the company's longest-tenured senior editor. He was named to his first top editor's position when he took over news operations at The Marietta (Ohio) Times in 1992.

Before being named FLORIDA TODAY's executive editor in January 2015, Gabordi served as the top editor at the Tallahassee Democrat for 10 years.

"Bob's energetic leadership will be deeply missed as he retires from FLORIDA TODAY, but I'm confident he will find new ways to contribute in positive ways to the community he has grown to love so much," said Randy

Lovely, vice president of community news for Gannett. "I wish him all the best and thank him for all his contributions through the years to the news industry, Gannett and the Space Coast."

Over the years, Gabordi has collected a slew of local, state and national journalism awards including nine nods from the Florida Society of News Editors for his column writing. He is a four-time winner of Gannett's president's ring, given to the company's outstanding performers.

"In addition to his many community contributions and to being a world class journalist, Bob is known for recognizing and nurturing talent when he sees it," said Cindy McCurry-Ross, regional editor of the USA TODAY NETWORK-Florida. "He has been a coach and mentor to many, many successful journalists. Our industry owes him a debt of gratitude for that. I personally am grateful for his partnership and team spirit and wish him congratulations for his remarkable career."

At FLORIDA TODAY, Gabordi pushed for more in-depth and "watchdog" journalism, making the health of the Indian River Lagoon a key focus. He accelerated efforts at "digital first" news delivery and pushed for innovations by exploring non-traditional news products such as the award winning Murder on the Space Coast podcast, which has received more than 840,000 listens, and 321LAUNCH, a smartphone app that offers a one-of-a-kind augmented reality rocket launch experience.

"Bob came in with a straightforward message: Tell the community what you're going to do, do it exceptionally well and tell them you did it," said Bellaby. "That approach has helped deepen our relationship

FLORIDA TODAY Executive Editor Bob Gabordi announced Jan. 22 that he will retire March 1. Gabordi, center, with News Director Mara Bellaby and USA TODAY NETWORK-Florida Regional Editor Cindy McCurry-Ross. Bellaby will become executive editor immediately following Gabordi's retirement.
MALCOLM DENEMARK/FLORIDA TODAY

with our audience, and that's a major credit to Bob's leadership."

Gabordi also expanded FLORIDA TODAY's already long history of community leadership and engagement. Under his tenure, FLORIDA TODAY championed an anti-corruption bill that was signed into law by then-Gov. Rick Scott in 2015. The measure makes it easier to prosecute public officials for bribery and bid rigging.

"In my 40 years of representing newspapers I have never met nor worked with anyone with more integrity more passion or more desire to get it right," said Jack Kirschenbaum, an attorney with Gray-Robinson who represents the paper. "Working for Bob, being FLORI-

See GABORDI, Page 8M

Mara Bellaby to succeed Gabordi as Florida Today executive editor

Britt Kennerly FLORIDA TODAY
USA TODAY NETWORK – FLORIDA

Veteran journalist Mara Bellaby considers her chosen field of journalism a calling, "a powerful tool to inspire and challenge."

She is thrilled, she said, to continue taking on that challenge, as the next editor of FLORIDA TODAY.

The paper's current news director, Bellaby assumes her new role March 1 upon the retirement of Bob Gabordi, who announced his upcoming departure at a Tuesday meeting of FLORIDA TODAY staffers.

Bellaby, 48, said she is deeply honored to "to step into carrying on this legacy of FLORIDA TODAY and follow in the footsteps of amazing, innovative leaders" like Gabordi.

"I'm grateful for that opportunity. Journalism is so

powerful. Journalism can do so much good; bring people together," she told colleagues.

"Journalism can bring hope, can challenge, demand change. And that kind of journalism needs to be thoughtful. It needs people who are passionate and committed and willing to take risks, and that is this newsroom."

Bellaby has been at FLORIDA TODAY for about 12 years, serving as an assistant metro editor and space editor before taking over as news director.

"I'm pleased that we have named someone to the executive editor position who is not just an accomplished journalist, but an accomplished journalist in the Space Coast community," said Cindy McCurry-Ross, USA TODAY NETWORK – Florida regional editor.

"Mara is passionate about making a difference and an innovator who always has her eye on the future."

Bellaby has worked closely with reporters covering

the environment, education, space and criminal justice but counts the entire newsroom as her team, having worked on stories, projects and initiatives with just about every journalist on staff.

She was space editor during the final flights and shutdown of the space shuttle program. In the last few years, she's been the lead editor on the award-winning "Murder on the Space Coast" podcast and on the development of the 321 Launch augmented reality app. She's also proud of her work editing two major series: "Aging Alone" and "The Long Goodbye."

Gabordi, who has led the newspaper since January 2015, said he recognized Bellaby's potential from the time he first stepped into the FLORIDA TODAY newsroom as executive editor.

See BELLABY, Page 8M

CHAPTER FIFTEEN

MY SUDDEN STROKE AND ENDING

People who I've never met in person come up and tell me I'm an inspiration. A woman I was recently introduced to said, "Oh, you are the miracle."

I wanted to be an inspiration for my play at second base. Or maybe what kind of father I've been. Or for my work in the community.

I wanted to think my work as a journalist helped create a miracle in someone's life.

I never wanted to inspire for how I responded to having a life-threatening medical condition. Fighting to live when I might've died is not the miracle I wanted to be.

To be honest, I'm not sure what to do when people say stuff like this. I'm not sure what to say beyond thank you. It's not what I ever imagined for myself. It is not who I wanted to be.

On Nov. 9, 2018, after an early morning visit with a back surgeon who gave me the good news that I could avoid surgery and continue physical therapy for the spinal stenosis in my back, I went back to my office at FLORIDA TODAY. Within minutes, I suffered a stroke.

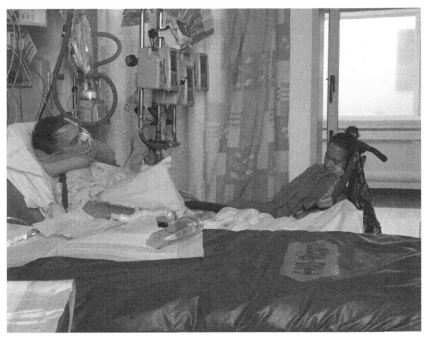

Just four days after suffering a major, life-threatening stroke, I found myself in stages between sleeping and being awake with family members at Viera Hospital. I spent a lot of time keeping Jessica company in hospitals. I guess it was her turn to the same for me.

Not just any run-of-the-mill stroke, either. Of course, not. Not me. I had a brain-stem stroke caused by a blood clot brought on by AFib, an irregular heartbeat. It's much more complicated than that, I guess, but that covers the basics.

I was overweight and for a couple of years had been neglecting my regular walking. I was drinking too much, stressing too much, and working too much. I was a mess and, if I thought about it at all, I would have kept my appointments with the cardiologist and paid attention to the warning signs.

But I didn't. That's how I found myself on the floor of my office, trying to get up and not really knowing what was going on. Two co-workers, Linette Sanchez and Mara Bellaby, saw me on the floor and called 9-1-1, which was there within minutes, carting me off in the back of an ambulance.

I'll never forget being carried on a stretcher from my office in the back corner of the building to the doors and the awaiting ambulance. Mainly, I'll not forget the look on the faces of my stunned colleagues, some crying, some ashen, all scared about was happening in front of them.

I wanted to stop and tell them it was going to be OK, but I was too scared myself, and – I recall thinking – maybe it wasn't going to be OK. I recall thinking about giving a thumbs up, but wondered if it was too cutesy or maybe a lie.

In the back of the ambulance, I thought about Steve Ellis, my former colleague at the Tallahassee Democrat, who died after a heart attack while working on a column at his home. His wife came in and found him on the floor and he argued about calling 9-1-1 because he wanted to finish the column.

I recalled standing in the middle of the Tallahassee newsroom, fighting back tears, telling our team Ellis had died. I wondered if someone would have to do that for me.

I did not want this to be the last time my colleagues saw me, that my legacy would be that I was the guy last seen being carried out the door

I hallucinated that the get-well-soon balloons were the heads of an army of people who came to suck information out of me. They had to go.

on a stretcher. That's why when I could I insisted on coming back to work, even though it was for a short period. I wanted to change that final image.

When I came back in early January for a short visit to pick up a few things, I was greeted at the door by the whole team, standing and applauding. It was a very cool moment.

I wanted to retire as a journalist, not a stroke victim. I don't know how else to explain it. But that's how I had always defined myself: father and husband, coach, and journalist. A counselor once asked me who I was.

"I'm a journalist," I answered. "Executive editor." It was not the answer she was hoping to hear.

"I asked you who you are, not your job description," she said.

But being a journalist was how I defined myself. It was who I was. Now I was just some guy carried out on a stretcher. That could not be the end of my story.

So, as the EMTs carried me out, I knew I had to find a way back, that God would not allow this to be the ending.

When I was in the ambulance, I remember looking at my numbers – my blood pressure looked good and my pulse seemed strong and I calmly tried to explain that to the EMTs. Finally, one looked at me and asked me to stop talking.

"Sir, we're trying to save your life and only have minutes. Could you please let us do our jobs?" one said, kindlier than those words might make it appear.

Sure, if you're going to put it like that, I said. I was only trying to help.

I remember arriving at Viera Hospital, where I had asked to be taken because I thought it would be easiest for my family. I remember going through the Emergency Room doors. I don't remember anything else for days.

I'm told that I quit breathing twice, which is why I had a breathing tube. Once, Donna's brother Don Hamernick and his wife Mary Hamernick were in the room when I quit breathing. They thought I had died.

I woke up to a room full of family, balloons, and flowers. All five of my children were there. My brother, Lou, and sister, Peggy Tourville Antonios, came from Connecticut. My grandchildren were in and out.

The balloons scared me, frankly. In my drugged mind, they were the heads of people floating around the room. I was clearly hallucinating, whether it was from the drugs or something else, I don't know.

I had the most amazing doctors and nurses at both Viera and Cape Canaveral hospitals, where I was transferred after developing blood in my urine. I was in ICU, then out of it, then back in again.

When I first awoke, I couldn't talk or swallow, thus the feeding tube that ran through my nose and into my stomach. I know I ripped out my tubes and made my nurse cry one night early on, when I thought I was being drained of information by some enemy army of occupation.

I couldn't stand on my own. That would take months of hard work.

But while still in Viera, I demanded my laptop so I could begin documenting my story for readers. My brain needed something to cling to and, as is always the case, I turned to my journalism. I knew if I could tell my story, it would be therapeutic for me and might do someone some good in the community.

There were so many cards and flowers that hospital workers asked my family to take some home. I fought against the feeding tube that eventually would be placed in my abdomen and into my stomach. But I was dreadfully hungry and – after failing a modified barium swallow test, which I never would pass – I agreed to the tube. It would stay in me for 15 months.

After about three weeks, I was well enough to go to Sea Pines Rehabilitation Hospital. I worked with amazing people there. For three or four hours every day I received physical, occupational, and speech therapy. I was visited by a psychologist regularly.

Physical therapist Corrine Smith taught me to walk again and to keep my balance. It was for only a few feet at first. But I was walking. And, as long as I could walk, I knew other skills would come back – or so I thought.

Finally, on Dec. 13 – some five weeks after Sanchez and Bellaby found me on the floor – I went home. They wouldn't let me walk out – I had to be in a wheelchair. But I would never use the walker they forced me to get. Once I left Sea Pines, I was on my own two feet. I donated the brand-new walker to Sea Pines.

Donna picked me up to go home. I could not have survived without her support. She was with me at Viera night and day around the clock, until after weeks, our family made her go home and get some sleep.

Donna was my inspiration to get better. I never saw her sad moments. The doctors made her cry when they told her that if I had to get a breathing tube again, I might never come off it. But all I ever saw was her smile when I made some small progress.

It was Donna and the kids who resisted bringing me my laptop but did so when I convinced them writing would make me happy. The doctors agreed with me that working my brain was a good thing. Sentences would take an hour to write. My fingers weren't doing what my brain ordered.

There were typos on top of typos and now, even more than a year later, I spend almost as much time correcting as I do actual writing.

But Donna believed in me, knew I would get better, and refused to let me quit. As I said in one of my columns, she was the "rock star" of my recovery.

My first column about what happened to me appeared on Nov. 26 in FLORIDA TODAY, but over the next few days it would publish across the state on other USA TODAY Network sites, including Tallahassee where I spent 10 years as executive editor. My email quickly piled up as I heard from many other stroke victims as well as people just grateful that I was writing about what happened to me.

It took me about three weeks to write what I normally do in a couple hours. It started this way:

"I always figured I'd die at my desk rather than retire."

I guess I almost did, so less than a month after this appeared, I announced that I would retire March 1. By the way, I went into the office and stood in front of a packed room for the announcement. I was still having trouble talking, and I still am, but made it through the 20-minute long presentation somehow.

I would continue to write, documenting my pursuit of normal health. I couldn't run a newsroom the way I felt I needed to do it and fight my way back to be a whole person. It was simply impossible.

Literally, I heard from thousands of people – readers in communities I had worked in, journalists from around the world, friends, co-workers, relatives, and complete strangers.

I heard from one young woman – well, first from her grandmother then from her – who had overcome a stroke she had when she was 12. The woman, Alex Dixon, who was now 21, and her family came to visit me to offer encouragement on my recovery soon after I got home from the hospital.

I wrote a column about her visit.

"This is a story of how her family came together for Alex, fought for her, refused to let others give up on her and supported each other. It is a story of how a loving, nurturing family can win when facing overwhelming odds. And it took the whole family, including father Marc and grandfather. Harvey, and many others; non-family members, too.

"The entire family called a timeout on their own lives to support Alex and each other. Grandma was a retired reading instructor and went to work teaching Alex about letters and reading again. Little sister Jessica, now a neuroscience and statistics double major at Florida State, assumed the role of the big sister in helping Alex. She says in the book her sister 'has become a miracle, my miracle.'"

I also continued to post on social media, of course. And photos of me told the story. The one of me and Jessica sleeping in my hospital room that had great meaning to me. Donna and I had visited Jessica in the hospital more than enough; this was her turn to visit me.

I wrote and I posted about my stroke and recovery because while there is no question it helped to tell my story, writing also helped me help others, again meeting my definition of what local journalism is supposed to do. I heard from so many people who spoke with their medical professionals to assess their own risk factors after reading about my stroke.

I was far from "in the clear" health-wise, especially through the first year. While I was in the hospital and doctors were trying to determine the cause of the blood in the urine, a growth was discovered on my kidney. Of course, there was a fear that it was cancerous, and it was not until October that my doctor felt comfortable ruling that out.

I worked hard to get back on my feet and walk again. I feared that when I had reduced my walking and gained weight, I had helped cause my stroke. At first it was short walks and never alone. Donna or one of my therapists would walk with me to the corner, where I would rest on a bench before walking home.

By January, I was walking enough to begin tracking distance: 28.2 miles for the month. But I would get stronger and go farther: 711.1 miles for the year. In 2020, I'm on pace for more than 1,000 miles. I walked on sidewalks, in the grass, on the beach, at parks, even in some 5K races. I didn't care that I couldn't win, but I never wanted to finish last and didn't.

I still was not swallowing enough to get the feeding tube removed or to stop ingesting the life-saving formula I had come to hate four times daily through the tube. It was the perfect food, the right vitamins, the right calories – I slowly lost more than 50 pounds. Despite the hard work of four speech therapists, I felt no closer to swallowing for a long time.

Swallowing is a complicated thing. Like learning your native language, be glad we come about it as tiny children; it's too hard for adults. A lot of things have to go right for us to swallow and get the food or drink to the right spot.

I had predicted when they put a feeding tube into my stomach that it would be gone in a matter of weeks. I've always had a special relationship with food. I love to shop for just the right ingredients. I love to make things like bread and pasta from scratch or put together an original recipe. I smoke my own salmon (I once almost caught one in Alaska). Or slow cook a piece of beef or pork on my Big Green Egg.

I love to serve food to others and watch them enjoy not only the food, but also the presentation. I sometimes surprised my co-workers with bread, trying new recipes on them, such as my Italian bread made with herbs I've specially grown in my garden. Sometimes I'd smoked piece of fish.

But mainly, I love to eat it. That's what made cutting weight as a high school wrestler so difficult. I love to eat. That and stopping exercising was how I gained extra pounds to begin with and probably a huge factor in how I ended up in that hospital bed with life-saving tubes running in and out of my body.

It wasn't a matter of weeks or even a few months. The feeding tube, meant to be temporary, was in me for more than 15 months.

It wasn't for a lack of trying. Re-learning to swallow was as hard as anything I've ever done. I worked the muscles until I would literally fall asleep. I did the exercises every day. Several times a day. In the car. In the shower. Watching TV. While on my daily walks. I practiced my swallowing exercises. I sang notes. I worked on using a big voice. I practiced in bed at night and first thing when I awoke the next morning.

One doctor told me the muscles in my throat were paralyzed and he didn't see much hope. I cried, then got over it and went back to work. The docs had a job to do and so did I. I worked even harder. After I began to swallow, another doctor told me he had given me a 50-50 chance of swallowing again, and the odds were only that high because he knew how hard I had been working at it.

I practiced and worked, and I documented my progress on social media and in my columns.

Slowly, I began to have some success last fall. Not that I wouldn't choke, even on my own saliva, let alone things I was trying to swallow. I told Carol Hermanowicz, my incredible therapist at the Melbourne Regional Medical Center, over the summer that my goal was to eat Christmas dinner with my family.

No, she said, let's go for Thanksgiving.

And so it was. For some reason, just before Thanksgiving, the pieces came together, clicked into place. Magic happened. I began to swallow more or less normally. Not easily. It was still hard work, and it might always be hard work. But it happened and my life – at least physically – resembles normal.

A miracle? Well, I don't know. It was plain, old-fashioned hard work. Just like with my journalism, those who I couldn't outsmart – which was just about everyone – I outworked. In this case, I outworked my stroke.

Inspirational? Well, let me put it this way, I really didn't know what else to do. Giving up or giving in to the stroke weren't options, so I fought with all my might. And I prayed for the strength to keep the fight going, to never give up. I knew I had a whole world full of people praying for me, too.

There was a lot of collateral damage. I gave up the job I loved so much and haven't found anything to replace it. I lost my life insurance. It even has been harder to get some people on the phone. As we struggle as a nation against the novel coronavirus that has taken so many lives, I have a new status: at risk.

I go on daily walks trying to keep my social distance. I still dream of telling stories and try to be supportive of the brave journalists still on the job helping local communities through this latest challenge. I know we will emerge stronger from this, too.

Just like with my stroke, we'll look back at this virus and know that it changed us, not always for the better. But in the end, we'll know that we won.

We won.

COLUMN: **Road to recovery: FLORIDA TODAY Executive Editor Bob Gabordi healing after stroke**

By Bob Gabordi
Executive Editor, FLORIDA TODAY
Published Nov. 26, 2018

I always figured I'd die at my desk rather than retire.

Being a journalist is what I love and what I was meant to do. But in minutes on Friday, Nov. 9, everything I was, everything I had dreamed of being, no longer existed.

My voice suddenly changed pitch and I began to slur my words. I tried taking a sip of water, only to feel as though I was drowning from aspiration. Soon, I was face-down on the rug in my office. I might have died right there if not for co-workers Linette Sanchez and Mara Bellaby's quick decision to call 911.

Maybe I had been ignoring signals of an impending stroke for days. I had been feeling off-kilter, steering a little to my left when I walked, even bumping into walls.

My blood pressure was up when I had checked it at my doctor's office, where I was treated for back pain. I guess we attributed all the signals to the back pain.

The ride to Viera Hospital in the back of a Brevard County Emergency Services ambulance was surreal. Seconds mattered, and these men wasted none of them, once hushing me as I babbled about the shock of it all.

The docs would later say that I had been experiencing atrial fibrillation but didn't know it. In AFib, as I understand it, there is an irregular heartbeat. The upper heart beats too quickly, which can cause clotting. Apparently, my heart unleashed a clot straight to the medulla in the brain stem with the accuracy of a champion dart thrower.

In AFib, the heart beat can feel like fluttering. AFib can and does happen often without noticeable results. The fluttering feeling is often ignored as nothing, which it is, until it is your whole life.

I've not been home since that morning some two weeks ago. I've not had food or drink through my mouth. A special tube has been surgically inserted into my stomach so that I can take in nourishment. I've developed a slight case of pneumonia due to aspirating.

I've stopped breathing on my own at least twice.

I have hallucinated at least twice, as well, ripping out tubes and wires, determined to hold off enemy invaders.

On top of that, a growth that has yet to be fully identified has been discovered on my kidney. I need to ask permission and wait for help to move from my bed or to use the urinal.

But it's not all grim.

My family has come from near and far to support me, Donna and Jessica. A brother and sister from Connecticut. Children and grandchildren. Dear friends from all over.

Literally thousands of people from the community and journalists from around the world have sent their love and support. So far, it has taken my family three trips home to cart all the flowers and balloons from well-wishers.

I have had amazing care and support that is beyond just medicine, starting at the shiny new Viera Hospital and continuing with specialized care at Cape Canaveral Hospital. Nurses, doctors, technicians, CNAs — all just amazing and loving people who reflect the goodness that is Brevard County.

I'm writing now because I'm about to enter rehab. I want you to come along with me so I can show you what it is like. I need you to be there with me to make it through.

Though I'm certainly not out of the woods yet and the risk of a repeat stroke is still relatively high, with your support, now is when I can begin to fight back in earnest.

My strength has already returned to much of my body. I can stand without assistance for short periods. I walk fairly well with the help of a walker. In another two to three weeks, I hope to be back on the type of food I've seen on endless TV commercials while hospitalized. I hope to be able to type most words correctly on the first or second try.

I crave crawling into my own bed or getting up for a drink of water in the middle of the night just because I'm thirsty.

I want to go home. Play with my dog. Cook on my Big Green Egg and make some of my world famous homemade Italian pasta, the first order of which is headed to Tulsa, Oklahoma, to a very special doctor who was visiting Viera Hospital and took great care of me and gave me hope.

More than that, I want you to get your blood pressure checked and take aggressive steps to moderate it if it is too high. I want you to ask your medical professional about your risk factors for AFib and what you can and should do to lower them.

Selfishly, I want good things to come from this. I want us to get truly serious about harnessing the love and knowledge in the community and really make Brevard County the healthiest place in Florida.

I'm headed to rehab at Sea Pines Rehabilitation Hospital. I'm told there is hard work ahead if I'm going to get back to being me. But we've made it this far and the plan is to win.

Join me. It should be a great ride.

Gabordi is executive editor at *FLORIDA TODAY*. His direct dial number is 321-242-3607 and cell phone is 850-591-2229. He is *@bgabordi* on Twitter and */bgabordi* on Facebook. You can also find him on LinkedIn. His email address is bgabordi@ floridatoday.com.

Support local journalism: Subscribe to FLORIDA TODAY at floridatoday.com/subscribe.

Christmas 2019: All together. Front row (left to right) Reece Gabordi, Cole Payton holding Rowan Ladd, Brady Gabordi. Back row (left to right) Declan Ladd, Madison Ladd and Finleigh Payton.

CHAPTER SIXTEEN

THE FAMILY

As I've said before in this book, this business is not easy on families. When my children were younger, teachers would send home messages for their Dad, the newspaper editor. Sometimes there would be notes, sometimes the messages were verbal. Rarely were they complimentary – such as "great column" – but even the compliments were not especially welcomed by the human carrier pigeons. They just wanted to be kids, like everyone else.

That's something I didn't realize so much: How having a Dad who was so well known in the communities we lived in affected them.

By the time Alex came along, I was starting to get it. He is the youngest of the five Gabordi children and was born almost 14 years after Rob, the first born.

Alex quit wanting to do stuff with me, like going to the grocery store, where there was a chance that I would be stopped by the mayor or – worse – a random reader who wanted to have a "work-related" conversation. I loved that stuff. Alex did not.

Jessica, of course, changed everything. She impacted us in ways that are difficult to understand, let alone try to explain. When big brother Rob applied for Marshall medical school, he asked me to read and edit an essay on why he wanted to be a doctor. It was about Jessica and his relationship with her. I had not expected that and began to cry tears of pride two paragraphs into the essay. I advised him to not change a word.

Research has shown mixed results for the impact of children with developmental disabilities on families, but mostly it shows families pull together. We were close and to this day they all call home at least once a day. I credit Donna, of course, for that, but Jessica was a part of it, too.

So, you might understand how angry I was when a school employee called me and implied a threat to Jessica's safety because of a column I had written. "Don't bite the hand that takes care of your daughter," the employee – a nurse, of all things – said.

That employee was removed from her job.

Jessica has inspired me to help educate governors in three states about children with disabilities, and more than once we have had to take on school employees, too. I nearly fell out of my chair when a school employee told us during a meeting to discuss Jessica's Individual Educational Plan, required for children with special needs by state law, that the money being spent on Jessica would be better used to educate a child who could learn and didn't I agree?

Jessica, of course, wasn't the only child of ours affected by having an editor for a dad. We moved a lot. I mean a lot. We went from being Yankees to Appalachians to Southerners, and I loved it all. You'd have to ask the individual family members what they thought. I think you'd get mixed opinions.

Let's see if I can trace the trail:

Cranston, R.I., to Danielson, Conn., to Norwich, Conn., to Ledyard, Conn., to Alexandria, Va., to Dale City, Va., to Marietta, Ohio, to Huntington, WVa., to Asheville, N.C., (two different homes) to Tallahassee, Fla., to Melbourne, Fla.

Of course, I had some side trips in which the family didn't move but thought we might: A couple months in Jackson, Tenn., and five months in North Hills, Pa.

One day, Rob – now Dr. Robert Gabordi, a surgeon specializing in breast cancer in the Tampa, Fla., area – said he was glad we moved a lot. It taught him about areas of the country he might not have known otherwise. I'm not sure he always felt that way.

In kindergarten in suburban Washington, he was at a school that had the children of embassy workers with dozens of different languages being taught. His buddy was Abdulla, which is not a name we ran into much when we moved to Marietta.

When we moved from Dale City to Marietta it was hard on the kids, especially Rob, who was in middle school. His buddy Nathan Thompson came for a visit a couple months afterward – the same time as a corporate on-site visit, which is when the executives would pile into a corporate jet and go tell the local directors what we were doing right and wrong.

Nathan and his father, an Army lieutenant colonel who had been with U.S. forces in Kuwait and Iraq, had been with us at Boy Scout camp along with John and Michael Coppersmith. John Coppersmith was a Metro Transit police officer. The other campers didn't have much of a chance when we executed precision raids in the middle of the night. The other dads made fun of me when I signed up for swimming lessons – until they saw my 20-year-old college girl swim instructor.

So, anyway, Nate was visiting us in Marietta the night of the corporate dinner, my first on-site as an editor. I was nervous about the visit, but it was going well, until Donna appeared at the door. The boys had gone to gymnastics and Nate had fallen awkwardly. He broke his arm and his parents were coming to get him in the morning.

I can't remember who said what next, but one of the corporate executives – Phil Currie, vice president/news, I think – spoke up and offered to take him home on the corporate jet. And that's what happened. Nate was thrilled, of course. His parents were grateful, and I felt closer to the corporate folks than ever. They had hearts. Who knew?

I've mentioned Donna and I had five children. For all I have put them through, I'm grateful they haven't written a book about me. But if this is to be about truth telling, I can't tell you often enough how hard journalism is on families.

That was especially true for a young editor with ambition to advance, while being a good father and husband. On the latter two, like I said, I'm grateful they haven't written a book on me.

It's not unheard of for journalists to have large families, but it isn't normal, either. I often had to be clear about that when I've told colleagues about the five kids.

"Five kids," they exclaim. "Same wife?"

Yes, and she has been the centerpiece of the family.

There are seven grandchildren, and we're counting on more. Alex, the youngest who is engaged to Jolynn Arias, hasn't started having kids yet.

He lives nearby in Orlando and has always had a gentle side to him. He won the "peacemaker" award in kindergarten. When he was born, Rob was thrilled to finally have a brother. He became kind of a mascot to the Huntington High baseball team. When the team all got crew cuts and dyed their hair blonde, we were surprised that they dyed Alex's hair, too.

When he was a baby, Rob propped him up in his car seat and drove him slowly around the park in my blue Mustang, top down, as a kind of offering to the high school girls. Alex was a chick magnet before he made it to kindergarten.

Alex was deeply affected by moving so much. He would throw up every morning on the way to school in Asheville. It was such an issue that Donna or I would drive him to school.

Gabordis play rough with each other. They did while the kids were growing up and they do now. Tracie, Rob's wife, took a trip to New York with Rob, Alex and me for my 60th birthday. She was still kind of new to us at the time.

Rob and I were bickering on the way out of the Mets game, trying to negotiate the No. 7 train of the subway. Tracie had had enough, and she let us have it. Rightfully. We were misbehaving badly. I don't remember her exact words, but the ones I do recall I won't repeat. She made her point succinctly: She was never traveling with us again.

Of course, she did.

Rob and Tracie have two kids so far, Brady and Reece. Yep, Rob is a Patriots' fan, too.

Rob must be an excellent doctor. His patients just adore him. I've been at events where women just hugged me and told me what a fine young man I raised. Some say that he saved their lives, but, more important, he treated them as people and not just patients. As someone whose life needed saving, I know how important that is.

Niki was the most like her dad growing up. When she married Josh, I told him in front of the crowd at the reception, "Remember, no give backs." Independent. Strong willed. My mother's temper. But she is an amazing mother and I love the woman she has become.

None of them has ever loved my job or the stress I dealt with. But I think Niki saw it most – or at least spoke about it the most.

When she was 10, I coached her baseball team as I did her brother's teams. She was a very good player, fast and smooth. One day, in the middle of the game, she walked the length of the dugout and stood in front of me.

"Dad, do you notice anything different about me?" she asked, one hand on her hip.

No, I replied.

"Well, I'm a girl, and the rest of them are boys. And I don't want to play with them anymore."

And with that, she was done.

No, she didn't want to play softball with girls, either, not after playing baseball. And that was that, until she became a coach. She coached her son's T-ball team in Kansas City and one of her players' father was Alex Gordon, star outfielder for the Royals. I flew out to help her with practice for a week, but it was pretty much all her after that. I guess the Gordon dad came out to help a little, too, and she made sure everyone understood she was the head coach and he – the guy with 13 years in the Majors – was the assistant. That's my girl.

Niki and Josh had our first two grandchildren, Cole and Finleigh.

Danielle was smart enough to fall in love with a sport I knew nothing about, soccer, and she was quite a player. We drove around the countryside for soccer games. I remember when we moved to Asheville, we were a little late to register for the advance play travel team tryouts, but the coach said she could come practice with the team. After the practice, the coach invited her onto the team. She was that good.

She was one of two freshmen girls at TC Roberson High to make the varsity her freshman year. The team was ranked No. 1 in the country by USA TODAY. They made it through the playoffs to the state championship game. I had cleared my plate and planned to take the parent bus for the big game.

It was May 31, 2003, and I was on the bus and ready to go when my cell phone rang. Eric Robert Rudolph, the notorious bomber of the 1996 Olympics, abortion clinics in Birmingham and Atlanta, and an Atlanta gay nightclub, had been captured in nearby Cherokee County after a five-year manhunt by the FBI.

I walked off the bus and found Danielle to explain why I wouldn't be going to the biggest game of her life.

"That's all right, Dad," she said. "We'll just have to go back again next year."

Of course, her team never went back to the championship game. TC lost the game in a shootout after regulation finished in a tie. I "listened" to it on the Internet on a live blog we did from the game.

Danielle would eventually injure an ankle that I'm convinced curtailed her soccer play, and although she continued to play in high school, wouldn't play at the University of North Carolina. I missed her senior year, something I have always regretted, because I accepted the job as executive editor of the Tallahassee Democrat. I spent 10 months without Donna, Jessica, Alex and Danielle.

By now, Rob was long gone to college and medical school. Niki eventually followed us to Tallahassee. She had already switched colleges once to be closer to us when we moved from Huntington to Asheville. And she did it again, transferring to Florida State to graduate as a Seminole.

Danielle did play and coach soccer again, although it was a University of Miami club team that went to a championship tournament while she was in law school. She boxed on the UNC club team, knocking out an opponent from the University of Maryland with a hard-right cross.

Of course, I was working and didn't see that, either, though I relish the photograph her mom took at ringside. I was on the phone with Donna as Danielle was boxing.

"Hit her, Danielle," I heard her mother scream. "Hit her. … Oh, not that hard."

Danielle and Matt Ladd, who we've known since Huntington days, have three kids. The irrepressible Madison, Declan and Rowan. Both parents are lawyers.

I don't think anyone ever threatened them directly over my job, although that would have been a way for me to go ballistic. I mean, except for the idiot nurse who made the comment implying a threat against Jessica. But people did call and while in the course of expressing their dislike or anger toward me, mention my kids or my wife. That was enough to get me to blow my top.

Donna probably put up with the most: Phone calls from busybodies, implied or direct statements about her husband, but she never once gave up on me.

Donna's story is woven throughout the book. I don't think there is any question she has been the glue that has held this family together. She's done this by maintaining a very simple approach to life. When I ask her why the grandchildren seem to gravitate more toward her than me, she says, "Well, I changed their diapers."

That makes reasonable sense. But she is more than a diaper changer. She has been a rock or, as I put it in one of my columns referenced earlier, the rock star of my recovery after the stroke.

The truth is my whole family has been there. All the kids, grandchildren, Donna, my brother Lou and sister Peggy, and brother Rick, who sent love and support from afar.

There is a photograph that I love most of me sleeping wired up in my hospital bed. Beside me in her wheelchair fast asleep next to me is Jessica, who knew better than most what Dad was going through.

This group of people, my children and wife, played a bigger role in my recovery than even the incredible medical professionals at Viera, Cape Canaveral, and Sea Pines Rehabilitation hospitals. They have always been there for me and, for better or for worse, I see myself in each one of them.

They know best of all what being a journalist has meant to me. They know my passion, because they have their own. They know how much I love what my profession does and the people who do it. It has never been easy, but like Tom Hanks says in the film "A League of Their Own," that's the way it's supposed to be.

"It's supposed to be hard," Hanks' character, Jimmy, says. "If it wasn't hard, everyone would do it. The hard is what makes it great."

COLUMN: My last column: Please support journalism and consider the other guy might just be right

By Bob Gabordi
Executive Editor, FLORIDA TODAY
Published Feb. 25, 2019

So, there I was, just finished speaking at a local school heading into the office, the same as most mornings, when suddenly I noticed the blue lights behind me.

One, two, three, four Huntington, West Virginia, police cars followed me into the parking lot of the 7-Eleven. Others came after them, I think.

At gunpoint, I was ordered out of the car and to put my hands on the trunk, which I did slowly, without comment or question. There were a lot of them, one of me, and they had guns.

After some time passed — you know, like forever — I heard one officer say, "I think we can let the editor of the Herald-Dispatch take down his hands."

"Excuse me," I said, trying to sound brave. "That's executive editor."

The best explanation I ever got for what happened was it was a case of mistaken identity. But so many things like that incident have happened over my 40 years as a journalist. And I'm not so sure there are a lot of hardened criminals who look like me.

This is my last column as an employee of Gannett and FLORIDA TODAY, and there is so much I want to express and stories I still want to tell. I retire March 1. But I plan to be around and to keep writing. It's just no longer up to me what gets published.

I know I'm a little emotional. It's a strange time for me. Words that usually jump from my fingers to the computer screen just aren't coming very easily right now. So, we're just going to have to see where this takes us as it happens.

Warning: I might ramble a bit.

I have no doubt that I've been blessed, not only by being surrounded by great journalists in my career, but also by being able to live and work in great communities. I hope you will continue to support their journalism; I think it's vital to our community's future well-being. I'm proud that Mara Bellaby is being promoted to replace me in Brevard.

My journalism career began in Cranston, Rhode Island, a place that once had bars over the windows of a local high school. It ends here in our little piece of paradise, where my wife and I wanted to be for decades and where we want to stay.

I have pushed people with my words. Intentionally so. I've wanted you to think and react. Mainly think. Too many people will only tell you what they think you want to hear. Too many of you are happy with that. That's easy and it makes me sad.

Honestly, I've never quite fit in wherever I've been. I've been too conservative in the liberal Northeast and too liberal in the conservative South.

I have my pet peeves and I've never been reluctant to point them out.

Let's start with people who build their political careers running against government while their only visible means of support is working in government their whole career. That kind of creeps me out, to tell you the truth.

I have the highest regard for our law enforcement officers, except those who think the phrase "to serve and protect" is just a slogan. Some of my closest relationships in the communities I've worked have been with law enforcement officers.

But two agency heads — one a sheriff and the other a police chief — said they wanted to hurt me. Later, one would spend time in a federal penitentiary and the other got a job working parking meters. In fairness, the latter said he was only kidding and that he said he wanted to kill other people, too. It was all right there in a state investigation.

There have been other "funny" moments over the years, too, like the time the naked guy climbed the fence and my family's back stairway to knock on our door at 3 o'clock in the morning. Or when the Marietta, Ohio, police officer didn't notice when someone bashed out our car window — even though the officer had been parked across from our house all night.

There have been poignant moments, too, like when we had to get West Virginia U.S. Sen. Jay Rockefeller to send a plane into St. Vincent to rescue a reporter who was in the cross-hairs of the island-nation's government.

That involved a Huntington couple the U.S. administration was willing to abandon but my newspaper — no, their newspaper — would not. They were to be hanged, but were eventually freed, thanks to that reporter, a young man named Mark Truby, and the newspaper that would not quit.

The family came to the newspaper building to celebrate on the downtown street that day. Journalism has always mattered, but never, it seemed, as much as on that day.

We called that series "Prisoners in Paradise" and it won major national awards. But none meant as much as a young girl's smile and her tears of joy as she thanked us for her mother's life.

There have been failures, too. Gary Bennett is still in a Florida prison with very little hope for justice. Lucille Showalter went to her grave in Connecticut without an admission from her son's killer.

Maybe I should just write about how fortunate I've been, both in my career and in life. But that seems rather obvious. I helped raise five amazing children, who have blessed me with six grandchildren and counting, and coached several hundred more to play baseball, including on a trip to the Babe Ruth World Series with a special group of Tallahassee 13-year-old boys.

I've gotten to talk with presidents, including Jimmy Carter, Ronald Reagan and George H.W. Bush, and movie stars, such as Bob Hope and Robert Redford. I got to meet sports legends such as Willie Mays, Keith Hernandez, Randy Moss, Buster Posey, Sam Cunningham, Charlie Ward and Bobby Bowden. Former Marshall and New York Jets quarterback Chad Pennington, a journalism major, was a favorite.

For 26 of my 40 years in this business I have had the great privilege of leading newsrooms in unique corners of the country. All have been special.

Working with the International Center for Journalists, I've been honored to host and mentor dozens of journalists from around the world, including Ukraine, Georgia, Russia, Malaysia, Romania,

Argentina, Syria, Kenya, Uganda, Ghana, Turkey, Armenia and, of course, Pakistan, where I've traveled three times.

These journalists and their struggles to be free are in my heart forever. As are the people of the communities where I have spent these last 40 years.

The outpouring of emotion and support, the well wishes and — especially — the prayers as I've dealt with health issues these last few months have been overwhelming. I cannot begin to thank you for that, but I'll try by giving back and continuing to speak out on issues our community faces.

Thank you doesn't cover how much gratitude I feel for the doctors, nurses and therapists who have worked so hard since my stroke to give me back my life, first at Viera Hospital, then Cape Canaveral Hospital and then Sea Pines Rehabilitation Hospital, and then the Visiting Nurses Association at home.

My wife Donna and I were not born here but we have chosen to live here. It's hard to find a good sunset to ride off into on Florida's East Coast, but I've always favored sunrises anyway. That's where I plan to be: like the morning light, always rising.

Gabordi is executive editor at FLORIDA TODAY. He retires March 1. His private email address is bgabordi99@yahoo.com. His cell phone is 850-591-2229. He is @bgabordi on Twitter and / bgabordi on Facebook. You can also find him on LinkedIn.

Support local journalism by becoming a subscriber to FLORIDA TODAY at floridatoday.com/subscribe.